A PEOPLE'S HISTORY OF BASEBALL

A People's History of Baseball

MITCHELL NATHANSON

UNIVERSITY OF ILLINOIS PRESS
Urbana, Chicago, and Springfield

Library of Congress Cataloging-in-Publication Data
Nathanson, Mitchell, 1966–
A people's history of baseball / Mitchell Nathanson.
p. cm.
Includes bibliographical references and index.
ISBN 978-0-252-03680-4 (hardcover : alk. paper) —
ISBN 978-0-252-09392-0 (e-book)
1. Baseball—United States—History.
2. Baseball—Social aspects—United States—History.
I. Title.
GV863.A1N368   2012
796.357—dc23   2011034116

For Joanne, Alex, and Jackie.
As always.

CONTENTS

Acknowledgments

ix

Prologue

xi

1

A Game of Their Own

1

2

The Sovereign Nation of Baseball

28

3

Rickey, Race, and "All Deliberate Speed"

67

4

Tearing Down the Walls

108

5

"Wait 'Til Next Year" and the Denial of History

146

6

The Storytellers

180

Notes

221

Bibliography

261

Index

271

ACKNOWLEDGMENTS

Many thanks to everybody at the University of Illinois Press who shepherded *A People's History of Baseball* to daylight: my editor Bill Regier, senior editor Tad Ringo, and everyone else who went above and beyond to make my book the best it could be. I would also like to thank the two anonymous readers, whose invaluable comments and thoughtful suggestions improved the book immensely, widening its scope and intensifying its depth such that would have been impossible without them. I likewise owe a debt of gratitude to my colleagues at the Society for American Baseball Research, particularly those on the SABR listserv, who provided guidance and a seemingly bottomless well of knowledge in response to my varied queries. To my wife Joanne, thank you for patiently allowing me to prattle on and on at the dinner table as I was working through the book. And to the late Howard Zinn, whose work inspired this book, thank you for demonstrating to anyone willing to listen that the received wisdom is hardly the only wisdom.

PROLOGUE

What is baseball? At first blush this appears to be a straightforward question. And in many ways it is. Baseball is a game. Nevertheless, the question persists: what is it, really? Football is a game, but it is not baseball. Neither are basketball and hockey. Putting aside the differences among balls, pucks, rules, and regulations, there seems to be something fundamentally different about baseball when compared with these other sports. All of them are games, but to many people, baseball is *baseball*. In a sense, it is something else altogether.

This sense perhaps comes from the notion that, aside from a game, it is also a concept. It is America's game—our national pastime—so therefore it bears significant emblematic weight. And it has historically borne this weight remarkably well. It has been used to inform us as to our national values and beliefs, to promote and reaffirm what it means to be an American, to define the essence of our country, practically from the time it first gained popularity in the mid-nineteenth century. Even in its shortcomings it has, in a way, defined us, represented us, and told us who we were. So, what is baseball? Symbolically and conceptually speaking, it is America. Through the game's historical narrative, larger themes emerge: ones focused on equality, patriotism, heroism, capitalism—the usual suspects within the American canon. And to be sure, all of those themes can be found in baseball, some of them in abundance. Therefore, in many ways, baseball's narrative is idyllic America's as well. Assuming we choose to see it that way.

Because we can also see it another way. Rather than see baseball through a patriotic, sepia haze, we can choose to see it through a more critical eye, one that permits us to see our collective selves at something less than our best. Through the growth and development of baseball we can see the corrupting potential of influence—the petty power struggles as well as the consequential ones—that have likewise defined our nation for well over two centuries. Though baseball as a game is sharply defined, constrained by tangible boundaries such as foul lines and a strike zone, baseball as a concept is a far more malleable entity. It can be, and has been, many different things, depending on one's viewpoint. To say that baseball is America is simple enough—assuming that we understand what "America" means to the one drawing the parallel.

A People's History of Baseball is baseball history from an alternative viewpoint. Herein are stories focusing on the concept of baseball but ones that challenge convention and play out differently than the oft-told tales because of the shift in perspective. Regardless, they have much in common with the more well-known stories in that beyond their differing perspective, they are just that—stories. Rarely, however, is a story merely a story.

Simply put, stories are oftentimes how we construct our world. As scholars of storytelling have observed, "[w]e understand, we 'know,' by relying on a stock of conventional stories—stories about how the world runs, how people are likely to behave in it, how certain causes are likely to result in certain effects. These stories are our ordinary understanding of the world."[1] These tales turn out to be useful in our comprehension of more general rules and principles. In short, we become indoctrinated to universal concepts of how our society "should" work through the stories we tell and eventually internalize. It is through this process that the concept of baseball (that is, the notion that our national game is somehow representative of basic American ideals and mores) flourishes. In this way, and to take as an example one of the stories discussed herein, how we understand the story of Branch Rickey, Jackie Robinson, and the breaking of baseball's color line shapes our perception of more universal principles, such as what it means to be an American. Because of the nexus between baseball and America, these baseball stories often serve as the symbolic examples that enlighten us on our beliefs regarding how our country operates and what it stands for.

Of course, not all stories are equally effective. To achieve significant symbolic status, a story must connect with its intended audience; it must speak to their values in order to produce the necessary resonance.[2] To do this, it must first be coherent: it needs to hang together such that all of the necessary elements fit neatly as if parts of a puzzle.[3] Next, it must ring true with the listener's own sense of how the story *should* play out. Interestingly, one thing it does not have to be is accurate or truthful in any way. In fact, fictional stories are oftentimes the most persuasive stories precisely because their freedom from the constraints of truth allows them to hang together so well and so neatly match their audience's expectations. As Aristotle recognized in his *Rhetoric* more than two thousand years ago, logical arguments or stories persuade not because there is something inherently true about logic but simply because people value and respond to logic irrespective of the truth underlying it.[4] "True" stories suffer in comparison because of the inherent contradictions and missing pieces present in messy, everyday life.[5] Consequently, not only is the veracity of a particular story an inaccurate measure of its persuasiveness, if anything, the opposite may be the case: the asymmetry of reality can prove to be a significant barrier to the resonance required for a story to achieve its goal. In this sense, the more resonant the story, the more suspect it becomes. Because patriotic, culturally affirming baseball stories have traditionally resonated very deeply within American society, they deserve their moment under the microscope. Discovering what lies behind their creation might prove illuminating.

Irrespective of the truth, as consumers of these stories, we tend to consider those stories that conform to how we view our world, or our country, as the truth anyway.[6] In fact, they do not even feel like stories to us. Because they resonate so deeply, we tend to believe that they also inform us as to the bigger picture—our country, our world, our beliefs.[7] In this way, popular, comforting, cheerful stories are oftentimes the most powerful stories of all.[8] By contrast, "counter-stories"—ones that challenge accepted, conventional beliefs—are often dismissed as (take your pick) manipulative, political, anecdotal, unprincipled, and/or unfair.[9] To a large degree, these criticisms are accurate; counter-stories are typically all of these things and more. But so are the others. In the end, all stories, whether they confirm our beliefs or challenge them, are manipulative, political, anecdotal, and, to the extent they are used to illustrate larger, universal truths, unfair. For in the end, all stories are just that—stories.

A *People's History of Baseball* is not about the baseball stories we already know but the ones we are much less familiar with—the counter-stories. At first glance, the stories challenged and retold herein may not even strike us as stories at all—the founding of the National League, baseball's relationships with the rule of law and the media, the integration of the game, midcentury expansion, and the rise and public rebuke of the Players Association. Rather, they feel like objective, historical narratives. As we now know, however, this makes them immediately suspect—not false per se but subject to closer analysis. The point of telling these counter-stories is not in the expectation that they will replace the conventional stories (indeed, this is far too much to ask—it is extremely difficult if not impossible for a counter-story to change the conventional story merely by highlighting its inherent weaknesses)[10] but rather, in the hope that they will help us achieve a better understanding of the stories we, as a culture, have internalized; to help us recognize that they are simply stories and not objective analyses of the facts that underlie them. Through these counter-stories we can reassess the stories of baseball as America and perhaps understand them, as well as what they represent, more thoroughly.

By challenging the perspective of these deeply entrenched stories of baseball and offering alternative ways of approaching them, the counter-stories in this book also reveal something else: that the conventional "concept of baseball" stories are not so much stories of equality, patriotism, heroism, and capitalism as they are stories of power—how it is obtained, how it perpetuates itself, and how those who have it use the weapon of storytelling (through, in this instance, the notion of baseball as America) to convince their audience that they are not wielding it when in fact they are, and in significant measure. In the end, however, it is important to remember that as counter-stories, they are inherently manipulative, political, and unfair. In other words, they are no different than the stories we already know.

A PEOPLE'S HISTORY OF BASEBALL

A GAME OF THEIR OWN

Practically from the inception of the game, baseball and America have been, in a symbolic sense, virtually synonymous. On December 5, 1856, the *New York Mercury* became the first newspaper to declare the fledgling sport to be our "national pastime;"[1] four years later nationally renowned lithographers Currier and Ives issued a print connecting the sport with the upcoming 1860 presidential election, declaring both to be our "national game[s];"[2] later, poet Walt Whitman would exult that baseball was "America's game," remarking that it "has the snap, go fling of the American atmosphere— belongs as much to our institutions, fits into them as significantly, as our constitutions, laws: is just as important in the sum total of our historic life."[3] Very quickly, it simply felt natural to speak of baseball and America interchangeably, using one as a metaphor for the other, ascribing values to the game and the men who played and administered it that seemingly rang true on the larger canvas of the expanding and exploding nation as well. All of this seemed inevitable and uniquely American—to be so fortunate to have a game that spoke so clearly to our national character and temperament. What other country could possibly boast of such symbiosis?

In fact, by the middle of the nineteenth century, there were scores of them. In many countries within the vast British Empire, along with many British-influenced societies no longer directly under British rule, people felt toward cricket as Americans were beginning to feel about baseball.[4] Victorian-era colonial rulers, steeped in the British public school ethos of the cultural and socializing influence of team sports such as cricket, used the game precisely for this purpose when confronted with prospect of "civilizing" the non-British "natives."[5] Just as in England, where the game was considered a vital rite of passage in the training of those molded to become the future aristocrats of the empire, colonial rulers in countries such as Barbados deliberately introduced and preached cricket as a "socializing and civilizing agent."[6] In fact, "[c]ricket was considered the main vehicle for transferring the appropriate British moral code from the messengers of empire to the local populations."[7] So central was cricket to the perceived character of the British Empire that it is not unreasonable to assume that had Whitman been domiciled in the Caribbean rather than New York he would have nevertheless issued a virtually identical ode, substituting only the subjects of his exclamation.

The link, then, between sport and society was not unique to America. What *was* unusual, however, was that despite its British roots and heavy British influence through the middle of the nineteenth century, America nevertheless gravitated to a much less developed game—baseball—and saw in it everything its numerous British-influenced societal kin saw in cricket. Other British-influenced societies had developed native games just as Americans had developed baseball; in this they were no different than America. However, these games largely failed to survive, or if they did, remained confined within the realm of sport. In America, the results were far different. Despite cricket's substantial head start and its historic role as a societal symbol, baseball quickly and forcefully supplanted it both as a game and as the national metaphor. This begs the simple question: why?

The answer lies, at least in part, in another deliberate social policy, this one on behalf of a group of status-conscious Americans who attempted to emulate the small-town values of the Protestant (WASP) establishment of the early and mid-nineteenth century in an effort to increase their societal standing. As baseball became more popular as the century progressed, these men, who would eventually be known as baseball club owners or "magnates," saw an opportunity to hitch their star to the game and use it as a vehicle for self-promotion. For them, the goal was acculturation into the closed world of the respected (but increasingly less influential) WASP elites—a club they, because of perceived shortcomings as a result of familial and/or ethnic handicaps, otherwise could never hope to join merely through the accumulation of wealth alone. Aided by their journalist allies, these individuals set out to promote the game and, in essence, themselves, as "true" Americans, aspiring to a status they were otherwise not assured of achieving because of these familial and ethnic handicaps.

They would achieve this status through their successful proliferation of what has become known as the "baseball creed." Although, as the following chapters attest, the creed has been malleable through the decades, molding and conforming itself to respond to whatever the pressing issues of the day happened to be, its essence has never changed: that baseball, not unlike cricket in places like England, India, and Barbados, to name but a few, is more than a game; instead, it stands in for America in name as well as in concept and is an invaluable tool in the teaching and promotion of American values and ideals. In its most overt and cheerleading form (which was characteristic of its earlier incarnations), the hyperbole was especially thick: the game was promoted as "building manliness, character, and an ethic of success"; it molded youngsters, helping boys become better men not only through playing but simply by watching the game; it contributed to the public health and was an agent for democratization.[8] All of this was neatly summed up by a journalist in 1907 who wrote, "[a] tonic, an exercise, a safety valve, baseball is second only to death as a leveler. So long as it remains our national game, America will abide no monarchy, and anarchy will be slow."[9] Through the baseball creed, these "new money" Americans were ultimately able to gain the status (if not the power) they were seeking, breaking through and eventually opening up the historically closed but rapidly changing American hierarchy of the late nineteenth and early twentieth centuries. Though initially hardly the "magnates" and "leading citizens" they portrayed themselves to be, eventually they were able to achieve the status they had spent years trumpeting to the American public they had already obtained.

This self-promotional effort was itself not unusual in the sense that social climbing through storytelling has always been, and remains, an

American tradition. In fact, America takes its name from a storyteller who hoped to achieve goals similar to those of the early baseball "magnates." Like many of the early "magnates," Amerigo Vespucci was a merchant with aspirations to rise above his station into the aristocracy.[10] Like them, he had obtained a measure of wealth but soon learned that while the closed caste of early sixteenth-century Europe permitted aristocrats to become merchants, it was not so easy for merchants to become aristocrats. More than wealth was required. What was needed was something money could not buy. Therefore, in search of this elusive goal, "[h]e sought to project himself as a magus in touch with the powers of nature, and he frankly wanted enduring renown."[11] Eventually, following in Columbus's path, Vespucci reinvented himself as a world explorer, spinning tales that exaggerated his navigational expertise, accomplishments, and daring. After his death, his legend grew until, by the time of U.S. independence, it reached fruition when he was hailed as a "preincarnation of the spirit of revolutionary America," replete with traits symbolic of the nascent, Enlightenment-era United States—a nation that, according to the story, had evolved to become the physical manifestation of the spirit of Amerigo Vespucci.[12]

The early baseball "magnates" sought through baseball what Vespucci found through exploration. That they would find it speaks not merely to their efforts at self-promotion, however. To their benefit came, at the same time, a furious attack on the entrenched power structure and societal elites by the growing American underclasses, which were becoming more diverse through immigration and less like the elites who nevertheless still dominated the ruling and societal classes. Together, these movements eventually were able to fracture the closed caste of small-town, upper-crust America, which had been designed to shut these outsiders out in their efforts to keep status, and therefore power, concentrated in the hands of the few.

A PLAYERS' GAME NO LONGER

In its earliest incarnations, baseball was a players' game; the concept of an "ownership" rank, as distinguished from a "players" rank, was one far off into the future. Instead, baseball (or at least a version of it) prospered largely as a game played between members of middle- and artisan-class clubs that themselves emulated the elite clubs that defined and designated the top rung of mid-nineteenth-century American society.[13] Although there was some mixing of the classes and, as such, a number of upper-class baseball players and even clubs, by and large, many elite clubs preferred cricket to baseball and would typically never even consider the members of these lower-rank clubs for admission into their elite societies. These elite clubs were run and populated instead by white, old-stock Protestants—WASPS—who, in many instances, formed their clubs for the primary purpose of segregating themselves from the masses in an effort to demonstrate and display their superior societal status.[14] Indeed, the choice of cricket as a unifying theme for their clubs was not accidental: transplanted Englishmen, who initially controlled cricket in the antebellum era, proudly practiced exclusive and snobbish attitudes toward outsiders and discouraged the participation of the lower classes. The WASP cricket clubs that sprung up in their wake merely adopted this attitude.[15] Through their clubs, these old-stock Americans discovered, in the words of sociologist and chronicler of upper-crust America E. Digby Baltzell: "an ideal instrument for the gentlemanly control of social, political and economic power."[16] In fact, it was this notion of exclusivity through club membership that made the American club unique, separating it from the likes of its forbears, the British club. For while the British club (contrasting with the American club run by Englishmen discussed previously) was created to bring together members with like interests in activities such as golf, sailing, and tennis, in furtherance of their pursuit of these activities, the American club was (as these transplanted Englishmen recognized), and is, designed to foster social exclusivity—sport was merely the by-product of this socializing purpose. In British clubs, sport was the purpose and sociability the by-product; in the American ones, just the opposite was the case. As Baltzell noted, after one graduated from the youthful preparatory societies of the boarding school and the university, "[p]roper club affiliation was, after all, the final and most important stage in an exclusive socializing process." In the end, it was club affiliation, more than mere accomplishment alone, that determined an individual's social status during this era.

As stated above, many of these elite clubs revolved around cricket. As for why these status-conscious clubs gravitated toward the transplanted Englishmen and their fondness for cricket, one only has to look at the nature of American democratic society. Without the protections provided through rigid class lines such as those that existed within the British Empire, the American upper class, suffering from a perpetual case of status anxiety, was drawn to the transplanted Englishmen's elitist attitude toward cricket (which itself likely emanated from their unease in residing within a society that lacked the formal social structure of their homeland) and was attracted toward this unambiguous marker of high social status. As a consequence, the game was not promoted throughout the larger population.[17] By restricting entry into their clubs, and by playing a game that they discouraged outsiders to take up through their refusal to promote it, club members were therefore able to transform cricket into a synonym for a distinct class rather than society as a whole.

This was quite unlike how cricket was, and is, viewed in virtually all other countries of British influence (Canada being another, albeit lesser, exception). In India and the Caribbean, for instance, people from all levels of society were encouraged to play the game, although "stacking" (the concept of "positional segregation" within teams) was often prevalent and in deference to the differing social classes taking part in a given match. (For example, bowling and wicket-keeping were performed by low-status players, while the captain and star batsmen were reserved for high-status "gentlemen.")[18] Despite, or perhaps because of, the presence of stacking (which was particularly prevalent in multiracial British colonies such as Barbados, Jamaica, and India), cricket was able to thrive among all levels of society within these countries. On American soil, however, given that cricket was quickly co-opted by the anxious, status-conscious upper-class clubs, it was never given a chance to take root. In the end, it was the democratic concept of social mobility that killed cricket in America: elites' fear of the concept that anyone, from even the humblest beginnings, could rise to the top of American society.[19] This caused them to take a game from the public sphere and confine it to their own social circle, where, through club membership, they maintained the ability to thwart interlopers by citing shortcomings such as family, racial, or ethnic traits as justification for the perpetual stratification of their societies. As a result, cricket in America developed a snooty image, which is precisely what these elites had intended.[20]

With these elite clubs, with their elite game closed off to the masses, those below the top rung of American society focused their energies on a variation of the emerging game of baseball (although some did dabble in both games for a time[21]). Through the promotion of the game by these lesser, although solidly middle- and artisan-class, clubs,[22] baseball soon assumed the societal role in America that cricket played in England as well as the myriad other countries of British origin. Eventually, just as cricket captured the interest of the various classes in those countries, baseball became a passionate pastime of all classes within American society. However, this was not the case initially, at least not with regard to the version of baseball being promoted by these middle- and artisan-class clubs. And, like the upper class's co-opting and cordoning off of cricket for their specific, status-marking purposes, this was by design.

The Knickerbocker Base Ball Club of New York, the club that is commonly believed to have, in 1845, first set down in writing its rules for the earliest incarnation of what we today consider baseball (although there is evidence that another club in fact did so eight years earlier[23]) was a club in every sense of the word in that it was select in its membership: among the members of their club of fifty-odd men between 1845 and 1860 were seventeen merchants, twelve clerks, five brokers, four "professional men," two insurance men, a bank teller, a cigar dealer, one hatter, a cooperage owner, a stationer, a United States marshal, and several "gentlemen."[24] In short, this was a collection of men who found themselves one station beneath the city's elite.[25] Just as with the upper-class clubs, interest in baseball was not the foremost admission criteria for this club; instead, it was the requisite standing within the community that was, in many instances, determinative. As the baseball historian Harold Seymour observed, "[t]he Knickerbockers wanted to restrict baseball to their own social class. For a while they limited their matches to clubs that used the Elysian Fields, hoping in this way to meet only their social equals."[26] As such, they mimicked the elite cricket clubs that existed for the primary social purpose of excluding the likes of them.

By design, whenever they convened, teams made sure that the game they played was one that suited their purposes—athletically and otherwise. Although there have been bat and ball games of one sort or another for as long as there have been bats and balls, the Knickerbockers, as well as the other "gentlemanly" baseball clubs that sprouted up in New York around this time, adopted a specific version of baseball that appealed to their societal aspirations. In short, in defining "base ball" they made sure that it spoke to their values and was, not insignificantly, a game commensurate with their limited abilities on the field.[27] Thus, their game, the "New York game" as it would come to be known, frowned upon the rough and tumble aspects of the New England version of the game, where, among other indignities, runners could be retired by being "plugged" or "soaked" by the ball, and where the taunting of poor play was the norm.[28] Instead, as the more sedentary men of the rising middle classes were prone to be, they created a "gentleman's" game where "manly" skills were on display; however, they defined "manliness" as "gentlemanly," such that, in the words of baseball historian John Thorn, baseball became more "a matter of decorum and bearing [than] courage."[29] Thorn continued, "[f]or common men of sedentary habits who would, if they had their wish, be leisured gentlemen, such as the Knickerbockers, it was more important to comport themselves well than to play well."[30]

The aspirational ethos of the Knickerbocker club and the New York game was soon adopted by the other "gentlemanly" baseball clubs that sprouted around the nation. A St. Louis "base ball" club, for example, boasted that its membership consisted of "some of the brightest young men of St. Louis, among them a number of whom have left the impress of their handiwork in almost every honorable calling," while a Cleveland club brayed that its members "were nearly all scions of the best families of Cleveland."[31] All of these clubs were following in the footsteps of the Knickerbockers, who, if the reports were to be believed, could call as members players from some of the most socially prominent families in New York.[32] Of course, the reports were not to be believed; if these members did in fact hail from such backgrounds, they were more likely to be members of cricket rather than baseball clubs. Still, the reports spread, in New York and elsewhere, as these striving white collar and artisan status seekers positioned themselves for hopeful ascension into the upper ranks of American society.[33] What was important to these clubs was that they marked and differentiated their members from the lower classes, the semi-skilled or unskilled workers, who, at this point, were not as ravenous over baseball—at least as the New York game defined it—as they were.[34] Indeed, in his study of early baseball and cricket, George Kirsch suggests that the antebellum attraction of artisans to baseball may very well be rooted in their declining societal status as a result of the Industrial Revolution. As they declined professionally, many of these artisans may have turned to baseball to distinguish themselves this way instead.[35] If the base ball clubs of the era had their way, this would have remained the case indefinitely.

In fact, it was not difficult for these middle- and artisan-class clubs to restrict baseball (as they defined it) to their own kind, at least initially. These workers, with their higher incomes and shorter work hours, simply had more time and money to join clubs and engage in recreational activities than did their lower-class brethren.[36] In addition, as immigrants poured into the country throughout the nineteenth century, they soon came to dominate the lower classes, and many of them were simply not interested in baseball given that it was most likely unheard of in their countries of origin.[37] Thus, despite the reports of baseball sweeping the nation throughout the mid-nineteenth century, the veracity of this boast depended greatly upon how one defined "base ball": the New York game did indeed capture the fancy of the rising middle class and artisan status-seekers, and though other bat and ball games were played by the lower classes, their games were far less formalized, and more brutal, than the New York game and were thus not considered "base ball" at all by those interested in promoting the more gentlemanly version of the game. Although there were blue-collar clubs and players who did play the New York game, by and large those above and below the middle and artisan classes had a much more limited interest in it. This would change as the century progressed, however, and the game became more democratic in its appeal as well as less gentlemanly in nature.[38]

Because the gentlemanly clubs were true "clubs," they were participant based, with socialization (and marking) of club members the primary goal and sport secondary. Soon, advances in the game of baseball (as well as the creeping influence of the competitive aspects of the lower-class games) changed all of this. The trajectory of the original Philadelphia Athletics provides a representative example of how the gentlemanly New York game morphed from a club sport to a competitive, professional one, giving rise to the concept of team "backers" and eventually "owners."

The Athletics Base Ball Club was an offshoot of another club, the Handel and Haydn Singing Society, located at Sixth and Spring Garden Streets in Philadelphia.[39] Several of the members were interested in the game so, in 1859, they decided to form a ball club. They elected a president of the club, William Emot, who eventually gave way to Col. Tom Fitzgerald, a Handel and Haydn member and controller in the Philadelphia public school system who was notable for being the first to require music as part of the curriculum of Philadelphia public schools. (Later, his pamphlet "Music in our Public Schools" became popular and influential both throughout the United States and in London.)[40] Very quickly, this recreational endeavor created by and for members of the singing society outgrew its gentlemanly constraints. As the Athletics improved, they played more games and traveled more often. Somebody would have to pay these increasing expenses; the players' membership dues could not cover everything. Soon, the concept of "backers"—members who contributed financially toward the club's expenses but did not play—took root.

More ominous were the under-the-table efforts to increase the quality of the club. In 1865 Al Reach jumped from the Eckford Club in Brooklyn to the Athletics, becoming in the process the first player to switch cities in order to play baseball professionally and the first true mercenary in the game (there were paid players before Reach but never one who traveled as far as he did for the primary purpose of playing baseball for money).[41] Although the game was still, technically speaking, an amateur, "gentlemanly" endeavor, this was quickly falling by the wayside as the Athletics skirted the rules by having one of their backers set Reach up in a cigar store above Fourth and Chestnut Streets (he eventually transformed this into a sporting goods empire).[42] Later, backers enticed other top players to join the Athletics, putting them in fabricated jobs to skirt the amateurism requirements. Pitcher Dick McBride was given a desk in the city's treasurer's office, a $1,200 salary, and no obvious responsibilities; other players such as Patsy Dockney were given similar enticements.[43] Although some players, such as Reach, actually worked at these "jobs" and transformed them into something legitimate, others did not bother to hide the fact that they were jobs in name only. Dockney rarely showed up for his, preferring instead to "play ball every afternoon and fight and drink every night" in exchange for his salary.[44] With Dockney, as with a rapidly increasing number of the Athletics players, it was very clear what they had been brought to Philadelphia to do, and they made little or no effort to hide this reality. In fact, even though the Cincinnati Red Stockings of

1869 are generally considered to have been the first professional club in baseball history, this is accurate only to the extent that the Red Stockings were the first *openly* professional team or the first all-salaried team; the Athletics most likely put nine professional players on the field a year earlier, in 1868.[45] All of the expenses—uniforms, travel, procurement of top players—now fell upon "subscriptions from the members and extra donations by particular and particularly able friends."[46] In a few short years, the Athletics of the Handel and Haydn Singing Society had become a quaint and fading memory.

By the late 1860s, despite being members of the amateur National Association of Base Ball Players (NABBP), professionalism had taken over the Athletics, just as it had many of their rivals, thus leading to a vicious cycle where they had no choice but to turn even more heavily toward professionals if they hoped to continue to compete and succeed. Thus, although top players could find a home within the Athletics' club, the less talented ones were fading into the background. If they hoped to retain an affiliation with the club, it would have to be by a means other than playing. Many members left the club altogether but some remained, choosing to continue their involvement by financially backing the club, becoming the "able friends" so needed to finance the burgeoning business of professional baseball.[47] In less than a decade, the exclusivity of clubs like the Athletics and others had evolved (or devolved, depending upon one's perspective) to the point where they excluded the majority of their founders and members.

The divergence between what the Athletics once were and what they had become was formalized in 1871 when the NABBP split into two entities, one amateur (the National Association of Amateur Base Ball Players—NAABP) and one professional (the National Association of Professional Base Ball Players—the National Association). Still, however, although in the National Association there was now a clear demarcation between players and owners, it remained a players' league; the owners, or "backers," lurked in the background as the players took center stage. This was evident through the National Association's rules and practices: a player, not a backer, was elected the first president of the league;[48] "revolving" (players freely jumping from one team to the next in search of greater opportunity and compensation) was permitted;[49] and the league was very loosely organized—any group of players could gain entrance into the National Association and become "professionals" so long as they were able to find a backer willing to pony up the $10 league franchise fee.[50] This loose organizational structure (clearly drawn up by those more interested in playing the game than running it) soon led to problems that destabilized it: gambling, rumors of fixed games, and incessant revolving (all consequences of the increasing competitiveness of the games—legacies of the lower-class games where the point was to win rather than to comport oneself well[51]) were rampant. All of this clashed with the pervasive Victorian values of the time that were passed down through American society by the WASP elites.[52] With the National Association vulnerable and calls for reform coming from all corners, the backers—the same people who just a few years earlier were pushed aside in their own clubs by the professional players they, ironically, initially recruited to help increase their visibility and, hence, their social status—saw their opportunity to reassert themselves and reclaim their positions of status. In effect, they staged a "coup d'état," appropriating the game from the players and forming, in 1876, the National League (NL), and claiming it for themselves.[53]

In the new National League, the players were relegated to subordinate status; this was going to be an owners' league, not a players' league. In 1879 the reserve rule was established, which prevented revolving (and allowed the owner to choose his players, rather than vice versa).[54] Of course, the owners were free to trade, sell, or release players at their whim. Players were likewise granted no voice in league governance and had no right of appeal of any decision rendered against them; the days of a player presiding over league affairs was long gone. Soon, the players were removed from every aspect of the game save for the actual on-field competition. The owner decided everything else: who was to play on "his" club, what they were to be paid, who was to manage the club, and how "his" ballpark was to be run.[55] Perhaps most significant, the National League owners reestablished the concept of the exclusive closed club: no longer could any team join simply by paying the requisite franchise fee. Now, the league was closed to everybody except those chosen by the existing owners to join them—only fellow "elites" could boast of club membership.[56] In all of these ways, the formerly subordinate club backers had transformed themselves into powerful, high-status team owners, and they stood front and center before America in their newly prominent roles.

Once established, these owners were eager to inform the American public, and most notably the WASP elites they aspired to join, of their accomplishments in service to the Victorian values they helped to protect and promote. They "nourished the legend that the NL saved professional baseball from utter ruin. Had it not been for the timely creation of the NL and the sagacious decisions of its leaders, so the fable went, the national pastime would have continued its downward slide into complete degrada- tion . . . the NL ostentatiously presented itself as the national pastime's main moral guardian."[57] In this way, by rescuing the game "from its slough of corruption and disgrace," as they boasted, the owners presented them- selves to the public as nothing less than American heroes.[58]

Disseminating this information was rather easy and effective given the similar interests of and close connections between these owners and the journalists who were increasingly assigned to cover their games. By the time of the birth of the National League, this relationship between baseball and the media was an established one, with the nationwide tri- umph of the New York game attributable in large part to the handiwork of baseball journalists. Beginning in 1853, the influential and high-brow weekly, the *Spirit of the Times,* promoted the New York game, complete with its attendant definition of "manliness," to its audience, defined by founder William Trotter Porter as "gentlemen of standing, wealth and intelligence, the very Corinthian columns of the community."[59] The ability of the Knickerbockers and their compatriots to regularly reach their targeted demographic in this way helped their version of the game ultimately prevail. Later, other newspapers similarly preached the values inherent in the New York game. In 1889, the *New York Times* announced that "[b]aseball is an intellectual pursuit, which is indulged in only by gentlemen of the highest mental caliber, and by those whose minds have undergone a singularly-stringent training in the matter of intellectual- ity."[60] Other newspapers wrote in similarly gushing prose of the inher- ent value of baseball overall. With regard to the reporting on specific teams, lavish journalistic praise was equally forthcoming, for this not only helped to promote the game, it promoted these papers' hometown cities, as well as their civic leaders.

In the late nineteenth century, particularly in the newer, less estab- lished midwestern cities, survival of communities into the future was far from guaranteed, so newspapermen saw it as in their interest to not merely report the news but to engage in boosterism as a means of convincing outsiders, as well as locals, that theirs was a thriving community complete with top-notch civic institutions and prominent citizens.[61] In this way, boosterism—an act of self-preservation—generated a by-product of bloated, fawning portraits of club owners (who were often the most visible ambassadors for their cities) that were far more aspirational in nature than rooted in fact. As such, the image of club owners as wealthy, influential, benevolent "magnates" (a term otherwise reserved for industrial and financial giants) flourished, despite the reality that these owners were most often self-made, well-to-do merchants or moderately prosperous businessmen: successful (to a degree) but hardly magnates on par with the industrial and financial behemoths of the era.[62]

Even in the more established northeastern cities, boosterism existed, although not to the same degree. In addition, there were two other factors that explained the close connection between the owners and journalists in the Northeast as well as elsewhere. First, even as far back as the late nineteenth century, many writers depended on the owners for their livelihoods.[63] Because owners often paid their expenses and hired them for additional promotional work, these journalists were not about to bite the hand that fed them. Second, the relationship between the media and the owners was occasionally incestuous, with many team executives former journalists.[64] In 1901, former *Cincinnati Enquirer* sports editor Ban Johnson helped to transform the American League (AL) from a minor to a major league and became the most prominent example of this, but these types of connections predated him by several years. The Spink family not only founded *The Sporting News,* it was intermittently involved in ownership of various St. Louis–area teams throughout the late nineteenth century.[65] Other newspapers, in the Northeast as well as the Midwest, were instrumental in forming or otherwise supporting their local baseball clubs in their effort to promote their towns.[66] For all of these reasons, newspapermen found it beneficial to promote their local teams and paint the owners as larger-than-life figures: "selfless philanthropists" operating their clubs in the public interest, conveniently ignoring their many ties to gambling and corruption that would have sullied this image.[67] Through the journalists, the owners' goal of portraying themselves as noblemen, deserving of status equal to the WASP elites, moved one step closer to realization.

THE NATIONAL LEAGUE AS BASTION OF WASP VALUES

Although baseball, by the time of the National League's formation in 1876, had been hailed as the country's national pastime for two decades, the didactic qualities of the baseball creed were not yet firmly entrenched. This changed over the next several years, however, as club owners took the connection between baseball and America deeper than it had previously been, from merely a game that exemplified the gentlemanly qualities of the nation's best citizens to one that defined the essence of the country overall—one that, through the simple acts of playing or watching it, was vital to the development of new Americans complete with the proper American values and ethics.

The seeds of this transformation were embedded within the insistence of the National League's "magnates" to instill Victorian values within the fabric of their newly created league in an effort to aid them in achieving their ultimate goal: namely, acculturation among the WASP elites.[68] Interestingly, and despite their identification as "magnates," the club owners by and large aspired to a much smaller and quainter societal position than the one assumed by the true magnates of the day. Taking their cues from the WASP elites, who dominated the small-town lifestyle of the early and mid-nineteenth century that was being eclipsed at that very moment, the club owners adopted and promoted their mores in the hope of achieving a similar, though rapidly vanishing, status. In many ways they looked backward rather than forward for inspiration, seeking the status and community position that had theretofore been available to men of moderate means in the more rural and locally focused America that dominated the landscape prior to the dawn of the Industrial Revolution.[69] Drawing upon the small-town values stressed by the WASP elites, ones that preached the virtuousness of the villager or the yeoman farmer (as opposed to the corruption of the cities and of the industrialists currently threatening the status of the Protestant establishment), the club owners attempted to sell, through baseball, a vision of America that would resonate with these increasingly marginalized small-town elites.[70] As such, the "magnate" moniker notwithstanding, the club owners did not aspire to become the equals of Rockefeller, Carnegie, and their ilk. For those men were, in the eyes of many small-town and rural residents, corrupted city folk, "soulless monsters of monopoly" who threatened the basic fabric of America.[71] The club owners aspired to become the antithesis of these men; they sought to promote themselves, and therefore their game, as bastions of purity and morality—everything the actual magnates were not.

As such, they molded their game (or at least the public perception of it) to become one that embraced and emulated the Victorian "blue laws" enacted by the northeastern WASP elites who still dominated many local legislatures and who considered such laws crucial, particularly in the wake of increasing immigration and industrialization, to the preservation of their heritage and way of life.[72] Consistent with the prohibitionist wave then cresting in small towns throughout the Northeast and Midwest,[73] the National League upon its formation banned the sale of alcohol at league games.[74] In addition, it prohibited Sunday baseball and mandated that admission prices be kept high precisely to discourage and, in many cases prevent, attendance from lower-class fans.[75] In devising its admissions policy, the National League was simply emulating the more influential New York cricket clubs, which likewise had begun to charge admission to their matches a decade earlier for precisely the same reason.[76] Together, all of this resulted, in the opinion of Chicago owner Albert Spalding, in crowds "composed of the best class of people . . . and no theater, church, or place of amusement contains a finer class of people than can be found in our grandstands."[77]

In appealing to this increasingly smaller demographic, the National League ignored a potentially growing fan base as club owners went out of their way to make their games convenient for only a relatively privileged few to attend. They provided passes for prominent local citizens—businessmen, politicians, clergymen—in the hope that their attendance would lure other well-heeled citizens to consider taking in a game or two as well. They even went so far as telephoning some of their desired patrons to inform them of field conditions in an effort to nudge them out to the game. As a result of their rules and behavior, National League teams drew a largely male, middle-class crowd. All the while, there was, as a result of immigration, an increasing multitude of ethnics who did not share the Victorian distaste for alcohol or Sunday baseball and who might have had an interest in attending a game or several if it were convenient and affordable.[78] However, by design it was not hospitable, so they stayed away. Thus, just as concerned cricket officials were able to successfully weed out the working classes from their matches, so were the National League owners able to bar many of these same people from their games.[79] The brave owners who tried to buck their brethren and appeal to this potential fan base quickly felt their wrath and served as examples to the others not to step out of line. In 1881, in an effort to appeal to its increasingly large German population, the Cincinnati club persisted in selling beer and playing Sunday games in defiance of league rules. It was promptly expelled, its large German fan base apparently not the demographic the National League was hoping to attract.

Very quickly, owing to the elitist approach of the National League, rival leagues emerged, hoping to court the very fans who would have been National League fans if only they were wanted. In anticipation of the 1882 season, the American Association was formed as a workingman's counterpart to the National League. The association was created by two sportswriters from cities with large German populations—St. Louis and Cincinnati—whose teams were squeezed out of the National League because of its alcohol policy. The new league halved ticket prices (only twenty-five cents to attend an American Association game), sold alcohol, and permitted Sunday baseball to attract the blue-collar fans whose only day off was the one day baseball was forbidden within the NL.[80] Later, in 1883, the Union Association was formed along similar lines.[81] Initially, the National League responded as expected: by falling back upon the supposedly elite status of the National League as a means of denigrating the upstarts. NL club owners dubbed the American Association "The Beer and Whiskey Circuit," noted with derision that the Union Association was being floated with "beer money," and alleged that the league itself was "being run in the interests of brewers."[82] When these appeals to Victorian values failed, the American Association quickly began to outdraw the National League because of its presence in larger cities—after its inaugural season the NL ignored the nation's two largest cities at the time, New York and Philadelphia, until pressure from the rival leagues compelled it to expand into these markets in 1883. NL owners resorted to taking credit for their rivals' success. Making lemonade out of lemons, they claimed that, as trumpeted in the 1883 *Spalding's Guide* (published by Chicago owner Albert Spalding), such success merely owed to "the revival of the public confidence induced by the gradual establishment of honest professional play under the auspices of the National League."[83] Eventually, however, the National League realized that it had no choice but to make peace with its rivals to survive financially. In 1891 the National League and the American Association merged and formed an expanded National League. Critical to this merger was a loosening up of the league's Victorian policies: in the new National League, each city was free to determine its own Sunday baseball policy.[84]

Still, despite bringing the American Association into its fold, the National League clung to its elitist aspirations; however now, in its effort to reach the broader, more ethnically diverse fan base it previously ignored, and which its battles with the working-class leagues at last compelled the expanded NL to address (if not embrace), the prescriptive qualities of the game itself became the primary status markers. Hence, baseball as an educational, socializing, and acculturation tool was stressed more than ever. From now on, baseball as promoted by the NL owners would no longer be a game merely for gentlemen. Rather, it would be a game that could teach anyone at all to *become* a gentleman—a model American citizen inculcated with the bedrock values of the nation. This appeal to the WASP elites, of baseball as a gateway toward the moral principles inherent in the Victorian blue laws, and as club owners as gatekeepers of this "proper" way of American life (and fit for admittance into their restricted club) was coming, however, at a time when the elites' club doors were closing on outsiders more firmly than ever before. Before the Civil War, it was possible, although not common, for citizens of ethnic ancestry (such as the early German Jews) to gain entry into the upper echelons of WASP society. This was largely because there were relatively few such candidates for admission because of the relative trickle of immigration during the early part of the nineteenth century; the few ethnics who were able to accumulate wealth during this time were not considered a threat en masse to the dominant WASP society.[85] After the Civil War, with the uptick in immigration, this began to change. By the 1880s, with immigrants flooding the American borders, discrimination against all ethnic Americans became rigid and institutionalized as caste barriers sprang up around the increasingly threatened (and increasingly outnumbered) WASP elites. As the nation headed toward the twentieth century, although WASPs maintained their dominant leadership positions across the country, they were becoming less and less representative of the population as a whole. In addition, although as a group they did not see their wealth decline during this time, they were nevertheless becoming marginalized by the ever-increasing number of big-city industrialists and financiers whose wealth and power dwarfed theirs.[86] Accordingly, they felt threatened and closed ranks to protect themselves and their status. By the late 1800s, their closed caste excluded hyphenated Americans of all types.

To justify this increasingly rigid caste, the WASP elites naturally sought to align themselves with their wealthier brethren and against the teeming masses by falling back upon the social science of the mid-nineteenth century (developed and practiced almost exclusively by them, given their near monopoly on higher education) which, not surprisingly, validated their exalted societal rank. Following on the heels of Charles Darwin's *The Origin of Species By Means of Natural Selection, or the Preservation of Favored Races in the Struggle for Life* in 1859, the concept of social Darwinism (commonly attributed to Herbert Spencer, although his views were actually rooted more heavily in Enlightenment ideas of universal evolution rather than the more savage "survival of the fittest")[87] emerged post–Civil War as a means to justify class distinctions. At its core, social Darwinism, or at least the crude understanding of it as practiced by social scientists calling themselves "evolutionists," was a radical concept, striking at the heart of biblical theory, which revolved around the assumption of the unity of mankind and postulated that all men were descendents of Adam and therefore were all "equally brothers under the fatherhood of God." These social Darwinists, which many Western thinkers post-Darwin fancied themselves to be,[88] believed the opposite to be true: in the words of William Graham Sumner, America's leading social Darwinist and presumed disciple of Herbert Spencer, "the millionaires are a product of natural selection, acting on the whole body of men to pick out those who can meet the requirements of certain work to be done. . . . It is because they are thus selected that wealth—both their own and that entrusted to them—aggregates in their hands. They may fairly be regarded as the naturally selected agents of society for certain work. They get high wages and live in luxury but the bargain is a good one for society."[89] Indeed, Andrew Carnegie, perhaps Spencer's most ardent American protégé, argued as much through his theory of philanthropy: by funneling a portion of his wealth into charitable endeavors, men such as him "guaranteed the greatest good to the greatest number."[90] In the words of Baltzell, these evolutionists "were convinced that the Anglo-Saxon millionaires who ruled the nation in their day were the 'fittest' men in the world."[91]

As a group, the social Darwinists sympathized with various forms of racialist thinking. As such, they were also strict segregationists. Beginning in the 1870s, many American scientists drew from social Darwinist thought to justify separation of the races. Many neo-Darwinists believed that little good could come from interaction between whites and blacks and supported state efforts to compel both segregation as well as disenfranchisement of black citizens.[92] As the baseball club owners looked to emulate the WASP elites, who themselves were by now supporting many social Darwinist theories as a means of self preservation, it was perhaps inevitable that the National League would itself become stridently segregationist as well.

An offshoot of social Darwinism was the eugenics movement, founded in 1883 by Darwin's nephew, Francis Galton.[93] As a group interested in the biological consequences of social policy, they warned the social Darwinists that the "fittest" were not, in fact, surviving. Instead, "while millionaires were making money, morons were multiplying; modern medicine was preserving the unfit while modern war was sending the best to the front and keeping the worst at home; and, above all, the old-stock graduates of Harvard and Yale were being rapidly outbred by alien immigrants."[94] Supported by the WASP elites, they called for extreme curtailment of further immigration in an effort to protect even further erosion of the rapidly fading WASP-centered society; the Chinese Exclusion Act of 1882 being but one testament of their significant sway. Through all of this—social Darwinism, the "evolutionists," and the eugenics movement—nativism hardened as a core, impenetrable principle among the WASP elites. As outsiders, like the baseball "magnates," banged on their doors demanding entry, the WASP elites fortified their clubs by falling back on lineage as their last line of defense of privilege, with nativist clubs or "orders" soon sprouting up like dandelions. In 1883, the Sons of the Revolution formed; this was followed by the Daughters of the American Revolution, the Society of Mayflower Descendants, and the Aryan Order of St. George or the Holy Roman Empire in the Colonies of America, among many other nativist clubs. In fact, of the 105 "patriotic" nativist orders founded between 1783 and 1900, seventy-one were founded after 1870.[95] Genealogy also boomed during the last decades of the century. Amid the immigration surge, there was likewise a "patrician scramble for old-stock roots" in an effort to separate the established from the newly arrived. This scramble was, of course, "intimately bound up with anti-immigrant and anti-Semitic sentiments."[96]

It was in this environment that the National League owners, themselves in many cases the targets of these anti-immigrant, anti-Semitic sentiments, sought to gain entry into the upper echelon of American society through their baseball creed. However, they appeared to be up against a brick wall: while they were busy promoting their game, and therefore themselves, as authentically American, the WASP elites were busy arguing the opposite. Ironically, although on the surface it appeared as if the baseball creed was an attempt by the club owners to ingratiate themselves with the WASP elite, in fact the creed was a direct challenge to everything the elites stood for. For the prescriptive nature of the baseball creed preached the acquisition of American values through baseball; the social science of the era, as practiced by the social Darwinists and eugenicists, taught the converse: that such values were inherent in some and unattainable in others, and that it was heredity that mattered, not environment. By contradicting the predominant social science of the time, by challenging the values and assumptions of the WASP elites through their contention that, via the baseball creed, even the lowliest immigrant could be taught to be an upstanding, moral, American citizen, the club owners were taking a seemingly curious path toward acceptance by the WASP elites. However, not only was this perhaps the only avenue available to these Americans of newer stock, the creed too was the product of social science—a strain that very soon, because of the changing face of the nation, would become predominant.

THE BASEBALL CREED PREVAILS

In the end, the "magnates" and their baseball creed could not fail to emerge victorious in this clash of American societal theories. This was because the baseball creed was consistent with and grew out of a larger, emerging social scientific theory—a new social science—which would soon become predominant and was in keeping with the changes taking place in late-nineteenth and early twentieth-century America. As immigrants continued to pour over the borders, despite the protestations of the social Darwinists and eugenicists, America became much less homogenous and WASPish than ever before. Inevitably, the hereditarian view of human nature held increasingly little sway in an increasingly multicultural America. In fairness to the social Darwinists, most millionaires and societal leaders in William Sumner's time grew up in an America much more rural than it had by then become. In their youth, when society was small, controlled, and homogenous, heredity mattered, both on the farms and in the families who ran them. Good genes meant good livestock and good farmers from one generation to the next. In this world, good families prospered, bad ones went to seed. Social Darwinism not only justified these old-stock Americans' place atop the social hierarchy, it was consistent with their life experience.[97] As America grew more urban, these old rules and values no longer held sway.

The industrialized America of the late nineteenth century bore almost no resemblance to the rural or small-town America to which the WASP elites were tethered. The slums of the big cities were debilitating and the issues that arose out of them were far too complex and pressing to be ignored and blithely explained away through the vehicle of oversimplified elitist social theories. Social Darwinism thus became vulnerable in this increasingly urban, heterogeneous America. Inevitably, a new social science emerged that appealed to the burgeoning immigrant masses in that it explained their predicament and offered them a path toward advancement in their new country. Very soon, it vanquished social Darwinism and the eugenics movement, which would ultimately fall on their own swords with the rise of Adolph Hitler and the Third Reich.

The new social science—evolutionary environmentalism—was advanced by John Dewey (he preferred the term "instrumentalism") and focused on cultural environment as the key factor in achieving success. Diminishing the role of heredity, Dewey preached that education, as with most of the crucial skills in life, was a matter of experience rather than innate logic. One of his followers was Clarence Darrow, who neatly summarized the new social science's focus on environment over heredity when he said, "[a]sking how people grew up may make all men equal yet." This focus rapidly caught on (coming into its own by the turn of the century) given that it was compatible with the goals of the U.S. education system at the time, which was primarily focused on the task of assimilating the children of immigrants into mainstream American life.[98]

Increasingly, studies measuring the importance of cultural environment were produced that rebuked the social Darwinists by showing that it was environment, rather than the "natural" factors stressed by the social Darwinists and eugenicists, that primarily accounted for group differences. One study of army recruits during World War I famously showed that northern blacks clearly benefited from their superior cultural environment when they tested higher than white recruits from the poverty-stricken Deep South.[99] Other studies showing that environmental factors were primarily to blame for youthful lawlessness were also publicized. In 1910 and 1911, the anthropologist Franz Boas gave a series of lectures at Harvard where he discussed the result of his latest work, an anthropological study of immigrants, where he studied the physical changes in certain characteristics of immigrants and their children as their environment changed from Europe to the United States, and what this might suggest regarding cultural adaptability. His conclusions cut to the core of social Darwinism and the eugenics movement: "The adaptability of the immigrant seems to be much greater than we had a right to suppose before our investigations were instituted," he concluded.[100] Time and again, these studies demonstrated that inborn racial or ethnic traits were outweighed by environmental factors. In sum, it was cultural conditioning that lay at the heart of the evolutionary environmentalism movement and offered hope to those who were not born into privilege.

The baseball creed, with its overt claim of just the sort of cultural conditioning the new social scientists were preaching, fit neatly into this paradigm. In reaching out toward children and immigrants, offering baseball as a way to acculturate into mainstream American life, the creed, bolstered by evolutionary environmentalism, turned a spotlight on the owners that portrayed them as true, respectable, praiseworthy Americans after all. It was not out of the blue that people such as sportswriter Hugh Fullerton gushed that "[b]aseball, to my way of thinking, is the greatest single force working for Americanization. No other game appeals so much to the foreign-born youngsters and nothing, not even the schools, teaches the American spirit so quickly or inculcates the idea of sportsmanship or fair play as thoroughly."[101] Rather, these sentiments were simply in keeping with the emerging social science of the era. Because of the seamless fit between the baseball creed and evolutionary environmentalism, many Americans by the turn of the century saw baseball as an accurate reflection of contemporary society. To an increasing number of them, nothing more than baseball spoke to and of the nation. That baseball and America were, by the early part of the twentieth century, gloriously entangled was summed up by Albert Spalding in 1911 when he concluded that the connection was obvious: it was like saying "two plus two equals four."[102] If baseball had become "America's game"—a vessel through which the soul of the nation could be found—then the owners had wisely positioned themselves as the gatekeepers of this source of discovery. It was no coincidence that baseball came of age at the precise moment when the new social science bloomed across the nation; the two were intertwined.

It was likewise no coincidence that in both the new social science and the baseball creed the emphasis was the same: faith in reform through environmental improvements. This was compatible with the aspirations of the increasingly large number of urban immigrants of non-WASP ancestry. Both evolutionary environmentalism and the baseball creed supported and rationalized these minority groups' search for acceptance and respectability. Both served the interests of the downtrodden (especially immigrants struggling to assimilate) by attributing differences to malleable factors such as cultural surroundings rather than immutable ones such as race or ethnicity. Both gave hope to these people by stressing that they could indeed rise through the hierarchy of American society and could, if they were able to improve their environment, realize the American Dream. In all of this, both stood firmly on the side of the future; social Darwinism and the eugenics movement were firmly rooted in the past.

As it became more widespread and accepted, the baseball creed was likewise forced upon, cruelly enough, even those who harbored few wishes to assimilate into the dominant culture. Perhaps inevitably, its rhetoric, infused as it was with the foundational principles of evolutionary environmentalism, gained much traction as well with those who believed in the forced cultural assimilation of Native Americans in the late nineteenth and early twentieth centuries. Indeed, Richard Henry Pratt, the founder of the Carlisle Indian Industrial School in 1879, was a proponent of the creed and believed baseball to be instrumental to achieving his goal of "civiliz-

ing" his Native American students.[103] Not unlike his British forbears in
the Caribbean and India, Pratt—substituting baseball for cricket—used
the game to enforce his lessons regarding the dominant white culture,
urging his students to "pitch in and learn to play!"[104] In addition to the
cultural whitewashing his Carlisle school practiced in its formal curriculum
(which among other things mandated haircuts, school uniforms in an effort to separate the students from their native clothes and jewelry, and
the repression of indigenous languages),[105] baseball was added to the mix
in 1886—four years before its more famous football program began in-
tercollegiate play—and quickly became another tool in furtherance of the
school's assimilationist policy. Significantly, the team wore uniforms with
the initials C.I.T.S. stitched on the fronts, initials that technically stood
for "Carlisle Indian Training School" but also suggested the word "citizen."
Pratt was very clear in pointing out that this was not a coincidence: "See
how near that (C.I.T.S.) comes to being an abbreviation of 'citizens,' which
they all are aspiring to become?"[106] For better or worse, the baseball creed
very quickly became ingrained within mainstream American culture.

As American society grew more heterogeneous and as the old-stock
WASP elites became less representative of the population as a whole, their
influence began to wane. Not all retreated to their exclusive country clubs,
but their presence in public life and their status as elite cultural scions,
although still significant, was hardly the virtual stranglehold it once had
been. Meanwhile, the rise of Adolph Hitler and the Nazi Party during the
1930s, with their emphasis on a "master race" and extermination of supposed genetic inferiors, ended forever the debate between the new social
science and the old. In Nazi Germany, social Darwinism and eugenics
were being practiced in their most extreme, most horrifying form. As a
result, practically all Western thinkers outside Hitler's sphere of influence soon discarded any sympathy or attraction they may have previously
had to these theories. Scholarship treading in these areas was no longer
recognized as legitimate; the debate was over.[107] The new social science
was now overwhelmingly accepted (although within it there were, and
always would be, disagreements between various threads). In the end,
the owners—societal outsiders throughout the mid- and late nineteenth
century—were able to elevate their game and, ultimately, themselves just
as they had hoped. Through the ceaseless promotion of the game through

the baseball creed, and its convergence with the emerging social science of the time, the owners' dreams had been realized.

Ironically, it was most likely the failure of these late-nineteenth and early twentieth-century owners to thoroughly convince the public that they were indeed noblemen that finally led them to achieve the status they so desperately sought. Although they preened and called themselves "magnates," most people recognized men such as department store and Cincinnati owner John Brush, meatpacking "moguls" and Washington Nationals owners George and J. Earl Wagner, streetcar developers and Cleveland Spiders owners Frank and Stanley Robison, as well as the numerous billiard parlor operators, saloon keepers, theater owners, and the like (many of them Germans, Jews, and other ethnics) who likewise invested in National League clubs for what they were.[108] As such, and perhaps to the club owners' initial consternation, much of the public saw right through their boasts. However, in a changing society, this was to their benefit. For in the owners, many Americans did not see a class of men blessed with privilege from birth but rather, something of themselves—men from hardscrabble pasts who demonstrated the social mobility possible in this land of opportunity. In short, they were precisely the sort of self-made men envisioned through the hopeful ethos of the baseball creed.

By their very presence, the club owners suggested that the creed and evolutionary environmentalism were more than just theories. In many ways, they were the real-life incarnations of the Horatio Alger "rags to riches" stories that had become increasingly popular during the Progressive Era.[109] This would be somewhat ironic in that the Alger stories embraced the small-town WASP ethos that most assuredly took a dim view of evolutionary environmentalism. However, their overriding message of indomitable hope for the hopeless spoke (most likely unintentionally) to many who otherwise may have been predisposed to be hopeless themselves.[110] All of this inured to the benefit of the club owners who, in retrospect, should not have been surprised to find themselves tethered to a strand of WASP culture, given that they had spent many years doing all they could to emulate it.

Their good fortune was not all of their own doing, however. Had the country's first adopters of cricket—the WASP elites—felt less status anxiety and more secure in their sense of place within American society, they may very well have shared their game with the nation, and perhaps cricket rather than baseball would have evolved into a national metaphor here as it has in other countries of British origin.[111] That they kept their game to themselves opened the door to a new game, one promoted by people seeking status and power rather than fearful of losing it, and one that came packaged with a rhetoric designed to help them achieve it. This rhetoric resonated with a country in transition—one with millions of new citizens who were strangers in a strange land looking for something to guide them, something to grab hold of, in their effort to become, at last, "Americans." It was on the backs of these people that the club owners were able to elevate their game and, in turn, their own status to the point where baseball became more than just a game but symbolic of America as a whole. The baseball creed would be the first widely embraced, culturally affirming story of baseball; it would hardly be the last.

THE SOVEREIGN NATION OF BASEBALL

Having achieved the status they so longed for, the baseball "magnates" relished every opportunity afforded them to demonstrate the superiority of their game and, as a natural extension, themselves. As they were to discover, once they finally kicked the door down and established their game as a metaphor of America, there was seemingly no end to the institutions looking to glom on to them, much as they once tugged on the coattails of the WASP elites. All manner of establishments were eager to defer to baseball, to exalt it, to revel in the overt patriotism of the game as a way of either defining themselves or proving their nationalistic mettle. Throughout the twentieth century, among the game's ardent cheerleaders were the federal judiciary and legislature, which, either through admiration or fear, repeatedly refused to challenge the superiority of baseball, much as they cowered from other powerful institutions. In time, the game (although not the players[1]) would become beholden to no one—a grim reality that, many decades hence, led to a seemingly inevitable debacle involving the game's newly crowned all-time home run king where, through the illusion of baseball as subject to the rule of law, the reality of its independence from it was only confirmed once again.[2] As far as the game was concerned, this was troubling enough; metaphorically speaking, the baseball debacle spoke of America here too, albeit this time of a nation miles removed from the sunny portrait painted by the baseball creed.

THE ROOTS OF MLB'S EXTRALEGAL AUTHORITY

Thanks to the hard work of the club owners and their attendant journalists, it was not long before the message of the baseball creed permeated the national culture so deeply that, by the era of the Black Sox scandal, a philosopher could express the sentiment of baseball as America without fear of serious rebuke: "I know full well that baseball is a boy's game, and a professional sport, and that a properly cultured, serious person always feels like apologizing for attending a baseball game instead of a Strauss concert, or a lecture on the customs of the Fiji Islands. But I still maintain that, by all the canons of our modern books on comparative religions, baseball is a religion, and the only one that is not sectarian but national."[3] As the self-appointed caretakers of this national religion, the owners of Major League ball clubs were thus accorded a responsibility and therefore an authority higher than that of mere law. Pursuant to this hierarchy, and as became clear in the aftermath of the Black Sox scandal, the courts may have had the dirty job of keeping the masses in line but it was baseball that saw to it that they were inculcated with the appropriate American values.[4]

Of course, that the baseball creed was little more than a cultural fiction (there has always been a substantial disparity between the ideology of the game and its realities) was irrelevant. The entrepreneurs who founded the National League did not, after all, prevent gambling, game fixing, and the other vices that existed beforehand. Regardless, the ideology impacted how people viewed the game—it was of little matter that the creed was sheer fantasy. By the second decade of the twentieth century, however, the disparities between the myth and reality of the game were exposed to the extent that the creed was jeopardized. The revelation of this disparity tested the metaphor of baseball as America and, ironically, resulted in an even more greatly elevated status of the game within American society.

For a while at least, despite the owners' inability to rid the game of gambling and gossip of game fixing, the cultural fiction of the baseball creed remained dominant as rumors of impropriety remained just that because of baseball's hesitance to investigate them. And if it was hesitant to confront these rumors directly, it certainly was unwilling to turn to the law to investigate and potentially punish its players. Consequently, players of "doubtful loyalty" were tolerated and continued to play Major League ball from one year to the next out of fear that exposure would damage the creed irreparably, resulting in a loss of societal status for the "magnates" who owned the teams and who had appointed themselves the gatekeepers of America's national image.[5] Rather than focus on all that potentially tarnished the game, the club owners did as they and their predecessors had always done and drew attention instead to all that affirmed their position as guardians of the small-town and agrarian values that were routinely served up as antidotes to the evils of the big cities and (ironically, as it turned out) the monopolists who thrived within them. Even the stadium construction boom of the early twentieth century offered the club owners ample opportunity to display their village bona fides. Besides the obvious amenities offered up by stadiums such as Shibe Park, Ebbets Field, Comiskey Park, and others, the stadiums were in keeping with the WASP sentiment of promoting rural values as a cure-all for perceived urban ills. Just as numerous cities were busily constructing planned parks, pools, and other approximations of "civilized" rural life within their boundaries, the new baseball "parks" and "fields" were likewise paeans to the virtue and morality of agrarian life, and many owners were not shy in promoting them as such. Offering vast expanses of uninterrupted greenery, they served as concrete- and steel-encased civics lessons amid the cacophony of big-city life and, in the words of one historian, "sign[s] of how rural virtues could redeem the excesses of the city."[6]

Eventually, and despite the romance and mythic virtue of their stadiums, the club owners had no choice but to confront the problems facing their game as rumors of fixes grew louder in the early part of the twentieth century. Even prior to the Black Sox scandal of 1919, rumors abounded. Shortly before the infamous World Series contest between the Cincinnati Reds and the Chicago White Sox that season, reports surfaced that two of the greatest stars of the game—Ty Cobb and Tris Speaker—conspired to fix a Detroit victory over Cleveland in an otherwise meaningless game.[7] Predictably, these reports were ignored. When, however, a few weeks later rumors began spreading that the World Series itself was fixed, tarring the pinnacle moment of celebration of America's "civil religion," baseball was, reluctantly, goaded into action.[8] Its response would cement its status as a de facto sovereign entity.

For months, the owners refused to investigate rumors that Chicago had conspired to throw the Series to Cincinnati.[9] It is likely that they would have been successful in stonewalling any investigation of the Series were it not for the tenacity of Hugh Fullerton, a sportswriter who clearly was not beholden to the game's ownership cabal (at least in this instance).[10] Fullerton covered the Series and grew increasingly suspicious as the games progressed. Later, as the rumors persisted, he pressed owners to take action to investigate the allegations, to no avail. He tried to publicly admonish the owners for their inaction through the media but found himself stonewalled when Chicago's largest newspaper—the *Chicago Herald-Examiner*—refused to run his stories, partly out of concern that challenging baseball's pristine status would hurt newspaper sales.[11] Eventually, Fullerton found an outlet for his stories and used it to apply pressure on the owners, contending that the image of the game had been sullied by the rumors and that unless the allegations were investigated, this would continue to be the case.[12] Still, he was ignored. Finally, he pressed the button that brought action, alleging that it was the status of the owners themselves that was at stake. Discussing the diminishing stature of the game, Fullerton asserted that, "fault for this condition lies primarily with the owners. Their commercialism is directly responsible for the same spirit among the athletes and their failure to punish even the appearance of evil has led to the present situation, for the entire scandal could have been prevented and the future of the game made safe by drastic action . . ."[13] For a time, they still refused to act, collectively rebutting his allegations as "improbable muckraking."[14] Eventually, however, the owners realized that they had no choice but to do something to protect the sanctity of the cultural fiction of the baseball creed.

In a grand gesture, AL president Ban Johnson publicly proclaimed that he was providing $10,000 in league funds and hiring two "special prosecutors" to investigate Fullerton's allegations, actions that were permissible under an Illinois statute that allowed interested private parties to intervene and assist in the criminal prosecution of certain cases.[15] Soon the Illinois State Attorney's Office indicted eight members of the White Sox and five reputed gamblers for conspiring to fix the 1919 World Series.[16] With the nexus of baseball and the American legal system now at hand, MLB owners recognized the reality that they needed to take bold and affirmative action to protect the game's image or risk losing control of it altogether while the game was knocked from its pedestal and treated just like any other nefarious business. The Black Sox scandal was merely the tip of the iceberg: if even a few of the numerous other rumors of game fixing were exposed through investigations by state and local prosecutors, the game's sacred status would be tarnished forever.

Upon Fullerton's urging, the owners dissolved the league's "National Commission"—a structurally weak tripartite body that ostensibly ruled the game—and replaced it with a powerful, autocratic commissioner.[17] To fill this position, they likewise followed Fullerton's recommendation and hired Kenesaw Mountain Landis—a longtime friend of the owners who demonstrated his fealty in 1914 when, as a federal judge, he presided over but refused to rule on the Federal League's antitrust suit against the National and American leagues, choosing instead to wait out the Federal League until it had virtually exhausted itself out of existence.[18] His public persona fit the role for which it was designed—protector of the American way of life—in that he had gained the reputation as a "hanging judge" who was not intimidated by powerful people or institutions.[19] Judge Landis famously fined Standard Oil a whopping $29,240,000 for antitrust violations (which was overturned, as were many of his rulings, on appeal),[20] challenged the authority of labor leader Big Bill Haywood,[21] and even tried to exercise jurisdiction over Kaiser Wilhelm I for Germany's sinking of the *Lusitania*.[22] He looked the part as well; with his shock of white hair and perpetual sneer, he had "the visage of an Old Testament prophet who ha[d] looked around and [was] not amused by what he'[d] seen."[23] And of course there was the name itself: rock solid, larger than life.[24] Not surprisingly, he was a proponent of the baseball creed, having remarked at one point that "[b]aseball is something more than a game to an American boy; it is his training for life work. Destroy his faith in its squareness and honesty and you have destroyed something more; you have planted suspicion of all things in his heart."[25] In Landis, the owners found the image necessary to elevate the game above the mundane once more.

Landis was not so easily convinced to accept the position, however. Perhaps taking into account the numerous times he had been reversed upon appeal, he was unwilling to accept such humiliations anymore, insisting that he would only take on the role if he were granted absolute power, answerable to no one either within or outside Major League Baseball.[26] Despite the owners' assurances that he would have this power, he refused to accept the job until a new Major League Agreement was drafted, one that cemented his authority and insulated him from the vagaries of the appellate process.[27] Left with no choice, the owners eventually relented and ceded the authority to him that he demanded.[28] With that, Landis stepped into his new role and proceeded to remove the stain upon the national pastime's image.

Although acting in his official capacity as the game's protector, Landis's investigation into gambling and game fixing within baseball was exceedingly limited in scope. Rather than tackling the numerous rumors that swirled around the game, Landis chose to investigate the alleged World Series fix only, proceeding on the "single sin myth" that the 1919 fix was the only instance of foul play within the game.[29] In this way, he could rather easily restore the game's image: simply punish the lone transgressors and return baseball to its lofty perch.[30] The potential morass involved in investigating the culture of corruption that led to the 1919 fix would be avoided because of its unwieldy nature. Very quickly, it became clear that Landis was out to "solve" the scandal rather than address the underlying problems that led to it, and to return the game to its elevated status as quickly as possible. In this way, he reasserted the cultural fiction of the baseball creed, evidence to the contrary be damned, that nevertheless was prevalent before Hugh Fullerton intervened and exposed it as myth. He was aided in this regard by the new Major League Agreement he had insisted upon as a condition for taking the position. Soon, through his handling of the Black Sox scandal as well as his indifference to other, similar allegations, he accomplished what the owners had set out to do when they hired him—return baseball to its elevated plane, immune from the reach of the law.

At Landis's urging, the finalized Major League Agreement bestowed unparalleled power in the hands of one man: Landis was to be the final arbiter of disputes between leagues, clubs, and players, the determinant of punishment for any conduct he deemed contrary to the best interests of the game, and the arbiter of disagreements over proposed amendments to league rules.[31] In a catchall provision he invoked numerous times throughout his tenure, and that provided authority for virtually any action he wished to take, the agreement permitted him "to take other steps as he might deem necessary and proper in the interest and morale of the players and the honor of the game."[32] And perhaps most important (and most indicative of the owners' desperation for the moral salvation of their game), the owners expressly waived any rights to challenge Landis's rulings in court, "no matter what would be the severity of the new Commissioner's discipline."[33] Taken together, the agreement anointed Landis with "autocratic power over everyone in baseball, from the humblest bat boy to a major league president."[34] Through the powers inherent within the 1921 Major League Agreement, Landis ruled from a perch high above the judicial branch. In this way, he was able to both restore public confidence in the game and diminish the role of the legal system in baseball's affairs all at once, which was a point he was not shy about making. "Just keep in mind," he once said, "that regardless of the verdict of juries, baseball is entirely competent to protect itself against the crooks both inside and outside the game."[35]

Landis wielded his power from the moment he assumed his new role. On August 2, 1921, the eight indicted players and five indicted gamblers were acquitted by a jury of all charges.[36] Despite the jubilation that erupted in the courtroom and of baseball fans across the nation, relieved that their heroes had been cleared of all wrongdoing, Landis was unmoved. The next day he asserted baseball's superior moral authority by banishing all eight players from the game anyway. Irrespective of the verdict, he proclaimed that "no player who throws a ball game, no player that sits in conference with a bunch of crooked players and gamblers where the ways and means of throwing a game are discussed, and does not promptly tell his club about it, will ever play professional baseball." In his newly appointed role as the moral conscience of the national pastime, Landis did not need to investigate the allegations on his own, nor preside over a hearing to reach his verdict. Rather, his job was to administer a "character bath" to the game, regardless of the vagaries of the legal system. In this he was widely hailed. By banishing the Black Sox, he effectively, in the words of one baseball historian, "reaffirmed professional baseball's position as a respectable social institution whose ethical standards were demonstrably superior to those of the law."[37] By staying true to his reputation as a jurist who administered "tough justice," his decision signaled the return of integrity to America's game. He took the law into his own hands and administered what many believed to be justice, regardless of the jury's verdict. In the end, to many Americans, truth had prevailed even though the law did not. The Black Sox may have been found innocent within the world of law, but Landis insisted that they face judgment in a higher court—his. In the process, the extralegal and sovereign authority of Major League Baseball had been firmly established. Landis's punishment of the Black Sox set the precedent for his tenure as commissioner, where he ruled not with a sword of justice but with an "extra-legal scythe" to be used at his pleasure and whim.[38] This was particularly true given the reality that, regardless of his actions, there was nothing anyone within MLB could do to check him—the owners had forfeited their right to access to the courts in the 1921 agreement.

A few years after the Black Sox scandal, Landis once again wielded his scythe in an effort to protect MLB's position as an institution with its own system of justice, separate and apart from that of federal law. In 1926, two members of the banned Black Sox alleged that a series of games between the White Sox and the Detroit Tigers in 1917 had likewise been fixed.[39] In fact, Landis had been made aware of this accusation four years earlier, in 1922, but chose to ignore it to protect the integrity of the "single sin myth" surrounding the 1919 World Series.[40] Now, however, with the accusation aired in public, Landis was forced into action. He held a series of "hearings" over the course of several days, where he served not only as judge but as prosecutor, defense attorney, and jury as well.[41] Landis permitted oral testimony only and refused to call independent witnesses or release publicly the detailed descriptions of the games in question, which would have revealed a suspicious pattern of play. (All that was made available for public consumption were the previously released box scores, which, by themselves, revealed little beyond the games' bare facts.)[42] He also treated the witnesses for the prosecution and defense differently: he required the testimony of the accusers to take place in the presence of the defense witnesses, who could then mold their subsequent testimony to rebut what they had just heard; the accusers, however, were permitted only sporadic opportunities to likewise respond to contrary testimony. In addition, although Landis encouraged the exposure of inconsistencies in the accusers' testimony through this procedure, he failed to follow up on likely misleading or inconsistent testimony presented by the defense witnesses. In the end, there was only one verdict that was possible—the verdict Landis orchestrated through his actions in organizing and presiding over the hearing. The players were exonerated and the single sin myth remained intact. Most important, the accusation was "resolved" by MLB itself, quickly and emphatically, before the legal system had time to intervene. In his handling of this affair, Landis made sure that he provided closure to the episode; there would be no replay of the Black Sox trial in open court, subject once again to the whim of juries and the requirements of due process.

Around the same time, Landis was confronted with yet another scandal, this one involving two of the greatest stars of the game. And once again, he administered "baseball justice" in an effort to maintain jurisdiction for misdeeds within the game in-house rather than in court. In 1926, the rumors of game fixing by Ty Cobb and Tris Speaker, which briefly surfaced in 1919 shortly after the games in question were played, reemerged.[43] Coming on the heels of the Detroit-Chicago "hearings," Landis once again had no choice but to take action. And once again he did so both swiftly and with finality. Two weeks after exonerating the Tigers and the White Sox, he did the same to both Cobb and Speaker. This time, however, he convened no hearings, heard no testimony, considered no evidence. Once again, he refused to release the game descriptions to the public, some of which hinted at the possibility that the game in question appeared to be proceeding in curious fashion. In issuing his ruling, and in tacit recognition that there was more to the matter than he was otherwise letting on, Landis proclaimed that although Cobb and Speaker were cleared of any wrongdoing, they nevertheless were to play for different teams in the upcoming season if they wished to continue to play Major League baseball.

The lack of consistency in Landis's rulings, as exposed through his handling of the three game-fixing scandals, indicated his desire to mold his verdicts to whatever he determined beforehand best protected the image of America's game. For instance, he expelled Buck Weaver of the Black Sox for merely having knowledge of the fix (there was no evidence that he took money or participated in it) in his effort to "cleanse" the game. However, he exonerated both Cobb and Speaker, who even if they did not participate in a fix of the game in question, at a minimum had knowledge of an attempt to do so, because exonerating them would protect the image of a game that had presumptively already been cleansed.[44] Landis massaged investigations, or refused to even conduct them, to ensure that his actions uniformly resulted in verdicts that exalted baseball, not in ones that damaged its reputation. In his twenty-four years in office, Landis banned thirteen men for various "crimes" committed against baseball.[45] He likewise fined numerous others for sins such as offensive language, barnstorming (exhibition tours) in the offseason, and other similar offenses.[46] All of this was done with a singular goal: to present a facade of a pristine, all-American game that jibed with the cultural fiction of the baseball creed. In so doing, and in reassuring the public that "a firm patriarchal hand of justice ruled over the nation's pastime," its societal role as an elevated, sovereign institution remained firmly intact.[47]

JUDICIAL ACKNOWLEDGMENT OF
THE EXTRALEGAL AUTHORITY OF MLB

The federal judiciary and legislature have historically been all too eager to play into this fiction, deferring to MLB and its "law of baseball" whenever possible, allowing it to manage its own affairs without fear of judicial or congressional oversight. Baseball's antitrust exemption is perhaps the most cited example of this phenomenon, but although the Supreme Court's subsequent refusal through the years to acknowledge the obvious—that at its core, Major League Baseball is a business no different than an ordinary shirt factory—is representative of the judicial hands-off treatment of our national pastime, the 1922 case that created the exemption (*Federal Baseball Club of Baltimore v. National League of Professional Baseball Clubs*[48]) was perhaps much less so. For, in many respects, *Federal Baseball* was very much a product of its time, although the national reverence for baseball also seems to have played at least a supporting role in the outcome of the case at both the circuit and Supreme Court levels.[49]

By way of brief background, Major League Baseball found itself before the justices as a result of its battle with a potential rival, the Federal

League, although at its founding in 1913, the Federal League claimed to be nothing of the sort. A year later, however, it expanded and, seemingly flush with capital, declared itself a third major league, a putative equal of the National and American. It sought fans as well as talent from its more established rivals and refused to honor the reserve clause—a unilaterally imposed term inserted in all MLB player contracts that bound each player to his team indefinitely. Instead, the Federal League used as its strategy the lure of larger salaries to entice National and American League players to abandon their contracts and jump leagues. The result was inevitable: despite the presence of the reserve clause, Major League player salaries increased rapidly as the established owners attempted to ward off the threat. By the close of the 1915 season, the by now clearly underfunded Federal League was buckling under the weight of the salary war it started. By December 1915, the Federal League was all but defunct: several of the Federal League owners had sued Major League Baseball and had accepted buyouts, while others were permitted to buy Major League franchises. The Baltimore Federal League club, however, opted out of the settlement (or was not invited to the settlement meeting, the record is not clear). The other Federal League owners subsequently attempted to settle with Baltimore but the club refused, choosing instead to sue Major League Baseball (among others) in federal court.

Technically, the Baltimore club filed suit under Section 4 of the Clayton Act, which was enacted in 1914 as a complement to the Sherman Antitrust Act. In its pleadings, Baltimore alleged that the defendants violated the act by monopolizing talent and restraining trade. At the trial level, Baltimore emerged victorious when the judge instructed the jury that the defendants engaged in interstate commerce and that, through the reserve clause en-forced through MLB's National Agreement (which in relevant part bound all MLB teams to honor each other's contracts), they violated the relevant portions of the Clayton Act. As such, the only question for the jury was one focusing on damages. The jury found that the Baltimore franchise suffered damages in the amount of $80,000 which, when trebled pursu-ant to Section 4 of the Clayton Act, amounted to a verdict of $240,000 in favor of the Baltimore club, plus counsel fees. Major League Baseball appealed the verdict to the District of Columbia Circuit Court of Appeals, which reversed the trial court's decision and set up the showdown at the

Supreme Court. In essence, the D.C. circuit court held that Major League Baseball did not engage in interstate commerce and, therefore, its actions could not be regulated by way of either the Sherman or Clayton acts. This time, it was Baltimore's turn to appeal, which it did, and which led to the now infamous *Federal Baseball* decision.

In *Federal Baseball,* the Supreme Court, in an opinion authored by Oliver Wendell Holmes, solidified MLB's antitrust exemption in 1922 that the D.C. Circuit court had created a year earlier. In all of one paragraph, Justice Holmes dismissed the business of Major League Baseball as "purely state affairs." Although he acknowledged that state lines were crossed in the giving of "exhibitions of base ball" and that money changed hands pursuant to these exhibitions, Justice Holmes nevertheless held that "transport is a mere incident, not the essential thing." Thus, baseball could not be considered interstate commerce and, as a result, could not be subject to federal antitrust law, which applies only to "commerce among the [several] states." Although this opinion has been almost universally derided by legal as well as baseball scholars, it was in fact hardly the outlier many have argued it to be. Instead, it was in many respects in keeping with both the political and judicial philosophy toward both trusts and the Sherman Antitrust Act (all rhetoric notwithstanding) at the time.

Despite national fervor over the ominous presence of large trusts in the latter half of the nineteenth century (as well as the growing national distaste for the magnates who controlled them, as discussed within chapter 1), the Sherman Antitrust Act itself was initially considered little more than a ceremonial concession to this growing national unease. Something had to be done on the political level to respond, at least superficially, to the outcry, and so the Sherman Antitrust Act was passed, although few governmental officials viewed it as a legitimate or even necessary check. Despite his reputation as a "trust buster," Teddy Roosevelt in fact held a rather generous view of most of them, considering all but the most obviously insidious a necessary function of a modern economy. "The man who advocates destroying the trusts by measures which would paralyze the industries of the country is at least a quack and at worst an enemy to the Republic," he remarked early in his presidency.[50] As such, he, not unlike many within positions of power during the era, was not looking for excuses to bring down trusts or break up monopolies. Instead, Roosevelt made, or at least attempted to make, distinctions between what he considered "good" and "bad" trusts. As he believed that trusts and monopolies themselves were not "bad" by definition, he limited the staffing of the Antitrust Division of the Department of Justice to a mere five attorneys with an annual budget of $100,000. In the words of historian Richard Hofstadter: "By definition, since only a handful of suits could be undertaken each year, there could hardly be very many 'bad' businesses. Such was the situation as T.R. left it during his presidency."[51] In sum, pursuant to Roosevelt's logic, because the burgeoning modern American economy could not be inherently "bad," neither could there be many inherently "bad" trusts. Enforcement against the few bad apples pursuant to the Sherman Antitrust Act would be the exception rather than the rule, his trust-busting reputation notwithstanding.

By the second decade of the twentieth century and into the era encapsulating the *Federal Baseball* decision, the White House's view of trusts had not evolved very much. President Woodrow Wilson exchanged Roosevelt's rudimentary definitions of "good" and "bad" trusts for the only slightly less rudimentary concepts of "free" and "illicit" competition, with "free" competition resulting in increased "efficiencies" and "illicit" competition resulting in unwanted inefficiencies. Like Roosevelt, Wilson believed in the necessity and inevitability of modern trusts: "the elaboration of business upon a great co-operative scale is characteristic of our time and has come about by the natural operation of modern civilization . . . we shall never return to the old order of individual competition . . ."[52] As for what distinguished an efficient from an inefficient trust, no one knew for sure. In practice, it seemed as if, nomenclature aside, Wilson was still operating on the level of Roosevelt's playing field of "good" and "bad" trusts. And within such a framework, many trusts and monopolies would be left unchecked by the Sherman Antitrust Act.

Not surprisingly within this environment, by the early 1920s a majority of the Supreme Court (whose members after all are nominated by the president) felt similarly, although they expressed their beliefs in more technical language. Of course, each justice had his own view on the matter and some justices were more wary of trusts than others, but as a whole, the Court was hesitant to check them. Justice Holmes, the author of the *Federal Baseball* decision, viewed the Sherman Antitrust Act with condescension, once remarking privately that it was "a humbug based on economic ignorance and incompetence."[53] Though his fellow justices may not have shared the extremity of his disdain, the test the Court fashioned during this era was one that resulted in many trusts and monopolies being held to exist outside the scope of federal antitrust laws. Unless the trust had a significant impact on interstate commerce, it would be allowed to stand; a mere incidental impact would not be sufficient.[54] This was consistent with the Court's more fundamental position that Congress' power to legislate pursuant to the Constitution's commerce clause was rather limited—a view that evolved significantly in later years. This test was perhaps rooted in the basic belief at the time that, as a general principle, trusts and monopolies were only "bad" (to use Roosevelt's term) when they significantly impacted local autonomy.[55] If they had only an incidental or indirect affect on it, they were not inherently odious and were as such beyond Congress' grasp.

Within this political and legal setting, *Federal Baseball* fit in neatly. Major League Baseball's trust (which resulted in this instance in the reserve clause that was at the center of the dispute between the parties) clearly met Roosevelt's rudimentary test as, even in the wake of the Black Sox scandal involving the fix of the 1919 World Series, baseball—America's game—could be nothing other than a "good" trust. (Popular sentiment at the time blamed the players and/or outside gambling influences rather than White Sox owner Charles Comiskey for the fix.) And it most likely would pass muster under Wilson's "efficiency" test as well, because the circuit court found persuasive the owners' argument that without the reserve clause, competitive balance within Major League Baseball would be ruined.[56] Likewise, as the owners argued and the circuit and Supreme Court agreed, the baseball trust not only did not threaten local autonomy, it complemented and contributed to it. As the circuit court noted, the game of Major League Baseball "is local in its beginning and in its end."[57] Without the trust, so the theory went, the local presentations of "exhibitions of baseball" (to use the court's terminology) would be impossible. The choice of language by first the circuit and later the Supreme Court was most likely not accidental: by repeatedly referring to the subject of the litigation as "exhibitions" of baseball, rather than the "business" or "industry" of baseball, both courts were clearly signaling that such events— mere exhibitions—could have nothing more than an incidental effect on interstate commerce. Certainly, the cultural significance of baseball played an important role in the courts' rulings. However, once the issue before the judges and justices was framed through the lens of baseball as a game rather than as a business (a choice that likewise owed much to the game's societal standing), the resulting decisions were far from aberrations.

The *Federal Baseball* decision developed into an aberration, however, through the passage of time, which saw Congress' power to act pursuant to the commerce clause broaden considerably, thus rendering Justice Holmes's logic quaint and antiquated. And it was all but officially labeled a dinosaur as a result of the Second Circuit's 1949 decision involving New York Giants player Danny Gardella.[58] Gardella, an outfielder who bickered with team management over his 1946 contract, eventually jumped to the rival Mexican League—a move that prompted Commissioner Landis's replacement, Happy Chandler, to impose a five-year ban on Gardella as well as twenty-two other players who similarly signed contracts with the Mexican League.[59] When Gardella attempted to return to MLB, he found himself blacklisted. He sued MLB for reinstatement and his case was thrown out at the trial level. On appeal, however, the Second Circuit remanded the case back to the trial level for a determination of whether baseball had developed into interstate commerce in the twenty-seven years since the *Federal Baseball* decision.[60] If the language of Judge Jerome Frank in his concurring opinion was any indication, the answer was obvious. In his concurrence, Frank took note of the "steadily expanding content of the phrase 'interstate commerce' in recent years," and concluded that the sweeping expansion of the term had rendered *Federal Baseball* "an impotent zombi."[61]

Four years later, however, when presented with the case of *Toolson v. New York Yankees*,[62] the Supreme Court ignored the Second Circuit's reasoning and refused to bring the business of baseball into the modern era. It was here, rather than in the more popularly derided *Federal Baseball* decision, where the Court more clearly embraced the special, some would even say "mythic," status of baseball and held, in a one paragraph per curiam decision, that irrespective of the law and common sense, it was not going to intervene in the business of baseball. Instead, it deferred to it and tossed this hot potato over to Congress by announcing that it was up to the legislature to bring Major League Baseball into compliance with the federal antitrust laws if it so chose.

The Court finally admitted the obvious in its 1972 decision in *Flood v. Kuhn*,[63] concluding that the rationale underpinning the *Federal Baseball* decision no longer applied, but to little matter. For although it announced that Major League Baseball was indeed a business engaged in interstate commerce, it nevertheless refused to overturn the decision and render the Sherman Antitrust Act applicable to it.[64] Instead, in a telling passage, the Court held that the *Federal Baseball* and *Toolson* decisions were "aberration[s] confined to baseball."[65] In *Flood* the Court acknowledged what it had hinted at nineteen years earlier in *Toolson*—that baseball was special; that at least some of the laws applicable to the majority of society simply were inexplicably inapplicable to our national pastime. The antitrust exemption was one way of acknowledging this reality but there were others for those willing to look for them.

Briefly, *Flood* involved an attempt by star St. Louis Cardinals outfielder Curt Flood to refuse a trade to the Phillies. In essence, his argument, like the ones in *Federal Baseball* and *Toolson* beforehand, focused on the anticompetitive nature of baseball's reserve clause which, in this instance, prevented him from becoming a free agent and compelled him to acquiesce to the trade. Flood argued that the clause violated the Sherman Antitrust Act and, as such, was illegal. If there was ever any doubt that baseball was not subject to the ordinary rules governing the rest of society, Justice Harry Blackmun's opinion in *Flood* removed any trace of it. Blackmun was a diehard Minnesota baseball fan (his best childhood friend just happened to be his chief justice, Warren Burger; together the duo were tagged the "Minnesota Twins") and when he was assigned the majority opinion in *Flood* by Justice Potter Stewart (a strident Reds fan and recipient of the infamous note during oral arguments held in the midst of the 1973 playoffs, which read: "Mets 2, Reds 0. V.P. Agnew Just Resigned!!!"), he took it upon himself to compose something that went well beyond the bounds of a constrained judicial opinion.[66] Instead, he ventured far and wide, engaging first in a long and syrupy retelling of the mythical history of America's game, giving shout-outs to those players he considered worthy of special note, invoking the work of Ernest Thayer's "Casey at the Bat" and the lore surrounding the game, and indulging in other references that focused on the Americana embedded within it. When Justice Blackmun turned to the legal issues involved, he fared just as poorly, choosing to ground his opinion in the lore of the game rather than the legal issues the

Flood case presented. The law, in the form of the Sherman Antitrust Act, and Congress's by now sweeping power to act pursuant to the commerce clause, was not enough to cause him to reconsider what he knew in his heart to be true: that baseball, being baseball, was simply different:

> With its reserve system enjoying exemption from the federal antitrust laws, baseball is, in a very distinct sense, an exception and an anomaly. . . . Even though others might regard this as "unrealistic, inconsistent, or illogical" . . . the aberration is an established one, and one that has been recognized not only in Federal Baseball and Toolson, but in . . . a total of five consecutive cases in this Court. It is an aberration that has been with us now for half a century, one heretofore deemed fully entitled to the benefit of stare decisis, and one that has survived the Court's expanding concept of interstate commerce. It rests on a recognition and an acceptance of baseball's unique characteristics and needs. . . . Other professional sports operating interstate—football, boxing, basketball, and, presumably, hockey and golf are not so exempt.[67]

And there it was: baseball was unlike anything else for the mere reason that it always has been. And in Blackmun's opinion, always would be.

The Supreme Court's continued adherence to the antitrust exemption may be the most well-known example, but it hardly stands alone in the federal judiciary's deference to our national game. In fact, it has been very willing to defer to MLB in a myriad of ways, treating it over and over differently from other businesses and even unlike other professional sports leagues. Of course, not every court has been similarly deferential, as the *Gardella* opinion attests. But in many instances, federal judges have appeared to genuflect in the presence of America's game. This was the case in 1931 when the Northern District of Illinois put its stamp of approval on the unique and powerful authority inherent in Judge Landis's commissioner's office. When asked to consider the legality of Landis's autocratic control over MLB pursuant to the 1921 Major League Agreement, the federal court did not hesitate to grant to MLB what it most likely would have considered an impermissible concentration of power in almost any other circumstance.

The facts of that 1931 case, *Milwaukee American Association v. Landis*,[68] were somewhat convoluted and labyrinthine and involved the repeated reassignment and optioning of a player who at one point was under contract to the St. Louis Cardinals but whose contractual status was now in doubt given that each team he was assigned to was either owned or controlled by the Cardinals.[69] In short, Commissioner Landis ruled that St. Louis' option of the player to Milwaukee of the minor league American Association was void and that the player must either be returned to St. Louis, transferred to another club not controlled or owned by St. Louis (unlike Milwaukee), or released unconditionally. Landis, who was no fan of the "farm system" as pioneered by Branch Rickey's Cardinals, wherein one club owned or controlled several minor league clubs and shuffled players throughout, took a strong stand against such joint ownership, ruling that, in this case, such shuffling was contrary to the "best interests" of the game, pursuant to the power granted him under the 1921 Major League Agreement. At issue before the court was whether Landis's "best interests" power held any legal weight when challenged in a court of law.

At the outset of the opinion, the court made clear that in fact it did. The court took notice of the broad swath of power granted to the commissioner by the owners in an effort to "preserve discipline and a high standard of morale," concluding that this "disclose[s] a clear intent upon the part of the parties to endow the commissioner with all the attributes of a benevolent but absolute despot and all the disciplinary powers of the proverbial pater familias."[70] With the Black Sox scandal less than a decade in the past, the court was willing to defer to MLB in its efforts to preserve a code of conduct above and beyond that required by the legal system. This, by itself, was not unusual or improper. However, the court then went further when, despite acknowledging the reality that the Major League Agreement permitted Landis the authority of an "absolute despot," failed to likewise acknowledge that this was at least potentially dangerous. Instead, it gave its blessing to this seemingly boundless grant of power, refusing to even consider the possibility that such unchecked authority could be abused, choosing instead to be comforted by the notion that the individual so armed would wield it wisely: "[T]he provisions are so unlimited in character that we can conclude only that the parties did not intend so to limit the meaning of conduct detrimental to baseball, but intended to vest in the commissioner jurisdiction to prevent any conduct destructive to the aim of the code. . . . So great was the parties' confidence in the man selected for the position and so great the trust placed in him that certain of the agreements were to continue only so long as he should

remain commissioner."[71] Given the deference to Major League Baseball
and its "law" as created and meted out by its commissioner, the court was
not uncomfortable ceding authority to a system that embraced the rule
of man over the rule of law—the polar opposite of the foundational tenet
of the American legal system. This deference would prove troublesome
more than a half century later when Pete Rose would find his legal rights
brushed to the side as a result of this inverted system of justice.

A further indication of the extent to which the court was willing to
defer to the authority of Commissioner Landis was its response to the
argument that the provision of the Major League Agreement wherein
the club owners expressly waived their right of access to the courts was
in violation of public policy in that it deprived the court of its jurisdiction. Once again, the court appeared to be untroubled by this unchecked
grant of absolute power to one man. While acknowledging that most such
provisions are "commonly held void," here the court held that submission
of a dispute to Commissioner Landis as arbiter was not, provided that his
decision was not unsupported by the evidence or "unless the decision is
upon some basis without legal foundation or beyond legal recognition."[72]
What was left unsaid was how these determinations were to be made if all
access to the courts was barred. In a roundabout fashion, the court soothed
itself by concluding that the rulings of the commissioner of baseball could
never be considered arbitrary or improper because they were necessarily
made in furtherance of his pursuit "to keep the game of baseball clean."[73]
When and if this pursuit trampled the rights of others who stood in his
way was not a question the court appeared willing to answer.

After Landis's death in 1944, MLB did in fact revise the Major League
Agreement, removing the prohibition of access to judicial review and reining in future commissioners' power by requiring that only conduct in
violation of a specific league rule could run afoul of the "best interests"
clause.[74] However, these limitations lasted only twenty years; in 1964
outgoing commissioner Ford Frick convinced club owners to strike these
changes and return to the office of the commissioner the broad array of
unchecked powers enjoyed by Judge Landis.[75] And once again, the federal
judiciary confirmed both that these powers had been restored in full and
that it would defer to MLB just as it had under Commissioner Landis.

In June 1976, Oakland A's owner Charles O. Finley attempted to sell
two of his star players to the Boston Red Sox and one to the New York

Yankees, rather than risk losing them to free agency at the end of the season.[76] Commissioner Bowie Kuhn nullified the sales, asserting that because they would debilitate the A's and upset the competitive balance of the American League, they were in violation of the "best interests" clause.[77] Finley challenged Kuhn's ruling in federal court, with the case eventually reaching the Seventh Circuit Court of Appeals in 1978. In upholding Kuhn's actions, the court recalled and reiterated Justice Blackmun's refrain in *Flood* that "baseball cannot be analogized to any other business or even to any other sport or entertainment."[78] Likewise, the court noted that baseball's commissioner was similarly unique in that in no other sport or business was there a comparable position; one designed to protect and promote the "morale of the players and the honor of the game."[79] "While it is true," the court announced, "that professional baseball selected as its first Commissioner a federal judge, it intended only him and not the judiciary as a whole to be its umpire and governor."[80] Moreover, the court tacitly embraced the baseball creed and the unique role of baseball in American society when it noted that in 1957, the Supreme Court held that, unlike baseball, the antitrust laws do in fact apply to professional football. This, the court reasoned, was a "substantive pronouncement" with regard to the nexus between baseball and the legal system in that it indicated that baseball was something special and should be treated differently by the legal system than other professional sports.[81]

The court then expanded upon the holding in *Landis* by ruling that the actions of the commissioner can even be arbitrary and in direct contradiction of his previous rulings without running afoul of either the Major League Agreement or the law.[82] A's owner Finley contended that, at a minimum, the commissioner's actions must be consistent with "prior baseball tradition" and that his power was limited to ruling only on those violations that were either immoral or unethical or that were in contradiction to posted league rules.[83] The court rejected these claims and thereby rejected any limitations placed upon the power of the commissioner to act, unchecked, pursuant to the "best interests" clause.[84] From the language of the court's opinion in *Landis,* it does not appear that this court was willing to go to such an extreme, citing as it did the requirement that the commissioner's actions be consistent with "legal foundation."[85] The *Finley* court's recognition of the power of the commissioner to act in an arbitrary fashion apparently rejected this most basic limitation.

The *Finley* court did, however, establish a two-pronged test to determine when it would be justifiable for the judiciary to intercede in baseball's affairs; however, this test was couched in an excess of language so deferential to the autonomy of MLB that it was unclear precisely when a court could intervene under cloak of this authority. Specifically, the court held that MLB must "follow the basic rudiments of due process of law."[86] In addition, MLB must follow its own rules and regulations.[87] Failure to adhere to either of these parameters would constitute exceptions to the nonreviewability clause.[88] Absent these facts, the court was content to steer clear of the legal business of baseball. "Any other conclusion would involve the courts in not only interpreting often complex rules of baseball to determine if they were violated but also, as noted in the *Landis* case, the 'intent of the (baseball) code,' an even more complicated and subjective task."[89] In myriad other circumstances, courts have been more than willing to intercede into the affairs of organizations with similarly confusing, Byzantine codes of conduct. But because those other organizations were not Major League Baseball, they were far less hesitant to do so than the Seventh Circuit was here.

As *Finley* was working its way through the federal judiciary, along came *Atlanta National League Baseball Club v. Kuhn*,[90] a case that demonstrated that when it came to judicial deference, *Finley* was hardly the final word. In this case, the Northern District of Georgia was presented with a squabble between Commissioner Kuhn and Braves owner Ted Turner that emanated from boasts made by Turner at an October 1976 cocktail party. At the party, Turner told San Francisco Giants owner Bob Lurie that he was willing to spend whatever it took to lure free agent Gary Matthews (who had just completed his option year with the Giants and who was soon to be a free agent) from the Giants to his Braves. The Braves had previously been fined for tampering with Matthews a month earlier and, as an additional punishment, Kuhn denied the Braves their selection in the first round of the January 1977 amateur draft. Lurie filed a complaint with Kuhn and Kuhn held that Turner's comments were in violation of the "best interests" clause on several grounds. As a result, although Kuhn did not void the Braves' signing of Matthews (which occurred between the date of Turner's boast and the date of Kuhn's hearing on the matter), he did suspend Turner for one year and reaffirmed the stripping of the Braves' first round draft choice in the 1977 amateur draft. Turner filed a complaint in federal court and, once again, the extent of the commissioner's "best interests" powers were examined by the judiciary. And once again, the judiciary read them to be remarkably broad.

Initially, the court seemed to push back against the extent of deference suggested by the *Finley* court when it rejected Kuhn's assertion that the trial court's ruling in *Finley* (which was to be subsequently upheld on appeal) held that the nonreviewability clause deprived the court of subject-matter jurisdiction.[91] Instead, and seemingly in conflict with that decision, the court held that the actions of the commissioner could not be arbitrary and that the arbitrary nature of a commissioner's decision was one for the courts to decide.[92] However, what it gave with one hand it then took with the other as, in exercising this judicial oversight function, the court demonstrated just how far it was willing to go in service to MLB; how deferentially it was willing to treat MLB as compared with any other professional sports league. This became blatantly apparent when the *Atlanta* court tossed aside as irrelevant another case involving a professional sports league that was factually similar in many respects other than the most important one: namely, that it did not involve MLB. For reasons implied but unstated by the *Atlanta* court, this apparently made all the difference.

Three years earlier, the Western District of Texas was presented with *Professional Sports Ltd. v. The Virginia Squires Basketball Club, et al.,*[93] a case that involved the powers of the commissioner of the American Basketball Association, which, at the time, was a struggling rival of the established National Basketball Association. In that case the plaintiffs, the San Antonio Spurs, purchased a player, George Gervin, from the Virginia Squires, for $225,000. Upon his review of the proposed purchase, the ABA's commissioner vetoed the sale, citing his authority under the ABA's bylaws permitting him to settle any and all disputes in which either a player or coach was a party.[94] Similar to the Major League Agreement, the ABA's bylaws stated that "his decision[s] in such matters shall be final."[95] The Spurs challenged the commissioner's authority to intervene in this sale and the court agreed that the commissioner had acted improperly. The court held that although the commissioner did have the power to act as an arbiter to settle disputes, he did not have such power when it was the commissioner himself who created the dispute.[96] Here, as the court noted, both teams agreed upon the terms of the deal; only the commissioner objected to the arrangement. As such, the court held that "[w]hile the by-laws clearly contemplate arbitration by the Commissioner of disputes between clubs when he is acting impartially, it would be unreasonable and unrealistic to believe that the club members ever intended to authorize him to settle disputes which he himself had instigated . . ."[97] Although the league's bylaws further empowered the commissioner to "cancel or terminate any contracts . . . for violation of the provisions of the Certificate of Incorporation and By-Laws or for any action detrimental to the welfare of the League or professional basketball," the court held that this "best interests" clause would not save him in this case, given that the commissioner's actions were taken without the required notice and hearing. The court held: ". . . the principles of fundamental fairness, as well as the by-laws themselves, contemplate a meaningful 'notice and hearing' in actions taken under these sections, and since proceedings of this nature could have the effect of depriving a party of some property right, these terms should be construed to require at least the minimum essentials of 'due process.'"[98]

The *Atlanta* court acknowledged the holding in *Pro Sports Ltd.* but concluded that it was ultimately inapplicable to the issues before it. In dismissing Braves owner Ted Turner's argument that both *Pro Sports Ltd.* and *Atlanta* involved disputes initiated by the commissioner himself, the court held that here, Commissioner Kuhn was not acting pursuant to his power as an arbiter (which presumably would be improper in this instance, according to *Pro Sports Ltd.*) but rather pursuant to his "best interests" power that authorized him to investigate any act, either upon complaint or upon his own initiative, alleged or suspected to be in violation of the "best interests" of the game, and to determine the appropriate punishment, if any.[99] The court, however, ignored the remainder of *Pro Sports Ltd.*, which contemplated the "best interests" clause of the ABA's bylaws by invoking the "principles of fundamental fairness" and by holding that any actions taken pursuant to this clause with the potential to affect a legal right must be accompanied by "at least the minimum essentials of due process." Unlike the *Pro Sports Ltd.* court, the *Atlanta* court ignored the bedrock principle of fundamental fairness by failing to take any steps to discern whether the Major League Agreement included any form of notice and hearing provisions in conjunction with the commissioner's "best interests" power, and if so, whether they were adhered to in this case at all, let alone in a "meaningful" way. Even the *Finley* court made passing mention of how "the basic rudiments of due process of law" must be followed;[100] however, when put to the test, the *Atlanta* court was not prepared to hold MLB to this requirement.

The dichotomy between *Pro Sports Ltd.* and the MLB cases highlighted the differences in treatment by the federal judiciary toward professional sports leagues in general and MLB. According to *Pro Sports Ltd.*, leagues without the power and sway of MLB were subject to the rule of law and could not contract their way around their legal obligations through unfettered grants of authority that infringed upon the rights of others. Regardless of the vagaries of their bylaws or the power bestowed in their commissioners, players as well as others operating within these leagues were nonetheless afforded at least some level of judicially protected due process—not constitutional due process but some level of fundamental fairness. The baseball cases indicated, however, that those operating under the MLB umbrella—players as well as noncompliant owners—did not enjoy this same right. In fact, taken together, the *Landis, Finley,* and *Atlanta* "best interests of baseball" cases stand for the proposition that MLB has the ability to waive the rudimentary due process rights of these individuals via the Major League Agreement regardless of any potential legal interests that may be at issue. This was evidenced in the Black Sox scandal of 1921 and would become clear once more in 1989 (even with the presence of the Players Association and a collective bargaining agreement) when Pete Rose faced a similar banishment from MLB. As indicated by the court's holding in *Pro Sports Ltd.,* the ABA, or any other professional league, would most likely face stern judicial resistance if it attempted to similarly punish a player after the cursory hearings held first by Commissioner Landis and later by Bart Giamatti.

BANISHMENT, PETE ROSE, AND
THE DANGER OF EXTRALEGAL STATUS

As a result of judicial deference to MLB in its decisions and procedures in furtherance of the business of baseball, the legal concerns relevant to banishment, where concepts such as fundamental fairness and due process should come to bear most heavily, have more often than not been swept to the side in MLB's never-ending vigilance in protecting and promoting its symbolic status. Not surprisingly, in the wake of these occasional "character baths," America's game has never failed to emerge standing (if not stronger than ever) while its victims were left crippled and oftentimes destroyed. Shoeless Joe Jackson and Buck Weaver are perhaps the poster children for this phenomenon, but as the Pete Rose affair attests, they are hardly the game's sole victims.

As the generation that could recall the Black Sox scandal died out, successive generations received their own lesson in baseball justice through the Rose affair, which in many ways was Black Sox redux.[101] However this time, by the late 1980s, there was over sixty years of precedent for MLB's exertion of extralegal authority. As such, the abuse of Rose's rights was far more blatant. Nevertheless, these abuses were easily brushed off by an entity that was confident by this point that it was highly unlikely that the federal judiciary was going to step in and challenge its authority.

The facts of the Rose case were relatively straightforward. In 1985 and '86, Rose, who at the time was managing the Cincinnati Reds, was alleged to have placed a series of wagers on 390 Major League games, including fifty-two involving his Reds.[102] Betting sheets were uncovered, complete with Rose's fingerprints, along with the betting records of Rose's bookies, including one of Ron Peters, a bookmaker from suburban Cincinnati.[103] If proved, this activity would violate Baseball Rule 21(d), which forbids any player, umpire, club or league official, or employee from betting on any baseball game. If the game was one in which the bettor had no connection, the penalty was a one-year suspension; if, however, the game was one in which the bettor "has a duty to perform," the penalty would be the ultimate sanction: permanent banishment from the game.[104] Upon receipt of this information, Commissioner Peter Ueberroth invoked his power to investigate and, in February 1989, hired John M. Dowd to conduct an inquiry into the allegations.[105] On April 1, 1989, A. Bartlett Giamatti succeeded Ueberroth as commissioner and the investigation continued, with Dowd focusing on the bookies, particularly Ron Peters, who was staring down federal charges of cocaine distribution and tax evasion and who was, therefore, in a vulnerable position himself.[106] To coax out his testimony, Dowd informed Peters that, in exchange for his "full and truthful cooperation with the Commissioner," Giamatti would agree to bring to the attention of Peters's federal district court judge the fact that Peters was "of assistance to us and that we believe that you have been honest and complete in your cooperation."[107] Peters agreed and then implicated Rose. Thereafter, Giamatti wrote to U.S. district court Judge Carl Rubin: "It is my purpose to bring to your attention the significant and truthful cooperation Mr. Peters has provided to my special counsel. . . . Based upon other information in our possession, I am satisfied Mr. Peters has been candid, forthright and truthful with my special counsel."[108]

Rose took exception to Giamatti's letter, claiming that it constituted evidence that Giamatti had prejudged the case, given that, prior to the hearing as well as the introduction of Rose's evidence in defense of the charges against him, Giamatti had apparently already concluded that the chief witness against him, Ron Peters, had been "candid, forthright and truthful." As such, Rose claimed that his upcoming hearing was little more than window dressing; he believed his fate to have already been determined. Therefore, he sued Giamatti in state court to prevent the hearing from going forward. Rose based his suit on several theories, the most pertinent of which drew from the dicta in *Finley* and was one based on a breach of contract theory where he claimed that Giamatti was contractually bound to conduct his hearing in accordance with the Rules of Procedure contained within the Major League Agreement, which stated that such proceedings should be run "in general like judicial proceedings."[109] He also alleged that the procedures to which he would be subject prevented him from properly confronting his accusers and from cross-examining them (particularly those named within what became known as the "Dowd Report").[110] Rose also echoed the court in *Pro Sports Ltd.* by raising substantive and procedural due process issues, claiming that public policy, as well as Ohio law, required "reasonable notice and a hearing with a fair opportunity to defend the charges."[111] Finally, he called on Giamatti to recuse himself from the proceedings, given his biased opinion as expressed in his letter to Judge Rubin.[112]

Wisely, Rose filed his case in state, rather than in federal, court; without the federal judiciary's history of deference behind it, he stood a better chance of at least having his voice heard. In June 1989, the state court granted his motion for a temporary restraining order, holding that despite the legal system's tradition of deference to MLB, here there was no choice but to step in given the strong likelihood that Giamatti had prejudged Rose's case and that the subsequent hearing would be "futile, illusory, and the outcome a foregone conclusion."[113] MLB, however, removed the case to federal court, where the Sixth Circuit eventually denied Rose's objection to the removal, thereby setting into motion the process for the "futile, illusory" hearing that could now finally take place.[114] Although Rose had one formal legal avenue still open to him—a hearing on his motion for a permanent injunction against Giamatti, albeit this time in federal, rather than state, court—federal district court Judge John D. Holschuh strongly hinted that he would abide by tradition and defer to the substantive and procedural rules as defined by MLB, irrespective of how it chose to implement them.[115] With state court closed off to him and the federal court loudly hinting that it would provide him no relief, Rose was effectively at the mercy of Giamatti. Therefore, on August 23, 1989, Rose consented to his permanent banishment from the game, signing a document in which he "recognizes, agrees and submits to the sole and exclusive jurisdiction of the Commissioner" to hear and determine this matter, as well as any other determined by the commissioner to be "not in the best interests of the national game of baseball."[116] In the end, despite the absence of a formal finding that Rose bet on baseball, let alone his Reds, and without so much as even the "futile and illusory" hearing contemplated by the Ohio state court, Rose was banished for life.

The agreement tossed a couple of bones to Rose, however: although it was technically a "permanent" banishment, it provided for the possibility of his reinstatement after one year.[117] More important, and perhaps in acknowledgment of the denial of due process and lack of a hearing prior to banishment, it contained potentially redemptive language: "[n]othing in this agreement shall be deemed either an admission or a denial by Peter Edward Rose of the allegation that he bet on any major league baseball game."[118] Combined, these two apparent concessions by MLB seemingly paved the path for Rose's eventual return to the game, and they most likely contributed to his acquiescence to the agreement and his dropping of his legal case, regardless of the ultimate futility of his pressing onward. Now, pursuant to the terms of the agreement, Rose could see his way out of the forest. Almost immediately, however, MLB made it very clear that any such path was illusory.

Upon the announcement of the agreement, Giamatti stated that irrespective of the language agreed upon by both him and Rose, he believed that Rose bet on baseball.[119] Instantly, for all practical purposes, the terms of the agreement had been changed unilaterally by Giamatti—to successfully apply for reinstatement, Rose would most likely have to admit that he bet on baseball. This was something that was not contemplated by the agreement and added yet another layer of injustice to MLB's handling of the Rose affair: not only was banishment carried out in the absence of a hearing with meaningful due process, both the banishment agreement as well as the terms of reinstatement were altered unilaterally and after the fact. To further complicate matters, eight days later, Giamatti died of a heart attack, thereby sealing Rose's fate.[120] Now it was extremely unlikely that future commissioners were going to take steps to undo the agreement of their predecessor, someone almost everybody admired immensely. This was made explicit in 1995 when (then-acting) Commissioner Bud Selig stated that he would not revisit Rose's banishment because "Bart Giamatti was one of the best friends I've ever had in the world, and I have great faith in his decision. His decision still stands, and as far as I'm concerned, his decision should stand."[121] Legal niceties and issues of fundamental fairness were not the issue in Selig's eyes. Instead, it was the reputation of a friend that hung in the balance. Because Rose was not also a friend, he was out of luck. In all of this, the law was irrelevant.

Taken together, the many stages of the Rose affair, as well as its ultimate resolution, were the story of an embrace of the rule of man over the rule of law—the polar opposite of the foundational belief upon which the American legal system rests. That Rose ultimately admitted in 2004 to betting on baseball was but an incidental footnote in the sordid tale, because it was the disregard for the process of justice that fouled the air, not the fact that Rose revealed himself to be an untruthful and incorrigible gambler; the disregard of the bedrock of due process that is ostensibly guaranteed for all—the innocent as well as the guilty. Yet somehow, despite the reality that baseball has been governed in the absence of such principles ever since the days of Judge Landis, it has remained a powerful metaphor of America. Rose's case illustrated that even the most basic concessions to the applicability of the rule of law as outlined in *Finley* were little more than dicta. When they stood in the way of "baseball justice," they were to be pushed to the side in the interest of protecting the image of the game. *Finley's* two-pronged test regarding the Major League Agreement's waiver of recourse to the courts called for judicial intervention when baseball's commissioner failed to follow baseball's internal rules or when he violated the basic rudiments of due process of law.[122] Giamatti violated both prongs of the *Finley* test, yet federal district court Judge John D. Holschuh strongly hinted that this was of little matter, considering that he was prepared to defer to Giamatti regardless.

Giamatti, like Landis before him, initiated and presided over a prosecution where he was the investigator, prosecutor, judge, and jury, acting in so many different capacities as to exceed, at least according to *Finley,* even the broad powers granted him within the Major League Agreement. In cases not involving powerful institutions such as baseball, courts have held that such concentration of power in one office raises serious concerns, as there exists obvious potential for abuse.[123] Moreover, the fact that the decisions made by this powerful individual are not subject to judicial review absent extraordinary circumstances is likewise a factor that, in non-baseball contexts, has raised the hackles of several courts, including the Supreme Court.[124] Obvious and odious are the institutionalized, structural biases inherent in such a system—one in which there appears to be no restraint upon a commissioner to punish individuals without proper review and safeguards, as well as one in which the commissioner himself is free to set forth the rules of procedure that he would then follow (or not, as the Rose affair demonstrated).[125] Yet in the Rose affair, the judicial system, as it has historically, chose nevertheless to defer.

After the Rose affair, the extralegal status of Major League Baseball was more assured than ever. Accordingly, MLB was free to establish its own rules and then break them whenever and however it wished. Indeed, it did just this the following year when Giamatti's replacement, Fay Vincent, commenced his prosecution of Yankee owner George Steinbrenner for payments made to alleged gambler Howie Spira in exchange for information detrimental to Yankee star Dave Winfield's charitable foundation. After Vincent's investigator's—John Dowd's—deposition of Steinbrenner, Steinbrenner discovered that Dowd had unilaterally altered the Yankee owner's deposition transcript, to the point (at least in the opinion of Steinbrenner's attorneys) of distorting his testimony. Although Steinbrenner filed suit over the matter, alleging (just like Rose before him) that this act violated the Major League Agreement's rule requiring that such proceedings "be conducted like a judicial proceeding, with regard for all the principles of natural justice and fair play," the federal court tossed out his complaint.[126]

Without the hammer of the law hanging over its head, it was not surprising, then, that MLB ignored suspicion and evidence regarding illegal drug and steroid use throughout the 1980s, '90s and '00s, particularly when to acknowledge such abuses would very likely dampen enthusiasm for the game and diminish its metaphoric value. This urge to bolster the game's image became increasingly acute after the labor unrest and resulting work stoppage that wiped out the 1994 World Series and threatened the popularity of the game. Upon its return in 1995, baseball was looking to reestablish its exalted status, much as it was in the wake of the Black Sox scandal. Eventually, it found the path through power hitters such as Mark McGwire, Sammy Sosa, and Barry Bonds, who threatened home run records and brought people back to the game, just as Babe Ruth had in the early 1920s. Absent the looming threat of legal action for noncompliance with existing federal law, MLB was free to ignore it, seemingly without consequence. Inevitably, players got bigger and home run records that had stood unchallenged for decades were smashed and then smashed again as the baseball record book was rewritten with each passing season.

All of this appeared to come to a head, however, on November 16, 2007, when, finally, accountability ostensibly arrived on baseball's doorstop through the vessel of federal intervention in baseball's steroid crisis. Regardless, despite appearances to the contrary, few things changed. In the end, irrespective of the thundering from the mountaintop, the steroid scandal revealed only that the relationship between baseball and the American legal system would remain as it had for nearly a century: disconnected, disjointed, and disturbing.

BONDS, STEROIDS, AND THE MITCHELL REPORT: CORPORATE CORRUPTION AND AMERICA'S GAME

Initially, November 16, 2007, seemingly portended a sea change in the culture of baseball, as well as its accountability under federal law. For on that allegedly fateful day, Barry Bonds, the game's recently crowned home run

king, was indicted on four counts of perjury and one count of obstruction
of justice stemming from his federal grand jury testimony connected with
the investigation of steroid use in sports in general and, in Bonds's case,
Major League Baseball in particular.[127] Pursuant to the indictment, federal prosecutors alleged that Bonds perjured himself when he denied ever
knowingly having taken steroids and human growth hormone, suspected
performance-enhancing substances.[128] This day was long anticipated, as
the federal investigation had dragged on for several months, with the
inevitable indictment the subject of a good deal of speculation within the
world of Major League Baseball. Now that it had arrived, it was largely
greeted with cheers from the commentariat: The *New York Times* hailed
it as "A Good Day for Baseball," promising that, as a result of the official
ferreting out of Bonds, "A Better One Looms" in the future.[129] Baseball, it
seemed, was finally being called on the carpet.

Very quickly, however, it became clear that the symbolic scope of the
Bonds indictment was going to be limited indeed, largely restricted merely
to the offending players and not infecting MLB itself—the culture in which
they operated. For although Bonds himself was vilified and grouped with
other high-profile, recently exposed perjurers such as entertaining magnate Martha Stewart and government official I. Lewis (Scooter) Libby Jr.,[130]
he was portrayed in many recountings of his sordid tale as somewhat of an
aberration: an immoral cog (although hardly the only one, as other players
suspected of steroid use would attest) in an otherwise righteous wheel.
In fact, the very indictment itself was perceived by many (as evidenced
through the hurrahs elicited in the *New York Times* and other publications)
as an indication of the integrity of the system: it may have had its flaws
but it eventually identified and spit out the wrongdoers. This was consistent with the congressional approach to the issue where, in the months
surrounding the Bonds indictment, a gaggle of high-profile players (Mark
McGwire, Sammy Sosa, Rafael Palmeiro, and, later, Roger Clemens, among
the noteworthy) was hauled before one committee or another in Congress'
furious attempt to appear vigilant on the issue, and scolded for the stain
they left upon America's game. Yet in its fury, Congress elected not to
call a single owner similarly to account. Unlike the players, no owner was
required to respond under oath with regard to what he knew and when
he knew it, nor asked to explain how he permitted his players to become,

literally, larger than life. This decision was hardly surprising. For to focus on the owners would be to call into question the integrity of the institution of baseball, something Congress, like the federal judiciary, has been historically loath to do. So it focused instead on Bonds and his compatriots, impugning their integrity with abandon, choosing to let the revered institution stand amid the ruins.

As it turned out, however, Bonds and his compatriots were hardly the root cause of the problem. For on December 13, 2007, barely a month after the Bonds indictment, another event much anticipated in the world of Major League Baseball took place: the release of the Mitchell Report.[131] In it, former United States Senator George Mitchell, acting upon the request of MLB Commissioner Selig, not only identified dozens of players who had taken steroids and other suspected performance-enhancing substances in violation of federal law over the past several years, but recounted MLB's historic indifference to this reality. Regardless, Selig encouraged the perception of the Mitchell Report as the symbolic closing of a chapter rather than the opening of one. To Selig, operating under the illusion of a "single sin" myth similar to Landis's nearly a century earlier, the history recounted within the Mitchell Report was irrelevant. Instead, the story as he spun it was an uncomplicated one: the offenders were identified, the pox upon the game exposed, and baseball had been cleansed. "This report is a call to action," Selig said as he raised his right index finger during the press conference in conjunction with the release of the report, "and I will act."[132] Selig's message was clear: the "action" he was referring to was directed primarily toward reining in the allegedly rogue players who had infected the game—the locus of the problem as he defined it and the ones who necessitated the quick "character bath" Selig was so eager to apply to the game through his crude interpretation of the Mitchell Report. They, much like Buck Weaver and Shoeless Joe Jackson before them, simply needed to be weeded out. Once that had been accomplished, the problem would be solved.

As Selig spun his tale, he created the simplistic fiction of a clearly defined "steroid era"—one that was a black mark on the game but ultimately just that: an era—defined by a minority of deviant players who, on their own, had compromised the integrity of the game—and that had now come to a definitive end.[133] Now that they had been identified and, just as important, properly castigated, baseball could once again assume its role as the quintessential American metaphor, just as it had in Landis's time. In his rush to, in effect, emulate Judge Landis and embrace this "single sin" myth for the twenty-first century, Selig made certain that accountability rested solely with the players, going so far as to suggest, shortly after the release of the Mitchell Report, that he was amenable to possibly striking yet another pose reminiscent of Landis in the Black Sox scandal by disciplining those named therein, in defiance of the recommendation to the contrary made by Mitchell himself.[134]

However, despite Selig's insistence, the history did matter. Contrary to Selig's one-dimensional take on the Mitchell Report, context was everything and in this instance, it revealed a much darker story of baseball—one that lay bare the consequences of the legal system's hands-off approach to MLB: the corrosion of America's game because of decades-long disregard of the law. Starting with only the most recent instance of MLB's cheerful legal ignorance (the one evidenced in Selig's charge to Mitchell upon handing the investigation over to him that asked him to focus his investigation on the years covered by baseball's 2002–2006 collective bargaining agreement—which permitted limited drug testing for the first time, irrespective of the reality that federal law applied to baseball even in the absence of such an agreement),[135] the Mitchell Report was essentially a detailed history of MLB's decades-long indifference to the pervasiveness of illegal performance-enhancing drugs and other activity in its locker rooms. In the end, it was not the revelation of the guilty players (many of whom had already been identified anyway) that was significant, it was the fact that so many could flout the law so blatantly, in locker rooms owned and controlled by corporate executives who, if anything, encouraged this illegal behavior. Far from the impotent report restricted to the fiction of "baseball law" Selig had requested, the Mitchell Report was instead a treatise that gave him and MLB much more than they had bargained for.

Right off the bat, the Mitchell Report destroyed the myth that Selig and MLB had perpetrated for years: the myth that the signing of the 2002 collective bargaining agreement somehow rendered 2002 a starting point in the discussion of illegal drug use within the game. By destroying that myth, the Mitchell Report invariably shifted the focus of the blame for baseball's steroid crisis from alleged outliers such as Barry Bonds and the others mentioned within the report, to MLB itself. By doing so, the Mitchell Report showed that the proper comparison was not between these so-called "aberrations" and people like Stewart and Libby—individual malfeasance within the structure of a just system—but between MLB and entities such as Enron, Lehman Brothers, and their compatriots in that what the steroid crisis ultimately demonstrated was *corporate* malfeasance amid a culture of corruption and a willful disregard for the law. Accordingly, as the Mitchell Report highlighted, in MLB it was the system itself that was corrupt, with the identified players merely symptoms of the problem rather than the problem in and of themselves. That Selig assumed that MLB had the authority to render the law meaningless was the root cause of the problem. Given the legal system's traditional deference to America's game, it was hardly an unexpected consequence, however.

Although Selig made no mention of it in his public proclamations, the Mitchell Report was in fact specific in its historical overview of both MLB's theoretical legal responsibilities as well as its practical avoidance of them. Specifically, in its "Summary and Recommendations," the Mitchell Report observed that Selig's assumption that the signing of the 2002 Basic Agreement with the Players Association signaled the commencement of MLB's responsibility with regard to illegally obtained steroids was "not accurate." Rather, "[b]eginning in 1971 and continuing today, Major League Baseball's drug policy has prohibited the use of any prescription medication without a valid prescription. By implication, this prohibition applied to steroids even before 1991, when Commissioner Fay Vincent first expressly included steroids in baseball's drug policy. Steroids have been listed as a prohibited substance under the Major League Baseball drug policy since then, although no player was disciplined for steroid use before the prohibition was added to the collective bargaining agreement in 2002."[136] The report further noted that this prohibition was binding upon the players even absent their express consent to it via a collectively bargained basic agreement. As stated within the report in its historical review of MLB's drug policies in theory and in practice: "Many players were suspended for drug offenses before 2002, even though none of these suspensions related to the use of steroids or other performance enhancing substances. Some suspensions were reduced in grievance arbitrations brought by the Players Association, but no arbitrator ever has questioned the authority of the Commissioner to discipline players for 'just cause' based upon their possession, use, or distribution of prohibited drugs."[137] Given that the Mitchell Report pointed the barrel of its gun at MLB, it was not surprising that Selig chose not to direct the public's attention to these sections of the Mitchell Report during his press conference, preferring instead to redirect the rifle toward the players.

As the report noted, in Vincent's 1991 MLB drug policy memo, he stressed that MLB expressly prohibited the use of "all illegal drugs and controlled substances, including steroids or prescription drugs for which the individual . . . does not have a prescription."[138] However, the response to Vincent's pronouncement of MLB's duties under the law was underwhelming. As Vincent recalled later, "[m]y memo was totally ignored by all. The point was to alert the baseball world to the recent inclusion of steroids as illegal prohibited substances under federal law. But the union did nothing to underscore my memo and I think the clubs ignored it as irrelevant."[139] The Mitchell Report found the ambivalence of team owners on this issue curious, given that, irrespective of the vagaries of "baseball law," federal law has always applied, at least in theory, to MLB outside the realm of the game's antitrust exemption. And here, the distribution of prescription drugs of any sort by individuals other than a duly licensed physician acting in furtherance of an individual determination of a proper course of treatment had been prohibited ever since the passing of the federal Food, Drug, and Cosmetic Act of 1938.[140]

Despite Selig's insistence that "baseball law" somehow limited the scope of MLB's responsibility to the period from 2002 onward, the report reiterated that, for as long as federal law has prohibited these substances, baseball was required to prohibit them as well. Regardless, and despite the Steroid Control Act of 1990, which increased the penalties for their illegal possession or distribution to levels similar to those applicable to narcotics,[141] MLB paid the law little mind. Theoretically, this was a clear abandonment of legal responsibility on the part of MLB. As a practical matter, however, it was something else. As trumpeted by the federal judiciary time and again through the *Landis, Finley,* and *Atlanta* cases, federal law had been irrelevant to MLB for nearly a century by that point; there was no reason for MLB to assume that the Steroid Control Act signaled any such shift in this reality. Indeed, willful ignorance of all sorts of laws had by now become the norm for MLB and the owners: they likewise routinely ignored foreign law in Venezuela and the Dominican Republic in the running of their baseball academies and paid little mind to foreign judgments issued against them.[142] Therefore, club owners were confident that not only could they blissfully ignore the mounting evidence of steroid abuse within the game from the 1980s through the 1990s and into the early 2000s, they could in fact reward the most blatant violators of the law with large contracts in recognition of their inflated statistical achievements attained, at least in some measure, through their possession and use of steroids and other substances in violation of the Steroid Control Act.[143]

The Mitchell Report did not stop there. Beyond rebuking Selig's implication of the superiority of "baseball law," it likewise made clear that MLB's frequent refrain that it had scant knowledge of the depth of the steroid problem prior to the release of the report was specious. The evidence to the contrary, as noted within the report, was overwhelming. Although many writers turned a blind eye toward the bulging bodies they increasingly saw before them in team locker rooms, others wondered aloud in print from time to time often enough to raise eyebrows across the nation, although apparently not within the Commissioner's Office. Before the Steroid Control Act was even passed, steroids had seeped into the sports pages. In 1989, in a well-publicized incident, oversized Oakland A's slugger Jose Canseco was arrested for possession of a handgun in a Detroit airport.[144] Pursuant to the search incident to arrest, steroids were discovered. The next year, Philadelphia Phillies centerfielder Lenny Dykstra arrived at spring training carrying thirty pounds of newly found bulk, which he credited to the work of "really good vitamins."[145] In 1992, *Boston Globe* columnist Peter Gammons reported that steroid abuse was "much greater than anyone lets on." He further wondered if a recent spate of injuries within the game could be attributed to steroid abuse "as players' muscle mass becomes too great for their bodies, resulting in the odd back and leg breakdowns."[146] *Los Angeles Times* and *USA Today* baseball writer Bob Nightengale was likewise suspicious and made his suspicions known in a series of 1995 articles emblazoned with headlines such as: "Baseball Still Doesn't Get It," and "Steroids Become an Issue in Baseball: Many Fear Performance-Enhancing Drug Is Becoming Prevalent and Believe Something Must Be Done," with the latter article picked up by wire services

across the country and revised and reprinted in *The Sporting News,* historically considered "The Baseball Bible," a few weeks later.[147] In the updated
article printed in *The Sporting News,* steroid use was called "baseball's deep,
dark, sinister secret."[148]

Regardless of these and other articles, and perhaps in a continuing
effort to keep its head buried in the sand while the game soared in popularity, MLB continued to profess ignorance. Even with much of the media
avoiding or ignoring the issue, the Mitchell Report was able to identify
eighty-five mainstream media articles that focused on the use and abuse
of steroids and other performance-enhancing substances within MLB
between 1988 and 1998.[149] Selig, however, throughout this period, repeated
his refrain, stating at one point that "[i]f baseball has a problem, I must
say candidly that we were not aware of it. . . . It certainly hasn't been
talked about much."[150] Selig's considered ignorance was a luxury he could
afford: the potential ramifications were nonexistent. Absent the threat of
accountability, Selig could continue to deny reality as the game descended
ever further into its slough of corruption and disgrace.

When not denying the existence of a problem, Selig spent much of his
tenure as commissioner throwing up his hands in helplessness and blaming
the Players Association for the game's predicament. In 2004, for instance,
he professed that, even had he known of drug and supplement abuse within
MLB, there was not much he could have done about it anyway because of
the presence of the Players Association and the constraints placed upon
MLB pursuant to the National Labor Relations Act (NLRA).[151] Although
he lauded the toughened testing standards enacted within the world of
amateur athletics, he concluded that such standards were not viable within
MLB.[152] Because drug testing was considered a mandatory subject of collective bargaining, MLB's hands were, according to Selig, effectively tied.
However, as the Mitchell Report stressed, the issues relevant to collective
bargaining were ancillary to MLB's ability to control the problem of substance abuse within the game and to enforce the law, which it could have
done had it so desired. Rather, it was MLB's decision to disregard the law,
which it knew it could do without consequence, that led to the culture of
steroid abuse as personified by Bonds and later, Roger Clemens.

The Mitchell Report noted that although MLB, through the Commissioner's Office, lacked the power to directly issue warrants and subpoe-
nas, it could have conducted investigatory interviews and compelled even

union-represented employees, such as those represented by the Players Association, to attend and answer truthfully.[153] This "interview right" is one enjoyed by all employers to ensure that their rules are being followed.[154] As the Mitchell Report observed, however, MLB "rarely required" its players "to participate in investigatory interviews regarding alleged performance enhancing substance violations."[155] Further, because steroid use was a violation of federal law, the report noted that, if it wished, MLB could have partnered with state and federal law enforcement agencies, which do have both warrant and subpoena power, and coordinated investigations through the indirect use of these powers.[156] However, prior to the investigation undertaken by Mitchell, MLB made little use of this avenue as well, choosing instead the path it has historically taken: one free from the potential encumbrances of the law. In short, by the end of the twentieth century, baseball and the law had become experts in dodging one another, freely, openly, and without repercussion.

As the Mitchell Report recognized, the course of undertaking an illegal drug–possession investigation of a suspected Major League player can and should be no different than investigations of employees in any other circumstance; the presence of the Players Association is, ultimately, a red herring. In nearly any other employment context, the ability to conduct drug testing is, although helpful, not a prerequisite for undertaking such a criminal investigation. Employers have always had other means available to them if they chose to investigate, identify, and rid themselves of drug offenders operating within their employ.[157] Technically, MLB is no different than any other work environment. Realistically, however, baseball's elevated symbolic status has made it different indeed. In its attempt to deflect attention away from itself, MLB repeatedly pointed an accusatory finger at the Players Association. What repeatedly went unasked in the process, however, was the foundational question of whether MLB even wanted to know the extent of the problem in the first place. Its failure to act in the many ways it could have suggests that perhaps it did not, for there was little to be gained and much in the way of status to be lost in the process. Without a sense of obligation and pressure from the law, it was simply more beneficial to allow the game to rot from the inside out.

In his response to the release of the Mitchell Report, Selig lauded the numerous (twenty) recommendations contained within; recommendations calling on MLB to use its powers of investigation, conduct background checks on clubhouse employees, cooperate with federal and state law enforcement, and the like.[158] He even stated that he would implement all of the recommendations that did not require collective bargaining immediately. Ironically and hollowly, Selig also called on Congress to classify human growth hormone a Schedule III controlled substance under the Controlled Substances Act, perhaps forgetting Fay Vincent's 1991 memo with regard to the classification of steroids as likewise a Schedule III controlled substance, which was met with a collective yawn by club owners.[159] Regardless, as the report made clear, MLB, not unlike Dorothy in Oz, had all of the powers outlined within the report at its disposal all along, and it was the reluctance to use them that was the problem rather than the absence of the powers themselves—the prevailing attitude that it was unnecessary, that there was too much to lose through compliance with the law and nothing to be gained. Freed from outside restraint and legal accountability, the Mitchell Report suggested that the core dysfunction at the heart of MLB had become none other than MLB itself.

RICKEY, RACE, AND "ALL DELIBERATE SPEED"

By the middle of the twentieth century, club owners were quite comfortable with their exalted status within American society. Presiding over America's game, they had become accustomed to being treated like royalty wherever they went: they were the well-regarded protectors of what had become the national civil religion,[1] the Sherman Antitrust Act still did not apply to them irrespective of the expansion of Congress's Commerce Clause powers, and the concept of due process and other mundane legal niceties were likewise notions they need not have concerned themselves with. Regardless of the nature of the engagement, the owners were the ones who invariably dictated the parameters of their involvement. If the Supreme Court would not tell them how to behave, few others stood much of a chance.

The burgeoning civil rights movement was something else entirely, however. Gaining momentum in the 1930s, it picked up steam during World War II until, upon the war's completion, its glare was fixated upon MLB, whose owners and executives (at least the ones paying attention) soon realized that eventually, they were going to have no choice but to accept integration.

Although powerless to stop the onrushing tide, they were nevertheless able to control something nearly as significant—how the story of the game's integration was going to be told and, ultimately, remembered. More than six decades later, their power in this regard still resonates.

The story they perpetuated is one familiar to nearly any American who has advanced beyond the sixth grade and is one of the most affirming morality tales in American history—the story of Branch Rickey, Jackie Robinson, and the integration of Major League Baseball in 1947. Pursuant to the story, the event was seen, and has been recalled, as an American tipping point: "Once the racial wall in the national game had been breached," the narrative goes, "it seemed indisputable that all other barriers to blacks should be removed as well."[2] Because baseball in America had mirrored the nation's racial practices for decades, the event was perceived as momentous and precipitous because here, baseball foreshadowed nationwide, federally imposed and endorsed desegregation, coming as it did seven years before the Supreme Court's landmark decision in *Brown v. Board of Education*.[3] According to the story, once Major League Baseball rejected the "separate but equal" fiction of the Court's 1896 *Plessy v. Ferguson*[4] decision, it was inevitable that the case was on its last legs.[5]

Meshing nicely with the predominant "great man" approach to American history (which focuses on the extraordinary acts of those few individuals deemed capable of altering a nation's cause on their own[6]), the story credits Brooklyn Dodgers president Branch Rickey as the mastermind behind baseball's "Great Experiment," as the integration effort came to be called, deftly maneuvering through the thicket of prejudice to bring equality to America's game at last. Although an extreme social conservative, Rickey has nevertheless been portrayed as a man who, for various reasons, harbored a social conscience that drove him to eventually introduce black players into the white game to "open up the baseball business to deserving new black talent."[7] In the process, he would achieve his goal of altering the course of not only baseball, but American history as well.[8]

Of course, the story goes, he could not do this alone. His mission required the fortitude of a player—the "right" player—who not only could excel on the field but off it as well; one who "would accept the responsibility of his race and who could bear that burden;"[9] one who would be able to ignore the taunts and jeers of teammates, fans, and opposing players; one who could turn the other cheek for the good of his people. "Are you looking for a Negro who is afraid to fight back?" Jackie Robinson is said to have asked Rickey, according to the popular retelling of this story. "Robinson," came Rickey's reply, "I'm looking for a ballplayer with guts enough not to fight back."[10] Once Robinson acquiesced to these terms, Rickey had found his man and, together, with the future of the black citizenry upon their shoulders, they succeeded in not only opening the door to black players, but keeping it open in perpetuity.[11] Pursuant to this story, Robinson, thanks to the actions of Rickey, is often cited as perhaps the most historically significant athlete in American sports history in that he not only changed a game, he changed the way Americans thought about their country.[12] Together, Rickey and Robinson, through the medium of baseball, joined hands to provide one of America's transformative moments. There is no purer moment of baseball as America than the one described in this story.

Inevitably, the didactic value of the story was seized upon almost as soon as it was told. In 1949, with the cold war heating up and the actor Paul Robeson questioning whether black Americans would willingly fight in a hypothetical war against the Soviet Union, the House Un-American Activities Committee called Robinson in to testify to the contrary, quelling such fears in the process.[13] At around the same time, a group of promoters sought to send the Brooklyn Dodgers and Cleveland Indians—baseball's two most integrated teams—on a world tour to promote not just baseball but America as well. To these promoters, it was considered "most important that the Negro race be well represented, as living evidence of the opportunity to reach the top which America's No. 1 sport gives all participants regardless of race."[14] For many, baseball was America; America was baseball. In each, the essence of the other could be found. America's superior moral vision was best expressed, consistent with this updated version of the baseball creed, on the field of play, sparking at the moment Robinson took his position at first base alongside his Dodger teammates for the first time. The Rickey/Robinson story is illuminative in that it is comforting and affirmative such that it confirms our faith in not only our country but likewise in those we have entrusted to lead it.

Although this story has gone relatively unchallenged for decades (for to challenge it is to challenge, in the eyes of the story's supporters, the essence of America itself), it is not the only story that can be told. The same facts and information that lead to the popular tale can also lead to a different one, one that is equally illuminating in that it shows men in a powerful institution—the "great men"—doing all they could to beat back a rising tide against them—the tide of integration—that threatened their status and way of life. This is not so much a story of equality but one where these powerful men fought to maintain control over the process of integration such that the resulting "story" was about equality only in its most superficial sense, with true equality having been delayed and denied to the majority of black ballplayers despite the success of Jackie Robinson.

The popular story of the integration of Major League Baseball is perhaps one of the most resonant and powerful in our culture. But, at its core, it is simply that: a story, one that, like most stories, is complete with gaps and inconvenient facts pushed to the side. It is in this marginalia that another story lies—one that fills in the gaps, reintroduces the facts, and tells a far different tale of the integration of our national pastime.

SEPARATE AND UNEQUAL

Because baseball has served as a metaphor of America practically from the time the first game was played, given the racial climate of the country in the mid to late nineteenth century, it should not be surprising that America's game would be, if it would be anything, white. As discussed in chapter 1, because of the early baseball "magnates'" desires to emulate the WASP elites, they promoted baseball as a game that harked back to the allegedly simpler times of agrarian and small-town America, one that possessed the "pastoral" qualities synonymous with innocence, virtue, and purity. These qualities have been associated with "whiteness" for centuries; in baseball, they had simply been splashed onto a new canvas.[15] The simple math of the era required baseball to be white to be pure. This was true in form as well as substance. The segregationist social theory of post-Reconstruction America likewise required separation on the ball field if the game was to be symbolic of "proper" national values.

For a time, though, the then–major league American Association (if not the National League, which instituted and enforced a whites-only policy from its inception)[16] as well as some minor leagues, permitted black players and, by some estimates, there were as many as fifty-five black players in professional baseball between 1883 and 1898.[17] Soon, however, with the retreat from Reconstruction and the emergence of Jim Crow gaining force, this practice ended as cries grew increasingly louder from all corners for segregation to be maintained in the name of purity. Occasionally, white players would object to the "colored element" in their games, with some, such as Adrian "Cap" Anson, refusing to take the field if a black player was involved in the game.[18] On at least one occasion, a group of white fans threatened mob violence if a black player took the field in an exhibition game.[19] In 1887, in response to the International League's (an upper-echelon minor league) fielding black players on six of its ten teams, the influential magazine *Sporting Life* asked: "How far will the mania for engaging colored players go?"[20] Not very, as it turned out. Heeding these cries, professional baseball became more vigilant in its efforts to segregate the game and to maintain segregation at all times, and by all means necessary.

The retreat from integrated baseball became complete in 1896 when the Supreme Court's *Plessy v. Ferguson* decision institutionalized state-sponsored segregation, declaring "separate but equal" to be the law of the land.[21] Ironically, once America's highest court had embraced the "purity" of which baseball had been striving, baseball began to shrink from this proclamation, at least in theory. Now, although there was nothing illegal about a segregated baseball league, Major League Baseball began to take great pains to deny the existence of a color line at all, choosing instead to operate under a thinly veiled cloak of, of all things, equality. This shift was borne out of necessity; the concept of baseball as America would no longer tolerate the old value system. The country's identity was changing; baseball's was required to change as well. As the twentieth century progressed, America was pulled into two world wars as well as several other conflicts. Its emerging role as an international leader required it to confront the hypocrisy of being the voice of freedom and equal opportunity abroad but of segregation at home. Soon, the mantra of racial purity, to say nothing of the social science, reeked when viewed in the light of the atrocities taking place in Europe. So another mantra was needed to replace it. As America repositioned itself as the beacon of freedom and equal rights for all, so did Major League Baseball, regardless of the facts behind this claim.

Ignoring the reality that permeated his league, Commissioner Landis (who established his fealty to the concept of segregated baseball early in his tenure by conducting in 1921 an investigation to assure himself that Pirates pitcher Moses Yellow Horse was indeed the full-blooded Indian he claimed to be and not an African American in disguise[22]) took every opportunity available to publicly deny the presence of a color line in the game, going so far as to discipline anyone under his jurisdiction who contradicted him. In 1941, Brooklyn Dodgers manager Leo Durocher responded to a reporter's question asking whether he would sign black players for the Dodgers by exclaiming "Hell, yes! I'd sign them in a minute if I got permission from the big shots."[23] Landis called him in, scolded him for commenting on baseball policy, and then issued his standard public statement, reiterating that his game had no such thing as a color line and that any owner was free to sign any player he desired.[24] This was a tactic he used repeatedly and one that survived his death in 1944. Two years later, a Major League Baseball joint steering committee issued a report on the state of the game drafted by Larry McPhail of the Yankees, a staunch opponent of integration. The draft report was notable for several things, not the least of which was McPhail's admission that Major League Baseball was officially segregated (and in his opinion, should remain so).[25] As this contradicted Landis's and MLB's longstanding stance on this issue, this statement was removed from the final version of the document.[26] Although, on one level, few people believed Landis's or MLB's statements regarding the nonexistence of a color line in the game, their proclamations were useful in at least providing the league with the appearance of equality, something it would not have if its leaders openly admitted the truth.

This appearance was a powerful tool as the first half of the twentieth century progressed. Despite the reality of the Jim Crow South as well as discrimination in the North, it was important for MLB to be something different, something higher, something better. "America" was still the theme of the game but now, "America" stood for something else. The mounting pressure to end the nation's apartheid, caused by international factors as well as the migration of many black southerners to northern white cities, redefined the concept of "America."[27] Purity was out, equality was in. And so in baseball, as in America, one fiction was replaced by another.

MOMENTUM TOWARD INTEGRATION

Regardless of the cultural fiction, the country was indeed changing and inching toward equality, toward the point where perhaps someday reality would match the myth. Much of this progress was the result of African American participation in World Wars I and II. World War I proved to be a significant early step for the simple fact that more than 400,000 black citizens served their country, although the vast majority of these were assigned to the Services of Supply Branch and never saw combat.[28] Black servicemen were among those on the first ships sent to Europe, acting as stevedores loading and unloading the vessels. They wore old Civil War uniforms and endured some of the worst living conditions imaginable on board. Later, other black servicemen arrived and, although the United States had no intention of allowing them to serve in the infantry (to allow them to fight and die along white Americans would be to acknowledge the fundamental equality of the races), the French government requested their services in active duty to help relieve their decimated and beleaguered troops. Unwilling to allow the four African American infantry regiments stationed in Europe to fight under the American flag, the United States eventually permitted these regiments to be attached to the French army instead. There, the regiments were supplied with French armaments, helmets, rations, and equipment and fought under French command.

Once ensconced as infantrymen—albeit as temporary Frenchmen—the regiments were the focus of concern of both the Americans and the Germans. On the American side, fears of potential postwar repercussions as a result of equal treatment by the French army led to the drafting of a document entitled, "Secret Information Concerning Black American Troops," which was an attempt to explain to the French why they should not treat these troops as equals, their personal feelings notwithstanding: "the French people must understand the position of Negroes in America. . . . Approximately 15 million Negroes in the United States presented a danger of race mongrelization unless coloreds and whites were kept strictly separated . . . the French people were accustomed to being friendly and tolerant toward Negroes; but such behavior deeply offended Americans as an attack on their national beliefs and aroused the fear that it might give American Negroes intolerable pretensions to equality . . ." From the Germans came propaganda leaflets dropped on their sector asking these African American troops why they were fighting the Germans when it was their own government that was discriminating against them: "What is democracy? Personal freedom; all citizens enjoying the same rights socially and before the law. Do you enjoy the same rights as the white people do in America, the land of freedom and democracy, or are you not rather treated over there as second class citizens?"

Regardless, the African American regiments continued to fight with the French army, with some performing so heroically as to be honored with the French medal of valor—France's highest honor. In early 1919, these troops returned home enlightened and emboldened, particularly after the United States refused to recognize the efforts of the soldiers awarded the medal of valor (such recognition would not come until 2003). Moreover, while they were feted with a parade in New York upon arrival, African American soldiers refused similar honors in the South when they were told they would march at the very end of the parade. Now awakened to the hypocrisy of which they had just taken part, many black citizens became more assertive in demanding their rights as Americans. This led to the Red Summer of 1919, so called because of the numerous race riots across the country (at least thirty-eight) partially fueled by white fears of returning black soldiers armed with a perceived "foreign (Bolshevik) ideology" that threatened the status quo.[29] As the summer ended and it became clear to these white mobs that African Americans would no longer meekly back down from conflict, the riots waned and were replaced with small-scale terrorism such as lynchings and burnings—acts that did not present the opportunity for an engaged battle.

In the years between the wars, the momentum toward equality increased. The migration of an estimated one million African Americans from the South to the North between 1916 and 1918 to replace white workers who had been deployed overseas exposed these people to (at least marginally) better individual rights than they had been accustomed to in the South. This migration north continued after the war as more people became exposed to the benefits of improved civil rights. In addition, the international success of athletes such as Joe Louis and Jesse Owens further highlighted the discrepancy between American ideals and actual racial practices.[30] By the time of the commencement of American involvement in World War II, black citizens were now more assertive—and more organized—than ever before. With an organized black leadership, this underclass now spoke with a unified voice. Civil rights activists warned that black Americans would no longer tolerate the indignities they suffered during the previous war. On September 27, 1940, the NAACP and other civil rights leaders met with military leaders to discuss the specifics of eradicating discrimination in the armed forces. Although their agreed-upon seven point program, calling for the integration of the military, was revised by President Roosevelt to eliminate the integration provision, it was significant in that it signaled the arrival of another source of organized black power—the black press. Calling Roosevelt's act "shameful," many within the black press pressured FDR to issue assurances that black soldiers would be treated as equals throughout the upcoming war. When they were not sufficiently appeased, they called for a march on Washington to protest treatment of black servicemen and workers by the military and defense industry. Concerned that such a protest on the eve of America's entry into World War II would be interpreted as a sign of weakness, Roosevelt succeeded in convincing them to call off the march by agreeing to enact the Fair Employment Practices Act of 1941, which banned discrimination in the government and defense industry.

Once American participation in the war began in earnest, African Americans enlisted, much as they had in World War I, only this time no longer under the assumption that military participation alone would bring change. Rather, by now many became convinced that political power was required. On this front, the black press became more vigilant in its effort to compel such change. Very quickly, this political muscle proved effective. In July 1942, General Eisenhower issued a statement of policy that broke with the past: unlike during World War I, when the United States attempted to enforce its segregationist policies abroad, now, in the European theater, the new U.S. policy dictated that "discrimination against the Negro troops [is to] be sedulously avoided." Moreover, no official position was to be taken with regard to the integration of social functions such as dances. Rather, the policy left it to local commanding officers "to use their own best judgment in avoiding discrimination due to race, but at the same time, minimizing causes of friction between White and Colored troops." Although full integration had not yet been achieved, rising black political power was beginning to have influence: African American rights were beginning to be honored and respected (at least in some instances), something unheard of only a few years prior. Further evidence of this comes from the court martial of serviceman (and future baseball pioneer) Jackie Robinson. On July 6, 1944, in Fort Hood, Texas, he refused a white bus driver's order to move to the back of the bus "where the coloreds belonged." Although the base provost marshal and the military police supported the bus driver, Robinson prevailed at trial. It is hard to imagine this happening during the previous world war.

Although most black servicemen were assigned to combat support units during the war, much as they were during World War I, these activities were no longer considered menial given the technological advances between the wars. Now, members of these support units built roads, bridges, hospitals; they became petroleum specialists in the intricate work required to keep all of the different types of vehicles, planes, and ships ready for action; they traveled all over the world to make what was uninhabitable livable in incredibly short time. Even so, the black press kept applying pressure on the government to permit black soldiers to fight alongside white ones, contending that the refusal to permit this amounted to a denial of equality. By December 1944, their strategy paid off when a manpower shortage resulted in the integration of the military for the first time: 4,562 black servicemen volunteered to enter training for combat, many of them accepting reductions in rank to private to do so. By war's end, the refrain that black citizens were somehow unqualified to fight for their country was rebuffed. Eventually, nearly one million black men and women served in World War II, in roles that caused the experience to be a transformative one on both an individual as well as communal basis. African Americans were now more empowered than ever to demand equality—their slice of the pie.

Eventually, the transformations taking place in the military trickled down to other parts of American life, most notably in New York. The city's powerful mayor at the time, Fiorello LaGuardia, actively courted the black vote, recognizing an emerging political force with the power to swing entire elections.[31] He established a committee to examine the city's racial climate, including the apparent discrimination against black ballplayers by the city's professional baseball teams, irrespective of the protestations of MLB to the contrary.[32] On the state level, the federal Fair Employment Practices Commission (which grew out of the Fair Employment Practices Act) inspired New York's State Commission Against Discrimination (which itself grew out of New York's Quinn-Ives Act, which imposed a fine of $500 or imprisonment for up to one year on any employer who refused to hire anyone because of their race).[33] After holding itself out as symbolic of America for so long, it was inevitable that Major League Baseball would become a convenient and frequent target of the early civil rights leaders.

Throughout World War II, the black and alternative press made the integration of MLB an issue. Much of the charge was led by Lester Rodney, a sportswriter for the Communist newspaper the *Daily Worker,* who had been pounding away on this front ever since he began writing for the paper in 1936.[34] He relentlessly brought the issue to the attention of his readers, highlighting the hypocrisy of the owners presiding over a segregated game that they nonetheless presented to the public as emblematic of the nation's highest and best qualities. His columns, even before the war, generated action: the Communist Party's 1938 New York City May Day parade (which at the time drew thousands) saw marchers fly "End Jim Crow in Baseball" banners; several Young Communist League members descended upon ballparks in various cities that summer handing out leaflets that drew attention to the issue;[35] and the TUAA—New York Trade Union Athletic Association (a consortium of approximately thirty area unions)—embarked on a 1940 campaign to gather one million signatures on petitions to end segregation in baseball (later the idea would morph into the "Committee to End Jim Crow in Baseball," which would continue to apply pressure on the owners). The TUAA later held an "End Jim Crow in Baseball" rally in New York's World's Fair Stadium in July of that year where it gathered thousands of signatures on its petition and treated fans to four baseball games between racially mixed teams.[36]

These efforts continued despite American entry into the war. Finally, in 1943, after relentless pressure from sportswriters Nat Low (who by that time had become sports editor for the *Daily Worker)* and Wendell Smith (of the weekly black newspaper the *Pittsburgh Courier*), the Pittsburgh Pirates were compelled to grant a tryout to two Negro League players, Roy Campanella and Dave Barnhill.[37] Although this tryout, as well as the others that soon followed on its heels, was little more than a publicity stunt undertaken solely to appease the black and alternative press (there was no possibility that the teams granting these tryouts were serious in considering these players, regardless of how well these tryouts went), these "shows" were more than had been offered previously, when team owners could ignore whatever cries there were for integration without fearing backlash. Later, during baseball's 1943 annual winter meeting, Paul Robeson addressed the owners, asking them to break from the past and integrate the game. Not surprisingly, team owners ignored him and his plea; under orders from Landis, they did not respond with a single question nor did they discuss his address afterward.[38] However, they did incur the wrath of Wendell Smith and Sam Lacy, a sportswriter for the *Baltimore Afro-American.*[39] Despite great resistance from MLB and team owners, this relentless pressure was starting to yield results.

As the war wound down, the pressure increased as the nation's attention turned inward and focused on domestic issues more acutely than had been possible during the war. On April 6, 1945, Joe Bostic, a black sportswriter, arrived at the Brooklyn Dodgers training camp with two Negro League players, demanding that they be given a tryout.[40] Bostic was a reporter for the *People's Voice,* a newspaper funded by Harlem Congressman Adam Clayton Powell, who in 1944 became the first African American New Yorker to be elected to Congress—a further indication of the emerging power of the black electorate in New York. Dodgers president Branch Rickey had twice earlier ignored Bostic's requests, turning him away at his office. Now, with the muscle of civil rights leader Powell behind him, Bostic was able to demand the tryout, get it, and inform his readers of it afterward. A few days later in Boston, at the urging of a Boston city councilman and Wendell Smith, another tryout was arranged at Fenway Park for the Red Sox.[41] Of course, these tryouts were shams but they were now occurring more frequently than ever before. Eventually, something would have to give, because there was no indication that these sham tryouts were doing anything to placate an increasingly restless and empowered civil rights movement. Later, on Opening Day at Yankee Stadium, the Congress of Racial Equality (CORE) helped to organize a picketing demonstration in an effort to enlighten the fans and castigate the owners of the game's most symbolic franchise.[42]

The summer of 1945 saw the pressure increase even more in New York City. The "End Jim Crow in Baseball" committee, supported by New York City councilman Benjamin B. Davis, picked up where the CORE demonstrators left off by picketing the city's three baseball stadiums, holding up photographs of dead and wounded black soldiers above the caption:

"Good enough to die for their country but not good enough to play for organized baseball."[43] Davis promised to make the integration of Major League Baseball a major issue in the coming fall election season.[44] Mayor LaGuardia also stepped up his integration efforts, asking for representatives of all three of the city's teams to join his "Committee for Unity" and to agree to comply with the Quinn-Ives Act (of which they technically were in violation).[45] He also urged his "Committee for Unity" to issue a statement announcing that integrated professional baseball in New York City would soon be a reality.[46] In response, the committee drafted a report that made note of all the recent developments in the city and concluded that the city's newly enlightened racial climate had made the city "the ideal proving ground for integration."[47] Within MLB, which by now was forced to confront the issue, a "Committee on Baseball Integration" was formed, although there is no evidence that it ever met, given that one of the committee members, Larry McPhail, "always had some excuse," according to fellow member Sam Lacy.[48]

Despite the fits and starts by MLB, there was no denying that the integration effort was gaining a foothold, at least in New York. And if it was successful there, then MLB would have no choice but to follow, given that New York was the epicenter of the league and home to its most glamorous teams. The black experience in both world wars, but particularly in World War II, compelled America to confront the segregation issue at last—there was no longer any way around it. Emerging black empowerment, combined with national and international pressures, were going to force the issue. Major League Baseball, as the symbolic face of the nation, was being pushed to the forefront of the desegregation cause because the growing civil rights movement showed no signs of relenting until integration was finally and fully achieved.

BRANCH RICKEY AND THE BATTLE
FOR CONTROL OVER THE INTEGRATION STORY

The "story" of Branch Rickey leads invariably to the widely accepted story of baseball's integration. Here as well, however, there can be more than one version of the tale. What is beyond dispute is that Rickey was a baseball genius. His innovations throughout the course of his long career, spurred by his dual passions—his desire to obtain a competitive edge and his desire to do so as cheaply as possible—revolutionized the game. His development of the farm system while running the Cardinals blended both passions very neatly in that the system provided the Cardinals with a perennial treasure trove of potential talent available only to them and at bargain-basement prices. This glut of talent forever on the doorstep of the majors had the further benefit of driving down the salaries of Rickey's big-leaguers, who were wary of engaging in pitched battles with him given the ever-looming threat of imminent replacement should they ever fall out of favor. By 1943, however, when Rickey left the Cardinals to take over the reins of the Dodgers, the farm system no longer provided such a competitive edge because of the simple fact that Rickey had been so successful with it in St. Louis that by now many teams were at least rudimentarily following his lead. Although the Dodgers had reached the World Series as recently as 1941, Rickey's keen eye for talent recognized the reality that the team was an old one and on the verge of collapse.[49] What was needed was an overhaul of the entire organization. The farm system would have to be rebuilt and restocked, but that would only bring the organization so far. Rickey realized that in order for the Dodgers to outrun their competitors in the National League on the field, he would have to outsmart his adversaries in the talent acquisition game. The farm system no longer gave him a leg up; a rebuilt one would, at best, put him on equal footing with his rivals. What he needed was something different, some new source of talent untapped by anyone else.

Shortly after arriving in Brooklyn, Rickey received permission from the team's directors to start scouting black talent.[50] Initially, Rickey had considered Latin American players but abandoned this idea because of the perceived obstacles faced by players who would have to overcome both a language as well as a racial barrier[51] (although he would return to the Latin American talent pool later in his career). Once his focus became clear, Rickey was single-minded in his pursuit. "The greatest untapped reservoir of raw material in the history of the game is the black race!" he said in 1945.[52] In this regard, his pursuit satisfied his passion for a competitive edge. And, if he could convince the public that these talented black players, currently being developed in the "Negro" leagues, were not under contract to their teams, they would be available to him virtually free of charge, thereby satisfying his frugal itch as well.[53]

Although historically Rickey has been portrayed as a social reformer, in fact he was far from it, even by his own admission. Rather, he was a sharp baseball man with an eye on the bottom line whose baseball instincts just happened to run right smack into America's burgeoning civil rights movement. Smart as he was (and no doubt much smarter than many of his baseball brethren), he recognized the rising tide and understood that MLB was going to have to integrate sooner rather than later—the symbolic status of the game made it such a convenient target for civil rights activists that it would have no choice.[54] Rickey had increasingly felt these pressures firsthand—it was the heat generated by the Quinn-Ives Act that boxed him into a corner that April morning when Joe Bostic arrived demanding a tryout for his players. He had no choice but to grant them one, even though he had no intention of signing them. Later, as Rickey was working behind the scenes on his own integration plan, he learned that Mayor LaGuardia was planning on making the integration of baseball the subject of his October 18, 1945, radio address.[55] Combined with the Committee for Unity's pending statement calling for the integration of baseball in New York, Rickey's hand was forced. Unless he acted immediately, he would lose control of the integration issue and possibly his competitive edge as well. Therefore, he convinced LaGuardia to change the subject of his address and hastily announced the signing of Jackie Robinson to a minor league contract on October 23, 1945.[56] Faced with the impending reality, Rickey masterfully managed to maintain control over the situation: "The Negro will make us winners for years to come," he said, once again in 1945. "And for that I will happily bear being a bleeding heart, and a do-gooder, and all that humanitarian rot."[57] In the midst of the moment, Rickey maintained that his was strictly a baseball decision. As the years passed, his story, as well as the official story, would morph into something different.

After the Robinson signing, Rickey began to emphasize reasons other than baseball for his actions. He became particularly fond of a story involving Charles "Tommy" Thomas, a black ballplayer Rickey coached at Ohio Wesleyan in 1903.[58] According to the story, Thomas was refused hotel accommodations when the team traveled to South Bend, Indiana, for a game. Rickey convinced the hotel clerk to allow Thomas to room with him. Once in the room, Thomas began to sob and, according to Rickey, scratch at his skin "as if he wanted to forcibly remove the stain of its color." "I never felt so helpless in my life," Rickey recalled later. In response, Rickey liked to say that he tried to reassure Thomas by telling him that "a time would come where there would be equal opportunity for all, regardless of race." The story closes on a heartwarming, if dime-novel, note as Rickey attempted to raise Thomas's spirits: "Come on, Tommy, snap out of it, buck up! We'll lick this one day, but we can't if you feel sorry for yourself."[59]

The Thomas story was an inspirational one and highlighted the humanitarian side of Branch Rickey, an apparent closeted civil rights advocate. However, it is one that was not told for the first time until shortly before Rickey signed Robinson, more than four decades from the date of its alleged occurrence.[60] Although Rickey and Thomas maintained a long-standing relationship that no doubt dated back to that time, and although it is likely that the story springs from a foundation of truth, the veracity of some of the specifics within it, particularly the most heart-wrenching ones, is open to question. In a court of law such testimony would likely be viewed with skepticism. As an American morality tale, it becomes fact simply because we would like for it to be. There is a difference between being sympathetic toward an individual's plight and being a crusader for integration. Rickey was perhaps the former but boasted that he was the latter. Because his story fit a comforting narrative, however, few sought to question it.

As the years passed and Rickey's legend grew, Rickey also stated that if it were up to him the Cardinals would have been integrated by the mid-1930s; it was only owner Sam Breadon who stood in his way. However, as with the Thomas story, no contemporaneous supporting evidence exists.[61] He likewise claimed to have been a supporter of integration ever since the alleged 1903 Thomas incident, but although he was an executive with significant input in player personnel decisions since becoming the general/field manager of the St. Louis Browns in 1913, he never once exhibited, at least publicly, any such indications prior to 1945. Many decades later, his children and grandchildren helped to further burnish Rickey's socially conscious image by recalling "stirring conversations at the Rickey dinner table . . . about Abraham Lincoln, the Civil War, and the unfortunate, continuing effects of slavery on American Negro life."[62] But with no corresponding, contemporaneous overt acts on Rickey's behalf in the several decades in which he was a very public executive with the power to act or, at a minimum, speak out on behalf of these causes (he was not a shy public speaker, nor one who ran from controversy, or from Commissioner Landis, as the 1931 *Milwaukee AA v. Landis* litigation discussed in chapter 2 attests), it is difficult to ascertain how much of these such stories are fact and how much are rose-colored, sepia-toned family legend.

To many who have tried to tackle the Rickey story and legacy in print, he remains a conundrum: an archconservative civil rights pioneer who opposed what he termed "radicalism" in any form and in any manner save this one instance.[63] He despised the *Daily Worker* as well as the agitation of the black press even though they were aggressively lobbying for what he repeatedly claimed was a fervent cause of his since the 1903 Thomas incident. Later in life, even after the integration of baseball, he supported Barry Goldwater in 1964 rather than staunch civil rights advocate Lyndon Johnson. When questioned as to his political stance, Rickey replied that a vote for Johnson would be "a step toward national degradation."[64] At every turn in his public life, Rickey stood in the corner of the socially conservative, with the exception of the Robinson matter. His actions in that one instance not only seem out of character but a direct contradiction to everything he believed in, and how he lived his life both before and afterward. For his biographers, it is difficult to shoehorn the Robinson episode into Rickey's life and still emerge with a coherent narrative. It is this riddle that causes many to throw up their hands and conclude simply that, in the end, Branch Rickey was a terribly complex man.[65]

The possibility exists, however, that he was in fact simple and straightforward, at least in his actions if not always his words. Perhaps he simply wanted to win baseball games and was willing to take whatever avenue existed that enabled him to achieve this goal at the lowest possible cost. This simple narrative does not require the elaborate twists and turns that the Rickey story traditionally takes. However, this narrative is hardly a symbolic one, hardly one that stands in for "America," so it is not surprising that it is not as widely embraced. Rather, the "Rickey as racial pioneer" story took hold because of its obvious appeal, infused as it was with delicious didactic potential. Sometimes, however, a story is more than simply a story. In this instance, the Rickey story would have a damaging effect on the integration effort in several ways, ultimately slowing the pace of integration in Major League Baseball many years. The effects of this story are still felt today.

BRANCH RICKEY AND THE
SLOW PACE OF INTEGRATION IN MLB

The popular Rickey story had both an immediate as well as a long-term effect on the game's integration movement. Initially, it distracted from and negated the integration movement that had developed significant momentum independent of him. Eventually, it set the movement back years.

Immediately, the story gave credence to Landis's longstanding lie that anybody within MLB could sign a black player if they so chose. As such, it justified the falsehood and permitted white America to gloss over the reality of racism both within MLB and, more important, within the nation. Although Landis's lie was a naked one, the Rickey story allowed MLB to escape greater scrutiny of its racist practices because it demonstrated that, at least superficially, Landis was correct. According to the story, one man did, after all, decide to sign a black player and no one within the game stopped him. MLB could defend itself by repeating the lie that the game was now, and always had been, open to everyone; it only took an individual with courage to make this possibility a reality. This fabrication glossed over the deep and longstanding institutionalized racism that was truly at the core of the issue.

More significantly, the story conveniently negated and ignored the enormous social pressures that the rising integration movement—spearheaded by the increasingly empowered and determined black and alternative presses along with progressive governmental leaders such as LaGuardia and Adam Clayton Powell—had on MLB and that, in reality, had more to do with bringing the game to the brink of integration by the end of World War II than anything having to do with Branch Rickey. This, in turn, resulted in the tragic consequence of the story: it wrested the integration issue away from these people and put it in the hands of MLB, to be doled out on its terms and through its good graces.

As African Americans, ballplayers and otherwise, understood all too well, there are real-world consequences involved in the seemingly academic distinction between grabbing something as a right and receiving it as a privilege.[66] With *Plessy v. Ferguson* still the law, black citizens in 1946 were left to appeal to white America's "better instincts" to achieve anything even remotely resembling equality.[67] Without legal or institutional acknowledgment of equality, the balance of power remained in white America's favor, permitting it to dictate the terms and conditions of any improvement in conditions.[68] African Americans were forced to become supplicants: "seeking, pleading, begging to be treated as full-fledged members of the human race."[69] World War II began to change this dynamic, at least incrementally. Although the law was still not on their side, their accomplishments on an international stage provided them with a legitimacy they had not previously enjoyed. This was evidenced by the increasingly aggressive black press, which found its voice during this period and was, therefore, no longer content to remain "in its place." Rickey's actions in 1945–46 had the effect of stopping this movement in its tracks as he did everything within his power to demonstrate and maintain control over the integration issue, thereby preventing it from ever gaining independent legitimacy through either law or institutional recognition. By doing so, he made sure that black ballplayers would still need to appeal to the "better instincts" of whites like him for integration to occur.

Although Rickey was alleged to have dramatically exclaimed, "they can't stop me now!" when Quinn-Ives was passed,[70] his actions thereafter were in many ways contrary to the intent of one seeking to promote racial equality. In actuality, rather than push for the passage of such equality laws, Rickey did what he could to prevent them from taking hold—to prevent the application of the stamp of institutional legitimacy on the equality issue that would have diminished his ability to control the nature and pace of integration. For once equality became a right, there would be no reason for black America to see any need to appeal to his "better instincts" to aid them in their cause. Rickey used his position on LaGuardia's Committee for Unity to convince influential community leaders to persuade the "End Jim Crow" group to call off its ballpark demonstrations;[71] he persuaded La-Guardia to postpone his October talk calling for the integration of MLB;[72] he made sure that MLB never became a test case for the Quinn-Ives Act, undoubtedly realizing that such a case could potentially cause him to lose control of the integration issue and his competitive advantage in signing black players in the process. Instead, he accelerated the timetable for his integration plans by hastily announcing the Robinson signing to stave off the onrushing tide.[73] By taking these actions, particularly those of postponing LaGuardia's talk and pre-empting the application of Quinn-Ives to baseball, Rickey prevented the integration issue from becoming defined as one of fundamental right, of natural law, and preserved it as something arising from choice, to be doled out by self-appointed enlightened people like him. It was this tactic that enabled him to maintain his competitive edge. At his core, Rickey was most likely neither a segregationist nor an integrationist; he was a baseball man. And as a baseball man, he would not be able to monopolize black talent if all three New York teams were required, pursuant to Quinn-Ives and pressure from the mayor's office, to sign black players. Very quickly, many other teams within MLB would have no choice but to follow New York's lead and his competitive edge would evaporate before it was even established.

Beyond these acts, aimed at maintaining his competitive edge, Rickey took further action to ensure that his edge would come at little or no cost. On May 7, 1945, Rickey called a press conference to announce that his Brooklyn Dodgers would be sponsoring a team, the Brooklyn Brown Dodgers, in a new Negro league called the United States League, which would challenge the legitimacy of the established, and revered within the black community, Negro National and American Leagues.[74] During the press conference, Rickey denounced the established leagues as "organizations in the zone of a racket," and made a point of noting that these leagues did not operate through the use of formal player contracts nor did they have a reserve clause that bound their players to their teams.[75] As for the rationale behind the formation of this league, Rickey later claimed that it was an elaborate cover operation that enabled him to train black talent for eventual admission into the Major Leagues without arising the suspicions of his fellow, presumably far less enlightened, owners.[76] Under cover of the United States League, Rickey could sign whomever he wished, train them, and no one would be the wiser as to his long-term plans.[77] What this league likewise brought him, however, was an opportunity to lay the groundwork for his eventual plundering of the Negro Leagues without compensation.

As an attorney, Rickey surely recognized the importance of establishing a foundation for future actions. Here, through his United States League, Rickey provided himself a platform to make his case to the nation that the Negro Leagues, despite their outward appearance as formal "leagues" with established teams complete with loyal fans and favorite players, were not leagues after all, nor were the clubs really "clubs" in the sense that Major League clubs were. Rather, the lack of formal contracts or a reserve clause, as well as the presence of unsavory characters filtered throughout the organization, rendered them, all appearances to the contrary, illegitimate. If such an argument could prove to be persuasive, then there would be no legal, ethical, or moral responsibility on Rickey's part to compensate these clubs later on when he would begin cherry-picking the top talent for his Dodgers.

Ironically, despite Rickey's strong words denouncing the corruption of the Negro Leagues, he harbored no hesitation in teaming up with many of these same bookies and gamblers to get his United States League off the ground.[78] If his comments were to be taken at face value, it is difficult to see why he would choose to perpetuate the immorality of the leagues he was challenging in his own league. Here again, however, his words and actions took different paths. In the end, he was not taking a moral stand; he was gaining a competitive edge. Understood in these terms, his actions seem reasonable. They were later borne out when Rickey plucked Robinson from the Kansas City Monarchs of the Negro American League and then ignored two requests from the Monarchs for compensation.[79] He later repeated this tactic in his signing of other top Negro League talent such as Roy Campanella, Don Newcombe, and others over the remainder of his tenure with the Dodgers.[80] Much as he had hoped, he was able to revive the Dodgers through a source of previously untapped talent that came virtually free of charge.

Rickey's actions did not escape the scrutiny of the black press. In reaction to his press conference announcing the formation of the United States League, several journalists took him to task, calling him a "pompous ass" or, worse, comparing him to the most reviled dictators of the time.[81] A. S. "Doc" Young wrote in the black daily, the *Chicago Defender:* "Rickey is no Abe Lincoln or FDR and we won't accept him as the dictator of Negro baseball. Hitler and Mussolini are no longer! We need no American dictator!"[82] One of Rickey's biographers characterized this criticism thusly: "Rickey must have chortled at the Negro activists' uninformed attacks on him . . ."[83] Perhaps these activists were not so uninformed. As they clearly recognized at the time, what was theirs was being taken from them and rebranded as something to be used for the benefit of white America. Surely this provided just cause for their outrage. Further, the sequence of events that took place in the ensuing months with regard to the method of integration, once it finally arrived, would justify their outrage, even if the story attached to these events would not.

THE JACKIE ROBINSON STORY AND THE MARGINALIZATION OF THE BLACK EMPOWERMENT MOVEMENT

In selecting the person to break baseball's unofficial color line, Rickey stressed that it could not be just any player. Rather, it had to be the "right" player, one who, as stated earlier, "would accept the responsibility of his race and who could bear that burden." In the famous story, echoed through the decades in its numerous retellings, Rickey grilled Robinson on the pressures he would face, playing numerous roles in the process, forcing Robinson to confront the types of people and prejudices he would likely face as the first black Major Leaguer. After three hours, in response to Robinson's question concerning the type of black player he was looking for, came Rickey's famous remark: "Robinson, I'm looking for a ballplayer with guts enough not to fight back." The wrong kind of player, according to this story, "would set the cause of true integration back generations."[84] It was for this reason that Robinson was asked during that meeting to turn the other cheek for the good of his race. And so began baseball's "Great Experiment" as it has come to be called.

This story, as well as the rationales behind the seemingly simple elements of it, has rarely been questioned, uplifting as it seems to be at first blush. However, once it has been dissected, another story emerges, one where the beneficiaries of this "experiment" appear to shift. Some questions immediately come to mind: namely, was it an experiment after all? Was there a need for a "right" player? What and who defines that "right" player? What if the "wrong" player had been selected instead? What would have happened if the pioneering player was an inferior talent and/or one who refused to refrain from retaliation? Would this have sent the integration effort back generations, as is commonly accepted? Or, could this have possibly had the effect of actually accelerating it? The answers to these questions raise the specter of some unexpected possibilities.

First, the title of the episode, "The Great Experiment," appears to be misleading in that an experiment supposes a tentative procedure or policy—something with the possibility of failure. However, given all that led up to Robinson's debut, there appeared to be little chance of this. The mounting pressures from several different sources, combined with the symbolic status of baseball, made integration a foregone conclusion by the mid-1940s. Regardless, the narrative not only stuck, it became linked with the notion that, for it to succeed, the "right player" had to be selected. This negated the idea that black citizens could claim equality as a natural right and suggested instead that it may be bestowed upon them dependent on their meeting certain preconditions acceptable to the dominant group. Implicit in this framework was the understanding (threat?) that if these conditions were not performed to the satisfaction of this group, equal rights and opportunity may properly be withheld.

With regard to the determination of this "right" player, at least in hindsight it becomes obvious that there was little chance that whoever was selected would not have succeeded, at least on the field. On one count there can be no dispute: Rickey had an acute eye for talent; there was indeed a treasure trove of talent available in the Negro Leagues, as would be demonstrated throughout the 1950s. By the end of the first decade of integrated baseball (1956), a black player had won six Most Valuable Player awards, seven Rookie of the Year awards, and the first Cy Young Award (Don Newcombe in 1956 when one award was given for both leagues). In addition, black hitters won batting, RBI (runs batted in), home run, and stolen base titles while black pitchers (few of them as there were) managed to lead their leagues in wins and strikeouts. More immediately, the two clubs that integrated first and to the greatest extent (the Dodgers in the National League and the Cleveland Indians in the American League) were instantly successful: the Dodgers won the pennant in 1947, and the Indians won the World Series the following year. In 1949 the Dodgers won the pennant again and were once more led by Robinson, who was the league's MVP, along with Campanella, who took home Rookie of the Year honors. Although the Indians fell to third place that season, they were led by Larry Doby, who led the team in both home runs and runs batted in. By the end of the 1950s, black players had won nine of the thirteen National League MVP awards issued since Robinson's debut (including the last seven), as well as nine of the thirteen Rookie of the Year awards. In retrospect, there were numerous black ballplayers who fit the mold of the "right" player, at least between the foul lines. Moreover, the abilities of Negro League players were well known to MLB insiders long before integration. In 1937 Joe DiMaggio told a reporter that the best pitcher he ever faced, bar none, was Negro League star Satchel Paige.[85] And DiMaggio was hardly the only one to recognize the talents of these players; Major League and Negro League players frequently barnstormed together in the offseason, and mutual admiration abounded.

In fact, the player Rickey selected, Robinson, was far from the most talented player then playing in the Negro Leagues. In college, at UCLA, he shared the football team backfield with Kenny Washington, who later became the first black player in the National Football League.[86] Robinson was also a talented collegiate basketball player and track and field star, becoming his school's first four-letter man.[87] Of all his talents, baseball was perhaps his weakest sport, although he excelled here as well in college and, to a much greater extent, in the Major Leagues. The fact that a player such as Robinson could excel in the Major Leagues in what was possibly his weakest sport immediately gave lie to the longstanding theory that black athletes were not good enough to play Major League baseball.

More important than on-field qualities were the supposed off-field qualities Rickey's "right" player was required to possess. However, there is little evidence that a more combative player would have had a significant negative impact on the integration effort. By many counts, at least northern cities (where most MLB teams resided prior to expansion) were demonstrating increasing tolerance for integration, as indicated by the findings of LaGuardia's Committee for Unity. A few years later, the federal Housing and Home Finance Administration concluded that Philadelphians would likewise be amenable to increased integration.[88] On the national level, the integration of the military signaled a recognition that change was coming in many forms; New York's Quinn-Ives Act was only one such example of this. Moreover, Major League players at the time, assuming they were products of their upbringing, may have been somewhat less prejudiced than is commonly assumed. Contrary to popular opinion, MLB was not dominated by white southerners during this era (in fact they comprised only slightly more than 25 percent of all MLB players in 1947);[89] the most populous states (California, New York, Pennsylvania, and Illinois) were the birthplaces of more players than any others.[90]

Regardless, Robinson was instructed to hold his tongue, and so he did. Despite fears of a backlash against the integration effort, Robinson's rookie season was a relatively quiet one as far as off-field incidents were concerned.[91] Later that season, Dan Bankhead became the first black pitcher in MLB, and with his debut came fears of potential brawls or riots given Bankhead's wildness—what would happen if and when he hit a white batter? True to form, Bankhead had trouble finding the strike zone—he ended the season with a 7.20 earned run average (ERA)—and, on August 26, in a game against the Pittsburgh Pirates where he gave up eight runs and ten hits in three innings of work, a pitch hit Pirate outfielder Wally Westlake. However, no confrontation ensued. Westlake took first base and the game continued.[92] Bankhead provided an interesting counterpoint to Robinson in that while Robinson excelled, Bankhead struggled, threatening every hitter who faced him with his dangerous combination of blazing speed and lack of control. Regardless, the struggles of Bankhead did nothing to affect the cause of integration, although he clearly was not the "right" player, according to Rickey's prescription.

Rickey's gag order itself was particularly troubling to Robinson personally and caused him significant grief for the remainder of his life. By not permitting him to speak out, Rickey exposed Robinson to unwarranted and ignorant allegations that he was an "Uncle Tom" for acquiescing to Rickey's edict. Indeed, Lester Rodney recognized the risks involved in even discussing the politics of the gag order[93] and avoided it (he avoided few other topics). In later years, Malcolm X viciously attacked Robinson for submitting to his "White Boss" in Malcolm X's attempt to marginalize Robinson from the civil rights movement of the 1960s.[94] Others who attempted to similarly criticize Robinson likewise confused the range of his options with Rickey's: while Rickey had many alternatives available to him during the 1940s and could have chosen a different path toward integration had he desired, Robinson did not; given that *Plessy* was still the law of the land and that baseball remained segregated, he found himself in the unenviable position of having little choice but to accede to Rickey's plan. As a result, through Rickey's "Great Experiment," Robinson not only was compelled to endure indignities from players and fans, but, as the culturally aware Robinson surely anticipated, from members of his own race as well.[95] The contrast in power between Rickey and Robinson left

Robinson with little choice but to grit his teeth and perform silently on the diamond. Although he would suffer the stings of this reality later in life, on the field he succeeded spectacularly.

By the end of his rookie season, Robinson was exceedingly popular. He not only won the 1947 National League Rookie of the Year award, a national poll ranked him as the country's second most admired man, trailing only Bing Crosby.[96] Very quickly he became one of the most sought-after celebrities in the nation, even traveling to and speaking in the South on occasion, and a popular pitchman.[97] Far from simply tolerating Robinson, large swaths of America embraced him surprisingly quickly. Although Rickey stressed that baseball's integration effort required delicacy, the overwhelming national response to Robinson appears to contradict this assumption.

Almost instantly, Robinson became a hero and symbol to many black and white Americans (although in some segments of the country he was vilified; death threats and catcalls were likewise a part of his existence but these represented a minority viewpoint, albeit a frightening one nonetheless).[98] Through one player, the "race question" was taken off the table, at least as far as MLB was concerned, as America moved on to other things. This was both good and bad; good in that it seemed to indicate that many Americans appeared willing to accept at least some initial steps toward integration, but bad in that it removed the pressure on MLB to integrate, thereby permitting it to control the pace and manner of integration for the next several years. In Robinson, America, both black and white, was presented with the "face" of integration. But, owing to Rickey's manipulation, the effect was something less than authentic. As a result, Rickey succeeded in presenting to America a distorted image—one that was more easily acceptable to white America. Rickey compelled Robinson to present a picture of what he believed the "right kind" of black citizen to be and in so doing, presented a powerful image to the nation. To white America, the image suggested a type of black American it should expect; to black America, the image instructed it as to the range of acceptable behavior in the presence of white America. Though this may have been a comfortable image for whites to accept, it was undoubtedly much less so for black Americans.

In actuality, Robinson was nothing like the image he portrayed in his inaugural season. He was combative by nature; a feisty, aggressive player who, as evidenced by his military court-martial, was a civil rights activist in the mold of the increasingly aggressive black press Rickey so despised. Although, by 1948, Rickey removed the muzzle from Robinson and allowed him to present his true self to the world (indeed, by 1949 he regularly lashed out at opponents and even umpires, eventually drawing the wrath of Commissioner Happy Chandler, who warned him to temper his behavior),[99] this is not the image of him that endures. By that point America had moved on. It had taken its snapshot of the integration of baseball and was content and comfortable with the story it told.

Through the use of language ("The Great Experiment," "the right player") as well as his machinations leading up to the moment of integration itself, Rickey managed to maintain control over the narrative such that the rate and method of integration came to be dictated solely by those who ran Organized Baseball. This resulted in an integration effort on a superficial level only; even after Robinson's debut, black players still could not claim that they had a "right" to play Major League baseball. Rather, those who were selected were merely permitted to play by a beneficent Rickey (as well as any of his brethren who *chose* to integrate along with him) and, accordingly, they were expected to be thankful for the opportunity rather than insistent. All of this negated the legacy of the black experience in World War II as well as the emerging civil rights mindset and movement. Through the enduring image left by the Rickey story of integration, black Americans were given the message that in order for change to occur, they should ask for it rather than demand it and to expect it only as a favor doled out on their behalf by those acting on their "better instincts." The various parts of the story effectively delivered the message that black citizens were not to stand up for themselves, not to demand respect and equality. Rather, just as Rickey instructed Robinson to turn the other cheek, they were to subjugate their individual rights for the eventual (time to be determined by others) rights of their race.

Ultimately, the Rickey story does indeed presage the landmark civil rights case, *Brown v. Board of Education,* just as many within the "baseball as America" camp have always claimed. However, in the message Rickey's actions delivered, it foreshadowed the most unfortunate aspect of that litigation: the "all deliberate speed" language contained within what is commonly known as *Brown 2.*[100] The denial of individual rights that sprang from this language highlighted the differences in how these rights were doled out to minority groups as opposed to how they were wielded by the dominant group. Both *Brown 2* and Rickey's actions eight years earlier had the effect of taking the integration effort out of the hands of those who were the victims of segregation and placing it instead into the hands of the very people who had practiced segregation for decades. And just as the "all deliberate speed" language delayed the integration of southern schools for years post-*Brown*, Rickey's actions ensured that post-Robinson, a truly integrated MLB would be decades in coming.

BROWN 2 *AND "ALL DELIBERATE SPEED"*

On May 17, 1954, the United States Supreme Court handed down its decision in *Brown v. Board of Education of Topeka, Kansas (Brown 1)*,[101] repudiating *Plessy v. Ferguson*[102] by announcing that, "in the field of public education, the doctrine of 'separate but equal' has no place."[103] Although technically a school desegregation case, *Brown 1* was, in reality, much more than that. Because the validity of school segregation hinged on *Plessy*, which was a case concerned not with schools but with railroad cars, *Brown 1* undermined the rationale for segregation in all public areas.[104] This was made clear in the immediate aftermath of *Brown 1* when a number of cases were decided per curiam on the authority of *Brown 1*, which overturned segregation laws in a variety of settings and crystallized the idea that *Brown* was applicable to the overarching concept of segregation, not its particular application to public schools.[105] Approximately one year later, on May 31, 1955, *Brown 2*[106] was handed down, which detailed how the process of integration was to occur. After taking note of the "substantial progress" taking place in some areas, the court held that "[f]ull implementation of these constitutional principles may require solution of varied local school problems. . . . Because of their proximity to local conditions and the need for further hearings, the courts which originally heard these cases can best perform this judicial appraisal. Accordingly, we believe it appropriate to remand the cases to those courts."[107] After placing the burden of desegregation on local courts and school boards, the Court announced the timetable for integration. Pursuant to *Brown 2*, the local courts were required "to take such proceedings and enter such orders and decrees consistent with this opinion as are necessary and proper to admit to public schools on a racially nondiscriminatory basis with *all deliberate speed* the parties to these cases" (emphasis added).[108]

The "all deliberate speed" language would prove to be a detriment to true integration in two ways. First, in deviating from the Court's common practice of issuing final judgments, the "all deliberate speed" language held that here, despite its ruling in *Brown 1* that "separate but equal" was no longer the law, segregation could nevertheless continue for an indefinite time into the future.[109] The language ensured that an entire generation of black students would attend segregated schools regardless of the language in *Brown 1*.[110] This was an unusual and damaging postponement of established legal rights.

In effect, through its delegation of the desegregation issue to local courts and officials, the Supreme Court placed the volatile issue of desegregation in the hands of segregationists—the individuals and entities that wound up on the short end of the *Brown* decision and those who were most likely to resist efforts to integrate.[111] Given this reality, it was not surprising that, through their manipulation of the "all deliberate speed" language, these segregationists would in fact delay integration as long as possible. For eight years after *Brown 2*, the Supreme Court refused to hear any case in which questions were raised with regard to pupil placement or that questioned the appropriateness of the various desegregation plans, as ineffective as they appeared to be even on their face.[112] As a result, those eight years saw little in the way of significant progress toward integration despite the strong language contained in *Brown 1*. By 1963, only 1.17 percent of black schoolchildren in the eleven former Confederate states were attending integrated schools, with most of this integration the result of white schoolchildren attending predominantly black schools.[113] Only 0.4 percent of black schoolchildren were attending predominantly white schools.[114] In all, of the 2,283 affected schools, 2,013 remained fully segregated.[115]

Second, the "all deliberate speed" language highlighted a distinction between how individual rights were parceled out to Americans, dependent upon their social status. Until *Brown 2*, constitutional rights were typically defined as not only present but personal as well.[116] Now, through the "all deliberate speed" language, the individual rights of black Americans were sacrificed in favor of a mass solution.[117] In effect, *Brown 2* told black Americans that while white Americans had individual rights, they had, at best, group rights.[118] The language gave credence to the curious notion that something could be unlawful yet still be permitted to continue for an indefinite time.[119] The natural result of this paradox was a lessening in respect for the rule of law, as was to be seen throughout the 1960s as the failure of *Brown 2* became more evident.[120]

As the 1950s progressed, it became abundantly clear that many local courts and school boards were doing everything in their power (and the "all deliberate speed" language gave them significant power) to prevent true integration. As the integration movement inched toward compliance, it likewise became clear that the "all deliberate speed" language permitted white southerners to dictate the pace and method of integration and to achieve "integration" on terms they could accept.[121] Rather than place the burden on those responsible for the constitutional wrong, "all deliberate speed" dictated that the victims of the violation would suffer the consequences of delay irrespective of the official acknowledgment of their harm.[122] By permitting this to occur, the Court reinforced the notion that, despite the strong language to the contrary in *Brown 1,* blacks and whites were still treated differently under the law, at least as far as equality principles were concerned. Although *Brown 1* spoke of individual rights, *Brown 2* decided that the best way to deal with the rights of black Americans was as a race rather than as individuals. "[I]t should go without saying," the Court remarked in *Brown 2,* "that the vitality of these constitutional principles cannot be allowed to yield simply because of disagreement with them."[123] Two paragraphs later, the Court repudiated this remark with its proclamation of "all deliberate speed." Together, *Brown 1* and *Brown 2* held that black Americans could be denied relief from a legal wrong they were found to have suffered so long as steps were being taken to prevent other black Americans—at some later date—from similar harm.[124] This was not how white Americans were treated under the law and, as time progressed, the paradox became more and more acute. As civil rights scholar Louis Lusky noted back in 1963, "[A]s each additional Negro child is forced into a segregated school, another person is denied equal protection under the laws and the Constitution is outraged anew."[125]

Eventually, the Court grew impatient with the pace of southern school integration and began to pull back from "all deliberate speed." Starting in 1962, the Court began hearing cases again questioning pupil placement and school desegregation plans.[126] By 1964, the Court announced that the time for "mere deliberate speed" had run out.[127] The next year, the Court stated that "[d]elays in desegregating school systems are no longer tolerable."[128] With the departure from "all deliberate speed" came accelerated integration at last. In 1964 Congress passed the Civil Rights Act of 1964 (which, significantly, called for immediate implementation; the era of "all deliberate speed" was now over), and in 1965–66 the U.S. Department of Health, Education and Welfare threatened to withhold federal funds to noncompliant districts.[129] As a result, the rate of integration rose to 6.01 percent in the former Confederate states—still nothing to shout about but significant progress nonetheless.[130] In the end, even though it was the Supreme Court that made the bold pronouncement of equality in Brown 1, it was Congress and the executive branch that ultimately compelled the integration of southern schools by placing immediate pressure on local school districts to integrate or suffer the consequences. Only once "all deliberate speed" had been abandoned, along with the concept of group rights over individual rights, did significant integration begin to occur. In 1970, the Court came full circle when it identified immediacy rather than patience as the touchtone for the integration movement.[131] By this point, "all deliberate speed" was officially a failure.

RICKEY'S INTEGRATION LEGACY:
"ALL DELIBERATE SPEED" IN PERPETUITY

Despite the shortcomings of Brown 2, the national desegregation movement was grounded in institutional bedrock—Brown 1's official pronouncement of racial equality irrespective of the subsequent "all deliberate speed" language—that blunted the long-term negative consequences of Brown 2 and allowed for the eventual dismantling of the offending language through official channels (that is, the Court, Congress, and the White House). Lacking a comparable institutional foundation, MLB, despite being seven years ahead of the nation with regard to the integration issue, ultimately lagged behind it. By taking action to prevent the application of either Quinn-Ives or the Fair Employment Practices Act to New York's Major League baseball teams, Rickey succeeded in guaranteeing that official declarations of racial equality in Organized Baseball would never come, thus leaving MLB in charge of the method and pace of the game's desegregation. This virtually ensured that integration would be done in a manner acceptable to Rickey and his colleagues—the very segregationists who maintained the color line for decades. This would alter the course of integration within the game thereafter.

As evidenced in the wake of the *Brown* decisions, there exists a fundamental difference between waiting for the establishment of a right and waiting for its enjoyment after it has been established.[132] Once equality had been etched in stone, as it was in *Brown 1*, the methods used to achieve actual integration could no longer be justified as beneficent gifts to the underprivileged class. Rather, they become the more mundane administrative machinery necessary to achieve what the law required.[133] At this point, these steps were now subject to critical assessment—not with regard to the "good intentions" that led to their enactment, but with regard to whether they did in fact achieve the results for which they were designed; that is, whether they succeeded in alleviating the offending discrimination.[134] Critically, if these steps were considered ineffectual, "self-help" was the next logical step.[135] Thus, it was the combination of *Brown 1*'s pronouncement and *Brown 2*'s administrative failure that contributed significantly to the turmoil of the 1960s and the increasingly militant black power movement.[136]

Post–*Brown 1*, the obstructionism and delay that followed struck at the integrity of the legal system, causing faith in it to erode and justifying illegal, militant tactics used to combat the abuses of the system.[137] At the heart of these actions was the concept that black citizens were being denied what was rightfully, legally, theirs. If those in power were not applying the law properly, then it was therefore not immoral to disobey the law, because it was the lawmaking system itself that was unjust, immoral, and, ultimately, illegal. That this militancy gained a foothold in the larger civil rights movement but never took hold within MLB is testimony to the differences between how the nation and MLB were integrated.

As a result of Rickey's efforts, there was never an official acknowledgment that blacks had a "right" to play Major League baseball; instead, they were merely granted the opportunity. The consequences of this distinction were significant—the lack of institutionally recognized equality within MLB meant that there existed no official, legitimized mechanism to address and correct the deliberately slow pace of integration within the game. Unlike the national civil rights movement, here there was no Supreme

Court to take action to solve the problem, no federal government with both the means and determination to step in and force an acceleration of the process. Rather, the only potential structure available for redress was MLB itself, an institution that had always professed ignorance with regard to a color line and that was never compelled to confront its denial. Within this organizational structure, MLB was free to continue its "deliberate" pace of integration for decades.

Amid the celebration over Robinson's entrance into Organized Baseball, overlooked was the reality that now, despite the cheers over the "integration" of the game, there were still dozens of qualified black players who were denied the opportunity to play Major League baseball solely because of their race. And among the persistent offenders of baseball's supposed open-door policy was Branch Rickey who, despite his claims, proved himself to be a less than enthusiastic advocate for black players during the remainder of his career. Immediately after the color line was broken, an informal quota system was established, wherein those teams that deigned to sign black players restricted their number at any given time.[138] In addition, the general rule for each team was to ensure that there was always an even number of black players to avoid compelling a white player to room with a black player on the road.[139] Rickey helped to create these norms (although he was not the only one) which, as was the case with many of his actions, were quickly copied by his peers.

In the spring of 1948, Rickey faced a dilemma over the placement of catcher Roy Campanella. Although Campanella was obviously ready to take over the position from Bruce Edwards, a solid catcher who injured his arm in the offseason and was unable to start the season, Rickey moved him to the outfield during spring training, a position Campanella was unfamiliar with. When, not surprisingly, Campanella did not perform well at his new position, Rickey sent him to the minors.[140] Although baseball historians have traditionally justified the move as merely part of Rickey's "master plan" to integrate all of baseball, the minor leagues as well as the majors (Campanella became the first modern-era black player in the AAA American Association), it also allowed Rickey to avoid the uncomfortable situation of having his popular white catcher unseated by a black player.[141] Rickey similarly manipulated his Brooklyn roster during the remainder of his tenure there, always ensuring that there were never "too many" black players at any one time.[142] Before the 1950 season he sold another superior black player, Sam Jethroe, to the Cleveland Indians so that white journeymen George Shuba and Cal Abrams could patrol the outfield in his stead, thereby maintaining the racial balance Rickey believed to be so important.[143]

Rickey left the Dodgers after the 1950 season to become general manager of the Pittsburgh Pirates, a team that had yet to break the color line. But although the architect of the "Great Experiment" was now running the club, he saw no reason to pursue integration for several years, despite his claimed deep-seated belief in equality and his alleged promise to Charles Thomas back in 1903. It was not until 1953 that Carlos Bernier, a dark-skinned Puerto Rican, became the first nonwhite to suit up for the Pirates.[144] In Rickey's fourth year with the club, Curt Roberts became the team's first black player.[145] Testament to his role as a baseball man rather than a civil rights crusader, Rickey by this point had turned his attention elsewhere in his efforts to improve the Pirate organization. Now that black players were no longer a source of untapped talent (although there were, as stated earlier, few integrated teams by this point and dozens of qualified black players still unsigned and available), they did not entice him as they did when he took over the Dodgers back in 1943.

As a man always looking forward for an edge rather than backward, Rickey believed, much as he had earlier when he concluded that the rising popularity of his farm system rendered that mode of talent acquisition old hat, that he would have to find a new source of readily available talent to remain one step ahead of his competitors. He found it in a place he had considered but rejected years earlier while with the Dodgers: Latin America. Rickey pried Roberto Clemente loose from his old team[146] and then focused the Pirates' scouting efforts on the Caribbean market, where he simply applied the method of labor acquisition he developed in St. Louis and Brooklyn to yet another virtually untapped market. In the words of David Fidler and Arturo Marcano Guevara in their study of MLB involvement in Latin America, he used the "boatload mentality" of player procurement, where the goal was "quality out of quantity as cheaply as possible."[147] Just as he had with his farm system in St. Louis and with his plundering of the Negro Leagues in Brooklyn, Rickey attempted to corner a relatively cheap market and reap the benefits. Here, however, the complication of a language barrier provided him with additional advantages in that not only were the contracts his players signed one-sided, many of the Latin American players were unaware of what they were even signing given that the contracts were not translated into Spanish. Even before he joined the Pirates, Rickey took advantage of the situation, signing future all-star shortstop Chico Carrasquel in 1949 to a contract he could not read and that was not explained to him.[148] After many years the foundation he laid in Latin America finally paid off, with players such as Rennie Stennett, John Candelaria, Omar Moreno, Manny Sanguillen, and Tony Pena fueling the resurgence of the Pirates in the 1970s.[149] As a baseball man, he proved once again that he was unmatched. As a civil rights crusader, his tenure with the Pirates perhaps demonstrated something else.

Apart from Rickey, racial quotas survived in baseball for years and on all clubs. Despite the immediate success of the integrated Dodgers and Indians, there was no rush to sign black players—on Opening Day 1949 these remained the only two integrated clubs. And both the Dodgers and the Indians, like every other club that subsequently integrated, practiced a quota system. In 1951, Minnie Minoso was cut from the Indians during spring training because they already had four black players. However, when another black player subsequently became injured at the beginning of the season, a "black" roster spot opened up and Minoso was recalled.[150] In 1952, after Brooklyn's staff ace Don Newcombe was drafted into the military, a "black" roster spot was created and filled by Joe Black, who was unlikely to make the team otherwise given that the Dodgers had already reached their racial quota.[151] Anecdotal stories such as these existed all over baseball as more and more teams dipped their toes ever so cautiously into the integrated pool even as evidence began to mount that their, at least stated, caution was simplistic and misguided. For despite the popularly stated concerns by management and other observers that integration needed to be done incrementally to avoid repelling white fans and inciting the white southerners who were (incorrectly) believed to dominate Major League locker rooms, the reality of integration told a somewhat different story.

Although there were players and fans alike who were virulent racists and who displayed their ignorance, many were not and did not. Paul Richards, manager of the White Sox during the early '50s, once told Lester Rodney that when it came to the players "we white Southerners, when we get rid of the poison, we're more natural about white and black," an observation that Rodney confirmed, to an extent: "The southern whites could kid around with their Negro teammates in a more natural way. I saw enough of that to make me feel that Richards was on to something."[152] Moreover, with regard to baseball fans, Rodney witnessed firsthand a genuine softening of racial animus in the wake of Robinson's arrival, along with an overall acceptance of black players across the nation, even in the Deep South. He recalled a 1949 exhibition game in Atlanta between the Dodgers and the Atlanta Crackers—the first integrated game in the state of Georgia. Despite pleas from the Grand Dragon of the Ku Klux Klan to call off the game, it not only went off as scheduled but, as Robinson, Campanella, and Newcombe took the field to heavy booing from the white stands, other fans, both black and approximately one-third of the white ones as well, stood and applauded the players in response. Rodney noticed similar reactions wherever he went: "There were blatant racists who yelled obscenities. Then there was a bigger body of fans who weren't happy about integration but wouldn't join the overt racists in shouting ugly stuff. Some with mixed feelings, like the ones in Atlanta, their 'normal' aversion to integration colliding with feelings about sportsmanship, which they also grew up with. . . . I'd say that late in Jackie's second year it was clear that the outspoken racists were a shrinking minority. Maybe some of them actually changed too, but even if they didn't they sensed they were on the losing side and they at least shut up."[153] Regardless, the club owners maintained their quotas.

Moreover, not only was there a limit to the number of black players allowed on each club, these players felt the pressure to be standouts for fear that if they were not, they would likely be cut and replaced by inferior white players.[154] These fears were not misguided—four years after Robinson integrated the Dodgers, all of the team's reserve players and relief pitchers were white.[155] The only black players on the 1951 Dodgers were the reigning MVP Campanella, twenty-game winner Newcombe, and Robinson.[156] This was not an anomaly and would be a trend that continued for decades, as evidenced by a 2007 study that found through 1986 (the end point of the study), black players were far more likely to be stars than white ones, the conclusion being that even in modern times, "lesser skilled black players still had a tougher time getting work."[157] Throughout the 1950s, although black players earned more money on average than white players, this was more a reflection of the reality that there were far fewer black players and that practically all of them were of star quality.[158] Although these players were rewarded for their productivity, white players were rewarded for merely getting older, regardless of productivity.[159] Black players were not permitted to merely age, because when their productivity dropped, they were likely to be cut. The Indians' release of black slugger Luke Easter in 1954 was evidence of this reality. Because he turned thirty-eight and his skills had declined, he was released and spent the remainder of his career in the minors (in 1954 he hit a combined .315 with twenty-eight home runs during stints in the International and Pacific Coast leagues). Meanwhile, similarly aging former white stars such as Phil Cavaretta, Joe Collins, Walt Dropo, and Eddie Waitkus were permitted to remain in the majors that season in complementary roles either as platoon players or pinch hitters.[160] Some would succeed in these roles; some would struggle. Yet these formerly productive players were typically given several opportunities to prove their worth in their new, reduced roles. Black players were rarely given even one such opportunity.

In short, there were very few black players receiving minimum salaries because the roster spots for these players were reserved for white players almost exclusively.[161] Here again, there is no shortage of anecdotal information that illustrates this reality. Returning to the 1951 Dodgers, they were presented with an interesting dilemma in left field. Although they had nine candidates for the position, the majority of these were left-handed. Eventually, they chose an elaborate platoon system consisting of six of the players—four left-handers, one switch hitter, and one right-handed hitter. All of them were white. Meanwhile, in the high minors, Jim Pendleton—a black, right-handed hitter—was tearing up the league. Although Pendleton was not projected to be a star, he was a solid player who could play several positions and would have been a valuable right-handed complement to the Dodgers' left field, left-handed dilemma. As the 1951 season progressed, five of the six members of the platoon struggled; only the left-handed Cal Abrams produced even capably, hitting .280. The Dodgers tinkered with the platoon all season, at one point calling up a white, right-handed hitter from the low minors who jumped right over Pendleton on his way to Brooklyn. When he failed as well, the Dodgers traded for an established player, Andy Pafko, and forgot about Pendleton, who wallowed in the minors for another year before being traded before the 1953 season.[162] Without the allure of star potential, scores of players just like Pendleton were routinely passed over by inferior white players for years.

Rickey's insistence on the "right kind" of black player likewise had a lengthy legacy, as dozens of black players were either never promoted to the majors or, if they were, found themselves traded frequently and disparaged along the way as being troublemakers for behavior that was frequently ignored in white players. Although Leo Durocher maintained a reputation of being color-blind (he is often hailed for sticking by a young Willie Mays despite Mays's early struggles upon being called up to the Giants in 1951), he showed a far less progressive face when his black players stood up for themselves or acted in ways Durocher believed to be indicative of the "wrong kind" of black player. Two of the three biggest black stars he managed (Mays and Ernie Banks with the Cubs) were hardly rebels and the third, Robinson, was a player Durocher openly feuded with during the only season they were together (1948).[163] Significantly, by 1948 Robinson was no longer holding himself back and began to assert himself. The feud between Robinson and Durocher spilled over into the 1949 season and beyond, when Durocher relocated to the Giants. Later, Durocher repeatedly had run-ins with those black players who refused to be subservient. His relationships with Lou Johnson and Oscar Gamble while managing the Cubs in the '60s showed a far different side of Durocher than the one popularly portrayed through his relationship with Mays.

Johnson was acquired by the Cubs in 1967 and brought with him a reputation for political consciousness. He became involved in the black power movement and was upset that MLB did not cancel games in April 1968 after the assassination of Martin Luther King Jr. After he tried to convince his black teammates to boycott the games in protest, Durocher responded by refusing to speak to Johnson and then helping to orchestrate his trade out of Chicago. He was soon exchanged for another black player, Willie Smith from Cleveland, who was much less of an agitator and of a personality similar to Banks and Mays.[164] Gamble was a young outfielder called up by the Cubs in 1969. Soon, he developed a reputation as a ladies' man, with many of his dates white women. Durocher confronted Gamble during a team meeting and insisted that he cease his interracial dating. When Gamble refused, he was traded to Philadelphia.[165]

Of all the stories, however, the one of Vic Power is perhaps the most resonant. By 1953 the most symbolic team of all, the Yankees, still had not integrated at the Major League level. They were managed by Casey Stengel, a man who believed wholeheartedly in the value of maximizing potential through the use of platoons.[166] This gave rise to the hope that the Yankees might finally integrate that season because Stengel was in need of a right-handed–hitting first baseman and Power, a right-handed prospect, was dominating the minor leagues in the Yankees' system. In fact, he was one of two top right-handed first base prospects in the Yankees' system, the white Bill Skowron being the other. Although Skowron looked to be the better power hitter, Power was more versatile (he also played third and second base, as well as the outfield), a better fielder, a faster runner, and was a better hitter overall. Rather than promote either, however, Stengel returned both Power and Skowron to the minors and, mimicking the Dodgers in 1951, went with an all–left-handed platoon at first base. In 1954, Stengel promoted Skowron as the right-handed complement to his platoon and shipped Power to the Athletics. In an attempt to justify the move, the Yankees claimed that even though Power was talented, he was nevertheless not the "right kind of Yankee."[167] As evidence of this, fingers were pointed at Power's style of play (too flashy, some claimed), his temper (he would not hesitate to speak out or even fight white players he thought had thrown at him or tried to spike him), and his penchant for dating white women.[168] The New York media proved to be quickly compliant in these sort of justifications, with *New York Daily Mirror* writer Dan Parker standing behind the Yankees' treatment of Power by asserting that "[t]he first requisite of a Yankee is that he be a gentleman, something that has nothing to do with race, color or creed."[169] Forgotten in this comment were the frequent transgressions of white players like Mickey Mantle and Billy Martin.[170] In the end, as Jackie Robinson observed when remarking on the treatment of black Latin American players during the 1950s, it was the double standard that doomed Power; he "refuse[d] to take second-class citizenship" and paid the price for doing so.[171] In 1955, the Yankees finally promoted a black player to their Major League roster: catcher Elston Howard, a talented but quiet player who rarely if ever spoke or acted out. Lee McPhail, the farm director for the Yankees at the time, later remarked, "[t]he Yankees were very anxious that the first black player that they brought up would be somebody with the right type of character. Elston was ideal."[172]

Although discrimination within the world of MLB is commonly thought of as a relic of the pre-Robinson era, and quotas, when they are thought of at all, are pigeonholed into the decade of the '50s, both have lingered into the modern game. In 1977, Minnie Minoso, by then a coach with the White Sox, experienced the effects of the quota system once again when he was reassigned, midseason, from an on-field coaching position to the public relations department concurrent with the White Sox's appointment of Larry Doby as their first black manager. Two black coaches on one team was apparently one too many.[173] "Stacking"—the practice of relegating black players to certain positions and excluding them from others (and popularized by those Indian and Caribbean cricket teams compelled to confront the prospect of players of high and low social status on the same field)—has also flourished and remains to a significant extent in baseball, with black players more likely to be placed in those positions commonly believed to be the ones requiring the greatest athletic skill and least amount of intelligence—positions like the outfield and first base.[174] In 1988, 78 percent of all black players played these two positions.[175] By 2008, only 5 percent of all pitchers and a statistically insignificant percentage (0 percent) of all catchers—the positions commonly believed to require mental as well as physical skills—were black.[176] On Opening Day 2007, there were only nine black pitchers overall on active MLB rosters and only four of these were starting pitchers.[177] Black coaches likewise have felt, and to a considerable extent still feel today, the sting of stacking. In 2010, only 23 percent of third-base coaches (who as a group enjoy significant prestige and are more likely to be groomed for managerial positions) were black, compared with 67 percent of the less prestigious, typically lower-paid, first-base coaches.[178] Moreover, there was not a single black pitching coach in 2010.[179]

Discrimination within the front offices of MLB is likewise still persistent, with the effects of this discrimination being felt on the field in the quotas and mindset that leads to practices such as stacking. In 2008, MLB could count only three black general managers—itself an achievement given that previously there had never been more than one.[180] Of team vice presidents (of which teams often have many), blacks accounted for only 4 percent of the total (eleven in all), with many of these in largely ceremonial positions and/or positions with little or no authority in player personnel decisions.[181] On the field, MLB remains, much as it has for decades, largely a white outfit. In 2007 60 percent of all players were white, while 8.2 percent were black—the lowest total in twenty-eight years[182] (the high-water mark for integration occurred in 1974 when 27 percent of all players were black).[183]

Ironically, the second half of the twentieth century has borne witness to fewer blacks earning their living from professional baseball than the first half, with Rickey's "Great Experiment," the demise of the Negro leagues, and the "all deliberate speed" of the subsequent integration movement each playing a role in this otherwise curious phenomenon.[184] Although there are undoubtedly many reasons why more black children and teenagers currently play football and basketball than baseball, one of them may very well be the treatment of blacks by MLB *post*-integration. This treatment has led to a perception that MLB, regardless of how fervently it promotes Robinson through commemorative days or by retiring his uniform number throughout the league, remains essentially a closed club. A black, former MLB scout encountered this perception in the course of his travels: "I think there's definitely a sociological element to what we're talking about. Now that two girls from Compton [California] dominate tennis (the Williams sisters) and a kid from Cypress [California] dominates golf (Tiger Woods), a lot of intelligent black people I know—professional, educated people—believe that the last bastion for white America is baseball. I'm talking about very intelligent people who believe that."[185] This perception is hardly the vision of baseball as America that most children are taught to take away from the story of Branch Rickey's "Great Experiment." This may be, however, its sad legacy.

TEARING DOWN THE WALLS

The civil rights movement on the left provided perhaps the most obvious, but by no means only, test of the owners' status and independence. On the right, the owners were increasingly pressured as well, as, in the midst of the post–World War II boom, challengers from all over the political spectrum wanted in on America's game and were less content than ever to sit on the sidelines and be dictated to by the self-appointed gatekeepers of American values. As a result of this pressure from all sides, but surprisingly, chiefly from people who in many ways were new and improved versions of themselves, the owners finally succumbed, ceding much of the status and glory they had worked so hard to achieve. Although the official date of death on the "owners-as-manor lords" tombstone is open to debate (likely candidates include December 23, 1975, the date of independent arbitrator Peter Seitz's ruling granting free agency to Andy Messersmith and Dave McNally, effectively killing the unrestricted reserve clause; and July 12, 1976, the date of the first collective bargaining agreement granting the players free agency, among others), the seeds of the owners' demise in status were planted years earlier, and in surprising ways. To make sense of it all, however, it helps to go back even further, to a time when the owners' might was seemingly limitless. Even then, as it turned out, although they were powerful storytellers, they were far less powerful in many other ways than they ever let on.

In fact, the peak from which the owners would ultimately descend was reached early in their existence, shortly after the turn of the twentieth century and marked by the begrudging consolidation of the National and American leagues under the Major League umbrella. After a two-year struggle, commencing on January 28, 1901, when Ban Johnson shook the baseball establishment by declaring his newly christened American League "major" and the equal of the arrogant National in all manner of speaking, the Nationals reluctantly accepted Johnson's American League into the fold, signing a peace agreement with the upstart league that doubled the number of Major League teams to sixteen. After the Baltimore franchise relocated to New York (to become the Highlanders and, eventually, the Yankees) in 1903, the Major League Baseball map was set: two leagues, sixteen clubs, ten cities. With this, the sixteen club owners pulled up the drawbridge and considered the matter of expansion, and the concurrent dilution of their power that came with it, closed . . . for good.

For decades they were unbreakable if not unchallenged: despite the occasional threat to their supremacy, the Major Leagues of the late 1950s looked very much like the Major Leagues that existed nearly six decades earlier. Although a few teams had recently relocated (to Milwaukee, Baltimore, Kansas City, Los Angeles, and San Francisco), the essence of the cabal that was Major League Baseball ownership remained unchanged. There were still sixteen clubs—no more. The tight ship remained united and closed to any and all outsiders. More important to these owners, the game itself remained just as it was back in 1876 when their forbears wrested it away from the players. Notwithstanding the minor annoyances of relocation, Major League Baseball was still an owners' game. The players were a necessary inconvenience but little more; it was the owners who made nearly every decision relevant to the game. The players were subservient, a secondary concern in all areas, save for the nine innings or so they trotted on and off the field 154 times each season. The owners' status as gatekeepers of America's game seemed perpetual as their fraternity was so entrenched in the national consciousness that several of them were household names: Topping, Webb, Wrigley, Stoneham, Crosley, Carpenter, Yawkey, O'Malley, and so on. Within twenty years, however, everything would change.

By 1980, the game of the 1950s was virtually unrecognizable. By then there were twenty-six teams and, perhaps even more shocking to those who controlled the game only a few years earlier, it was now firmly the players' game; the owners were still huffing and puffing but to no avail: the players had already blown the house down. Within a few years the players would be more popular than ever while most owners would be unrecognizable even to fans of their own teams. Just as was the case with the gentlemanly club game back in the mid-nineteenth century, these financial "backers" had been pushed into the background once more; their reign was over, they were gatekeepers no more. All of this surely must have caused at least a few of them to scratch their heads in wonderment over how things could have gone so terribly wrong for them so quickly. For by the late 1950s, everything was seemingly in their favor: they were members of a closed club complete with their judicially created antitrust exemption designed to keep unwanted competitors out, a reserve clause that inhibited player movement except upon their whim, and a de facto exemption from a whole host of other federal laws that, in essence, permitted them to dictate how to run their game and manage their affairs without fear of significant congressional or judicial intervention. Yet, despite all of these advantages, they managed to lose control of the game with alarming alacrity. Which begs the question: what happened?

The popular answer to this question is a simple and straightforward one: Marvin Miller happened. According to this theory, Miller's stewardship of the Players Association radicalized it, causing it to find its voice and attack ownership, bringing the owners to their knees in the process. Indeed, many owners to this day cite Miller's ascendancy to the helm of the Players Association in 1966 as the moment a radical element entered the game, changing it forever (and to their way of thinking, not for the better). However, the rise of the Players Association, while significant, is only part of the story—and an aftershock at that. Instead, the owners' downfall can be traced to events that predated Miller's arrival on the scene and ones that had nothing to do with the players or their nascent union. For the owners were felled by people seemingly much like themselves—moneyed elites—who differed only in the amount of true power they wielded. It was these businessmen who started the owners on their downward spiral toward anonymity, men who wanted in on the national pastime and who may have looked just like the owners from the outside but who were in actuality the products of a post–World War II corporate revolution that changed the very nature of American business.

By initially challenging the sixteen club owners' domination of the game and then ultimately infiltrating their ranks from the 1960s onward, these new-age corporate executives transformed the ownership ranks from a cozy, cohesive club to a ragged collection of widely disparate entities with agendas that rarely extended beyond their own self-interests. As such, this new collection of ownership interests were unable to agree on virtually anything. By the early 1960s, these powerful corporate interlopers forced MLB to expand for the first time since Ban Johnson arrived on the scene sixty years earlier. Despite all of its apparent legal advantages, MLB was compelled to initially add four teams and then, in 1969, four more. All of this because, in the end, the old cabal of sixteen club owners was revealed to be far less powerful than previously assumed. As a group they were exposed as an anachronism, a relic from the prewar era whose time had clearly passed. Now, their fraternity forcibly broken, the unity that had once defined them had been broken forever as well.

Within this environment, the sweeping societal changes then taking place in 1960s America—the aforementioned corporate revolution along with the more widely publicized student and civil rights movements— would, taken together, further debilitate an already destabilized owners' group, which, as it turned out, was held together through weakness rather than strength. Amid all of this upheaval came Marvin Miller, who tapped into the festering resentment of the hundreds of players who had endured but hardly prospered at the hands of the owners (and who themselves were not immune to the attitudinal changes taking place during the 1960s), and who was able to harness all of this energy and run roughshod over his wounded prey. By this point, however, the owners were in no position to put up much of a fight against a union that—taking its cue from the student uprisings and civil rights movement of the era—now mirrored the owners' fraternity of old: tight, focused, and determined to stake its claim as the new gatekeepers of America's game. After a series of one-sided battles, the Players Association succeeded in wresting control of the game from the owners.

While the owners would carp and complain, blaming Miller for every ill that befell them, their bleats were ultimately misguided—by the time Miller arrived on the scene, the owners were already on the steep decline as a powerful force within the game. Society had moved on without them, leaving the old guard behind as ghosts, ethereal visions of the past. Miller may have been their public nemesis but they were undone by other forces—namely, by powerful new-age incarnations of themselves. In the end, even taking Miller out of the equation, this once seemingly powerful collection of old-guard owners never stood a chance.

THE THREAT OF CONTINENTAL EXPANSION

Throughout the six decades between the birth of the American League and the challenge to the established Major Leagues in the form of what came to be known as the Continental League in 1959, there had been other attempts to break the tight fraternity that was Major League Baseball. All of these uprisings had one thing in common: ultimate failure. The Federal League challenge in 1914–15 died at the hands of Judge Landis—a friend of MLB who drove a stake through the Federals' heart by refusing to rule on their antitrust lawsuit until the league was bled dry. Landis was rewarded for his service with an appointment as the game's first commissioner while the challenge itself not only failed but actually was instrumental in seemingly creating even greater cohesion than before: the game's antitrust exemption rose from its ashes. A threat from south of the border in a well-hyped and supposedly well-funded challenge from the Mexican League in the mid-1940s likewise died under its own weight; in the end, the league was hardly as prosperous as it claimed, and stories of double-dealing and unfulfilled promises quickly limited its influence and diminished its power until it too had been erased as a formidable opponent (although, through the *Gardella* case, as discussed in chapter 2, it did expose the lunacy of the game's antitrust exemption—albeit to little ultimate avail). Shortly thereafter, MLB faced a challenge from the Pacific Coast League, which took advantage of the recent West Coast population surge to try to shoehorn its way into MLB's cabal by becoming a third major league in the late 1940s. Although much discussion and even congressional hearings ensued (hearings that included threats to MLB with the removal of its antitrust exemption should it continue to resist expansion), MLB was able to successfully fend off these challengers as well by 1951.[1] The issue of expansion was not closed, however, as MLB realized that it would continually be under the threat (hollow as it was) of removal of its antitrust exemption unless it did something. Indeed, between 1951 and 1960, Congress held hearings on baseball's "horsehide cartel" in seven of those years—always threatening, never acting.[2] Eventually, five teams relocated during the fifties, including two—the Dodgers and the Giants—to California, with MLB classifying each relocation as an "expansion" to satisfy its critics, congressional and otherwise. Still, after the dust cleared, MLB looked as it had for over half a century: sixteen clubs, sixteen owners. Geographic expansion may have been achieved but true expansion remained elusive. Despite the moves, the fraternity remained as closed and as tight as ever.

Baseball's entry into the Los Angeles and San Francisco markets may have solved the problem raised by the earlier Pacific Coast League challenge but it created a new one in the process. Owing to the loss of the Dodgers and Giants, there was now only one team in New York, where there had always been three. Moreover, America's largest city was now left without a National League team, whereas it had previously comprised a quarter of the senior circuit. Among the forlorn was Branch Rickey, the former president of the old Brooklyn Dodgers. On May 21, 1958, he authored a front-page story in the *Sporting News* calling for true expansion within MLB and the creation of a third major league.[3] This idea caught hold in cities that were envious of their brethren in Los Angeles, San Francisco, and the other markets that had recently welcomed relocated franchises and likewise desired Major League baseball.[4] Very quickly there was a movement underfoot—centered in New York, which simply could not stomach the desertion of the Dodgers and Giants. Fortuitously, New York was led by Robert Wagner at the time, a Democratic mayor facing reelection during a period of Republican upswing nationwide (Eisenhower had been reelected president two years earlier). Seizing a political opportunity, Wagner created a committee, the Mayor's Baseball Committee of the City of New York, to bring the National League back to the Big Apple. He appointed four Democrats to the committee, the most notable being its chairman,

William Shea, a political insider with a strong sports background. The makeup of the committee was crucial: given its connections and political leanings, this political/commercial alliance could possibly overcome the traditional deference given to MLB and at least give a third league a fighting chance in Congress. The political math was in its favor: although the sixteen club owners were overwhelmingly Republican, Congress was still controlled by the Democrats.[5] If the right coalition of cities could be brought together, there could be enough Democratic votes from states hungry for Major League baseball to put some actual, as opposed to merely theoretical, pressure on MLB to finally expand.

After initial attempts to follow MLB's traditional "expansion" blueprint by simply luring an existing franchise to New York failed, Shea and Rickey joined forces in an attempt to form a third major league.[6] On July 27, 1959, the Continental League was formally launched via press release with the proclamation that a new major league with at least eight teams would begin a 154-game season in 1961.[7] In that release, the Continental League announced itself as a formidable foe for the baseball establishment: the first five cities to sign on (New York, Houston, Toronto, Minneapolis–St. Paul, and Denver) were all major markets seemingly capable of supporting a Major League franchise. In addition, Branch Rickey was shortly thereafter named commissioner of the Continental League, thereby giving it additional heft and credibility.[8]

Regardless, MLB responded to the Continental League much as it did to the Pacific Coast League challenge earlier—by ignoring it. However, Emanuel Celler, the New York congressman who chaired the House Monopoly Subcommittee, took particular interest in the interplay between MLB and the Continental League given that he represented the district that had recently lost its beloved Dodgers. Soon he, joined by his counterpart in the Senate, Estes Kefauver, chairman of the Senate's Antimonopoly Subcommittee, officially stepped in. Very quickly, both houses of Congress held the threat of removal of baseball's antitrust exemption over MLB's head if it failed to act on the issue of expansion.[9] That Shea was on the side of substantial political clout was not lost on him: he made a point of announcing that he was keeping Congress informed of every step of the Continental League's progress and even egged MLB on a bit when he informed it that there were really only two avenues open to it: "help us or suffer the consequences."[10] Although Shea hoped to proceed with the cooperation of MLB, he made it clear that if none was forthcoming, he was prepared to proceed on his own, as an outlaw league.[11]

It took a while for MLB to get the message that this time, it would have to act, and in a manner that produced tangible results on the issue of expansion for a change. Rather than prepare for the reality of the threat the Continental League represented, Ford Frick, now the commissioner of Baseball, instead took umbrage at Shea and the Continental's forwardness, responding that "Baseball is not going to be sledge-hammered into putting a team in New York because of the threat of a third major league."[12] Two months earlier, upon anticipation of the official formation of the Continental League, Frick and the owners met in Columbus, Ohio, to draft a series of conditions (ten in all) that MLB would require to be met in order for a proposed league's application to be considered acceptable.[13] Implicit in these conditions was the owners' belief that the issue of expansion, much like nearly everything else up to that point, was one completely within their control: a new league would need to bow to them if it wished to proceed in any manner at all. In short, the owners' self-assessment, brought to the fore in their dealings with the Continental League, was that "[t]hey were regal. The third league was a supplicant to whom they might be willing to condescend to assist."[14] The reality of the situation would hit them in short order.

By January 1960, the full slate of Continental League teams was completed when Buffalo, Atlanta, and Dallas–Fort Worth were added to the roster. Faced now with a head-on assault, MLB attempted to bluff its way out of the jam: a consortium of National League owners met with the intention of producing a statement that it would work in conjunction with the American League to facilitate expansion by 1961. Rickey, however, was not fooled and implored his brethren to fight on despite this seemingly conciliatory step. Contending that the National League's actions were merely a con, Rickey added, "The N.L. will not extend to expand internally and they will not expand internally in 1961 or any other time."[15] Instead, Rickey believed, they would do what they could to undermine the Continental League and forestall expansion indefinitely. Taking Rickey's advice, the Continentals pressed forward and in May 1960, hearings commenced on a bill proposed by Senator Kefauver that would limit the scope of MLB's control over its players. If passed, the expanse of the reserve clause would be severely curtailed in that each MLB team's control of players would no longer be unlimited; rather it would extend only to one hundred players overall in its entire major/minor league system. Of these, all but forty would be subject to an annual draft by all interested clubs, including those within the Continental League.[16]

In the end, the sovereign nation of baseball prevailed, at least technically. On June 28, 1960, the Senate did as it had always done, threaten but no more; it sent the Kefauver bill back to committee, where it effectively died.[17] The antitrust exemption survived, and baseball was still intact. But not really. Frightened by the prospect of more hearings or, even worse, exposure of its reserve clause in court (something MLB feared more than anything; their own lawyer warned them as far back as 1946 to avoid litigation of this issue at all costs[18] and they zealously heeded this advice ever since), MLB capitulated. On July 18, 1960, less than three weeks after its Pyrrhic victory, MLB announced that, for the first time ever, it would expand in earnest.[19] Within two years the tight fraternity had four new members, two in the National League and two more in the American, such that by 1962 MLB had expanded 20 percent despite its vigilant opposition. Seven years later, MLB expanded again, adding four more clubs just as it had pledged to do as part of its 1960 peace accord with the Continental League. As a result, by the end of the decade, MLB was one-third larger than it had been at the outset.

The forced expansion of MLB was the first indication that the ownership cabal was perhaps not as powerful as previously assumed. In the end, true power won out. The tight fraternity was finally cracked and, once it was, the old guard's solidarity was irrevocably broken. This was evident in many ways, but perhaps none more striking than simple statistics. In 1959, twelve of MLB's sixteen ownership votes came from the top twelve markets (75 percent). In 1969, only sixteen of twenty-four votes came from these markets (67 percent).[20] This percentage continued to shrink with expansion once again in the 1970s, which was significant in that large-market teams such as the Yankees had an increasingly smaller influence over the league. As such, it was becoming more and more difficult to keep everyone "in line" and voting as a unified bloc. Moreover, by 1963, either through expansion or recent transfers in ownership, six of ten AL owners were men who were not members of the fraternity a mere three years earlier (in the NL it was four out of ten).[21] Thus, at joint league meetings, half of the decision makers were people new to one another. This dynamic only added to the increasing difficulty of maintaining group cohesiveness.

The changes and turnover in ownership only increased throughout the next several years, such that by the 1970s club owners were coming and going at an unprecedented rate. Though there had always been some turnover in ranks, pre-expansion turnover was nothing like it was after the challenge of the Continental League. Something fundamentally changed in the nature of club owners; they simply were not staying in the game as long as they used to. Although the irony was most likely lost on most of the ownership group as it existed during the mid to late '70s, despite their charges of renegade behavior leveled at the players as a result of free agency, it was the owners who were carpet-bagging like never before. All of this had disastrous results for their once tight fraternity: in this atmosphere it was almost impossible for the owners to develop a meaningful bond; before long, club membership would be shuffled once again. Without fraternal allegiances, everybody was out for themselves. Concepts such as deference and cohesiveness were a thing of the past. Without an institutional memory, owners meetings became pitched battles between self-serving owners interested only in what benefited them today—yesterday or tomorrow be damned.[22]

THE CORPORATE REVOLUTION

Turnover and expansion were not the only causes of the dissipation of ownership's collective power. In addition, the very nature of the people who owned clubs from the 1960s forward also changed significantly, causing a shift in primary allegiance from the once-sacred ownership fraternity to the varied interests involved in owning each individual club. This likewise rendered group cohesiveness near impossible in that now, there were many more interests at the bargaining table other than simply the sixteen (or twenty or twenty-four or thirty) men and women physically present on the owners' side. In short, the people at the ownership table by 1980 were far different in temperament and background than those sitting in those same chairs in 1960. They were the products of a corporate revolution in

America that, although not publicized nearly to the degree as the student and counter-culture revolutions of the same era, changed the fundamental nature of corporate America and, naturally, baseball's ownership group as well. Ironically, these new owners were far more powerful, in a global sense, than their predecessors but it was their power that caused them to fray as a group and become, collectively, weaker.[23]

Traditionally, owning a Major League baseball team was a relatively simple, straightforward proposition. The economics were rudimentary— the vast majority of revenue stemmed from gate receipts, along with a trickle from radio.[24] Expenses were minimal given that salaries and ticket prices were low. In this atmosphere, owning a baseball team was little more than a vanity investment. Just as in the nineteenth century, these nonplayers sought a connection to the game more for the status it brought them than the income it generated. Making money was not, and could not, be a primary motivation, considering there was not much generated. As the economist Roger Noll concluded of the pre-expansion, pre–free agency era, professional clubs had "revenues ranging approximately from those of a large gas station to those of a department store or large supermarket."[25] In this atmosphere, owners had the luxury of considering themselves amateur sportsmen. "Mr. [Phil] Wrigley never took a penny out of the ball club, never took a dividend," said Cubs business manager E. R. "Salty" Saltzman. "He didn't care much about profits; he just didn't care to subsidize losses."[26] Because being a member of this elite fraternity was what mattered most, cohesiveness and solidarity among owners was not a problem.

Of course there were always divisions among owners, and squabbles and grudges abounded. However, when it came to the proverbial "big picture," the operation of the business of baseball, they had every incentive to act in lockstep. To do otherwise would cost them money many of them simply did not have.[27] They could strike out on their own, sign the best prospects without regard to price, and take on veteran players with higher contracts to help them in a playoff push, but these tactics were risky. If these moves failed to translate into success on the diamond, they would not see much of an uptick in ticket sales, and then they would be left with bloated expenses without any way to balance their ledger sheets at the end of the season. Or, they could be content with life in the second division, smaller crowds, and barely a whiff of the pennant race and be assured of meeting their reduced expenses. The first option could bring them a nice profit or, if things went south, a mountain of debt that might require them to sell their club and leave the ownership fraternity they prized above all else. The second option virtually guaranteed perpetual membership in the fraternity regardless of how their club finished in the standings. Given the choice, it was no wonder so many of them took the latter route.

Self-interest (as opposed to self-promotion and status) was not much of a concern to these pre-expansion owners because, unless they did something foolhardy such as expend precious resources toward putting a competitive team on the field, their ledgers would be balanced by factors that had little to do with the play of their team on the diamond. Given the meager expenses in the game at the time, it did not take much in the way of attendance for a club to break even at the end of the year regardless of how it finished in the pennant race. A club could average as few as 1,500 fans per game during the week and still break even because it would receive the income necessary to pay its bills in the few games (night games, Sunday games, games against the Yankees in the AL or whoever happened to be ruling the NL at the time) annually that drew large crowds. For decades, a club could draw as few as 500,000 fans a season—with the majority of these fans showing up only for the aforementioned premium games— and still remain comfortably in business.[28] In this atmosphere it was not uncommon for owners and general managers to consult each other on salaries, player movement, and other internal decisions.[29] Maintaining a competitive advantage was not something that was always in the forefront of their minds.

Rather than fight the system (that is, the Yankees) and sweat, most American League owners found it more advantageous to give in to it, to take orders from the Yankees and make sure that their votes aligned with the Yankees' interests. In return, the Yankees subsidized their seven putative competitors.[30] The Yankees' tally between 1921 and 1964 is a testament to this devotion: twenty-nine pennants, twenty World Series championship rings in that forty-three-year span. Even in the National League, the Yankees held influence; their "brand" inured to the benefit of every other Major League team (not to mention the fact that the Yankees were often willing trade partners for teams looking to dump high-salaried players to balance their ledger sheets at the end of another disappointing season). The aura of the Yankees of Ruth, Gehrig, and DiMaggio spilled over into every Major League city. In this atmosphere, cohesiveness was not hard to achieve. Thus, it was mutual weakness that necessitated the codependence that drove these old-guard owners into each other's arms.

The old-time, pre-expansion owners were exemplified in the two-headed beast that ran the Yankees for much of their golden age: Dan Topping and Del Webb. Topping was considered the "sportsman" of the pair, not unlike Bob Carpenter of the Phillies and Tom Yawkey of the Red Sox. Although he dabbled in business, he was independently wealthy and effectively an amateur aristocrat.[31] With this background he answered to no one. His money was his own; he was privileged to spend it as he pleased. Webb, on the other hand, was a businessman through and through. By the early '60s one would not be incorrect in calling him a mogul—his construction empire spread across the nation and was involved in hotels, casinos, and ballparks along with military contracts. However, his was a typical prewar corporation in that despite its size, it was organized very simply. Given that his corporation was essentially involved in only a single line of business—construction—Webb was able to maintain a strong, authoritarian voice.[32] Like Topping, Webb was able to be a firm decision maker. The many businessmen-owners like Webb operated as the heads of similarly organized, relatively simply constructed corporations focused on one or, at most, two lines of business. Topping himself was the beneficiary of this simple, streamlined organizational structure: his grandfather, Daniel Reid, was known as "The Tin Plate King," having amassed his fortune in the tin industry.[33] Even those owners whose resumés were broader than either Webb's or Topping's typically stuck to a straightforward, relatively simple business model. Powel Crosley, owner of the Reds, was a little bit Topping, a little bit Webb: he was born into some money but then became an industrialist on his own. At times over the course of his professional career he was involved in radio manufacturing and broadcasting, household appliance sales, and automobile production along with his interest in the Reds.[34] However, one would hardly call Crosley's empire a conglomerate, or even an empire for that matter. Rather, it would be more accurate to say that he dabbled in a little of this, a little of that, over the course of his life. And in all of it, his was the final word.

This business model underwent a radical transformation beginning in the middle of the twentieth century but picking up steam by the 1960s such that by the 1970s and 1980s, such autonomy by any one individual was practically unheard of. This rendered it near impossible for any one owner to make firm decisions on the spot without fear of the ramifications beyond the owners' caucus; there were simply too many other interests to consider. This diminution of authority in the individual could have no other effect but to fray group cohesiveness.

The destruction of the small, single-industry corporation through the concentration of economic power was the outstanding feature of the post–World War II American economy.[35] During the 1950s this concentration accelerated such that very quickly a dwindling percentage of American corporations accounted for an increasingly overwhelming share of net corporate income. The transformation of America from a land of many simple, single-industry corporations—family businesses—to one of relatively few mega-conglomerates dispersed across multiple lines of business was swift and staggering. According to historian Richard Abrams: "By the end of the 1960s, the 100 largest industrial corporations held a greater share of total assets than the 200 largest had in 1950, and the largest 200 held about the same share as the largest 1000 did in 1941."[36] The result of this flurry of activity was obvious: between 1955 and 1970 the largest companies—the "Fortune 500"—practically doubled in profits and assets. As for how this came about, the answer was simple: mergers and acquisitions. 3,900 smaller companies were swallowed up by the two hundred largest in the decades following World War II, such that by the '60s, almost all large manufacturers were operating in more than five separate industries. Smaller single-industry companies, the mom-and-pop shops that formed the backbone of the American economy in the early part of the century and the ones that bred many MLB owners during this period, were gobbled up by increasingly larger, diverse conglomerates with complicated corporate structures and large boards of directors replete with divergent and often conflicting interests.

This transformation profoundly changed the nature of American business and, therefore, the management side of Major League Baseball. Decision making now was a much more complicated process. There were multiple interests to consider, many of them competing with one another.

As this new corporate influence seeped into baseball during the 1960s, the days of sitting across the table from a fellow owner and making major decisions on the spot were dwindling. To be sure, there were several members of the old guard left: the O'Malleys, the Carpenters, the Yawkeys. But over time they came to be outnumbered by the products of the revolution until they were little more than relics of an earlier, simpler time; plantation owners in the land of the corporate boardroom. When they finally departed, the old days were gone for good.

Most Americans were either unaware or indifferent to the corporate revolution going on all around them, which was changing the fundamental realities of their daily lives. Media attention was focused elsewhere: on Vietnam, the cold war, the hippies in San Francisco, and the sit-ins in Berkeley. In baseball, attention was similarly diverted to an issue that was easier to cover, easier to paint in black and white: Marvin Miller and his suddenly agitated Players Association. All of these uprisings were significant, sometimes colossal in their impact, but the corporate revolution affected them all in a quiet yet profound way: this revolution affected the decision-making process with regard to all of the others. And how a response is made often dictates the response itself.

In the Continental League, MLB got a taste of the changes that awaited it. There was some direct corporate ownership involved in the Minnesota franchise (Hamm's Beer) along with other individuals who pledged to keep their interest in their club separate from their corporate interest, but it was folly to think that a prominent individual in a leadership position in a large, publicly held conglomerate could completely divest himself or herself from the interests of their corporation simply by keeping the two legally separate. To be sure, MLB had already seen some of this infiltrate the game prior to the Continental League (Gussie Busch of the Cardinals being one obvious example), but as the '60s wore on baseball would see more and more of it. As new owners arrived on the scene of the now expanded National and American leagues, they were, in one sense, far more powerful people than their predecessors: they were in most cases far richer and far more influential politically, given the realities of running a multinational conglomerate (it is far easier to get the collective ear of Congress when your business operates in all fifty states rather than in one or two). But it was their individual power that eventually brought the owners down collectively; having to answer to so many interests other than their baseball brethren simply made group cohesiveness impossible.

The corporate influx only grew more pronounced as the decades passed. Eventually, huge conglomerates such as Disney, Time Warner, the Tribune Company, and others owned controlling interests in ball clubs.[37] All of these investors had varied agendas, some baseball related, some not. Although the transition from plantation to boardroom ownership was completed by the 1990s, the new wave began disrupting and fraying the old guard from the moment it arrived several decades earlier.[38] With all of the varied interests now present at the owners' table, the ability of a powerful team such as the Yankees, to say nothing of the commissioner himself, to dictate an agenda became increasingly difficult. How to persuade a conglomerate? There were simply too many layers of private agendas associated with each club to contend with; each one now had its own large, institutional problems to consider.[39]

Starting in the '60s, the economics of baseball changed; very soon clubs would no longer be the financial equivalent of supermarkets. The corporate revolution amped-up the American economy and made everything bigger and more expensive, including Major League baseball clubs. Significant debt service now became an issue: clubs needed to consider it whenever making significant decisions.[40] No longer could they simply fall blindly in line behind the Yankees; they had their creditors and shareholders to consider. Big money meant the arrival of big, powerful people and interests in the game, but people and interests with agendas that rarely considered the well-being of their putative competitors. The old guard always considered themselves a powerful lot, but the source of their collective power was rooted in weakness rather than strength. When they were confronted with true power in the Continental League, they buckled. When this power later infiltrated their ranks, the result was not enhanced power but, ironically, a dissipation of it. And it would be further eroded by the influences of television and other professional sports.

THE TELEVISION REVOLUTION

Because baseball held a decades-long virtual monopoly on the professional sports dollar, there was little incentive for MLB owners to put much thought into how their teams (as opposed to the image of the game overall) were perceived by the public. Up through the game's alleged "golden age" of the 1930s and beyond, it did not much matter if a team's fans were disgusted with the play on the field; there were few other avenues available to them. Boxing and horse racing were also popular through much of this era but because those sports were fundamentally different in nature, they did not seem to exert much pull on those otherwise inclined to attend a baseball game (or at least enough of a pull to cause club owners much consternation). If a sports fan of that era wanted to attend a game complete with a perpetual rooting interest, local ties, and all the emotional energy these factors generate, there was a pretty good chance that it would wind up being a baseball game. Judging from the meager attendance figures across the MLB spectrum outside New York, however, this monopoly was hardly something for club owners to crow about. Regardless, the few fans who did spin the turnstiles for the majority of the games, and the larger hordes who attended on Sundays, night games, or other special events, were more than enough to keep most teams in the black year after year. Ballplayers such as Babe Ruth and others may have been willing to employ public relations people to spur interest in them and massage their image[41] but many owners could not see a reason why they would need to engage in any sort of PR themselves. After all, baseball was, by default, the national pastime, the status of the owners as spokesmen for the nation's mythical village values was practically reverential and, on top of all this, most owners were at least breaking even financially. There seemed no need to bother with this extra expense. This mindset endured into the 1950s until the postwar societal and economic changes finally forced club owners to confront the way their game was marketed and perceived. The changes that resulted would further alter the dynamic among club owners, contributing yet again to the fraying of their once-cohesive group.

The sixteen-team monopoly on the sports dollar was shattered in rapid order. By 1962 there were four more MLB teams; more significant, by the end of the 1950s, interest in the NFL blossomed such that in 1960, less than two years after the famed "greatest game ever played" between the Baltimore Colts and New York Giants in 1958,[42] a new professional football league, the American Football League, was in business. Although the AFL claimed to be in competition with the NFL for fans and interest, it was also competing with MLB for many of these same people. There were many reasons why sports other than baseball emerged as rapidly as they did during the early 1960s, but the biggest one of all was the box now sitting in more people's living rooms than ever before: television.

Like most innovations, MLB club owners were, as a group, not merely cautious but downright belligerent to television when it first appeared: Yankees General Manager Larry McPhail unsuccessfully attempted to block the sale of television rights to the 1947 World Series, fearing that ticket sales would suffer as a result.[43] Branch Rickey was similarly hostile: "radio stimulates interest. Television satisfies it," he pronounced a few years later.[44] Regardless, television spent the 1950s infiltrating American households such that by the 1960s it became an untamable beast. The proliferation of television and the many new stations that popped up one after another meant that there were now seemingly endless hours of programming slots that needed to be filled. And few things proved to be a more natural fit with television than sports. Very quickly, baseball was no longer alone at the top of the sports pyramid.

Out of sheer necessity, television generated so much sports coverage (and was a more than willing partner with those other sports such as football and basketball, whose leadership embraced rather than scorned it) that a broadening of interest by the American sports fan was inevitable.[45] In a sense, television knocked baseball down a peg by democratizing the world of professional sports. The NFL and NBA may not have had the history that MLB enjoyed, but by broadcasting football and basketball games into living rooms across the country, television rendered these sports as important and meaningful as the national pastime. If the Bears-Redskins game was on TV, then it must be significant; if the Reds-Phillies game was not, then perhaps it was less so. It is hard to imagine the NFL or NBA achieving such national prominence on their own. Professional football had been buzzing on the periphery of the national sports consciousness for decades. It was only when television entered the picture that it was able to enter the national sports conversation that baseball had to itself for so long. It was more than a coincidence that pro football's "greatest game ever played" occurred at the dawn of the television era; in fact it was the nationwide distribution of the game that seared it into the hearts and minds of so many people.

Television soon drove professional sports rather than vice-versa. Along with the expansion that occurred in the traditional four major sports leagues, new leagues such as the American Basketball Association and the World Hockey Association soon joined the upstart AFL in the fight for attention. All of this expansion was fueled by television, which needed the games to fill out its broadcasting schedules. College football and basketball also found comfortable homes on television. And in all of these broadcasts the same message was conveyed to the sporting public: these games were as important as baseball games. Whereas previously, baseball had the entire summer to itself, now it was competing with an ever-earlier commencement of the pro and college football seasons in the late summer and the ever-lengthening basketball and hockey playoffs in the late spring. In a very short time, television put tremendous pressure on MLB to vie for attention: in 1959 there were forty-two professional teams in the four major sports, in 1972 there were 107.[46]

Perhaps MLB club owners in the mid to late '60s cared as little about on-field success as their predecessors had in the 1930s but now, because of television, they had no choice in the matter: either they competed or they suffered the consequences. This time, however, their chief competitors were no longer the Yankees or Dodgers or anyone else in either the American or National leagues, but rather the teams within their city or region that were battling them for the limited sports dollar. This local competition became fierce across the nation because of the explosion of professional sports during the decade; in 1959 only New York and Detroit could boast of teams in all four major sports and no city smaller than Boston had more than two teams. By 1969 there were fifteen cities that had either three or four professional sports teams.[47]

Beyond the numbers, baseball found itself handicapped in the television era because of the layout and nature of the game, as well as its own historical indifference with regard to the product put on the field. Football and basketball were seemingly made for television; basketball for its small court and nonstop action and football for its grid that ideally matched the contours of a television screen, along with the camera-friendly reality that all of the action at any one time was limited to a small portion of the field. Baseball, on the other hand, was a game played on an ever-widening field; it was impossible to cover more than a small section of it on television at any one time. Worse, by focusing the camera on the locus of the apparent "action"—the pitcher, batter, and catcher—the nuances of the game (the positioning of the fielders, the leads of the runners, the signals from the dugout) were lost.[48] What resulted were broadcasts of games that failed to engage viewers to the same extent the more obviously television-friendly sports did. If baseball was going to compete with football and basketball, those who ran it were going to have to finally concern themselves with the product on the field as well as how it was presented to the public. Because of television, baseball was finally forced to step up its game.

The Yankees paid a particularly heavy price in this newly competitive atmosphere. Their demise in the mid-1960s can and has been traced to a variety of factors—poor management (they were sold to a conglomerate, CBS, in 1965), bad trades, and poor player development. But it is also likely that at least some of their decline can be attributed to the increasingly competitive nature of their MLB rivals attributable to television. After all, although prospects such as Jim Bouton, Mel Stottlemyre, Al Downing, and Bobby Murcer failed to develop into the next generation of Yankee superstars, there had always been prospects that had flamed out. Prior to the '60s, however, the Yankees were always able to replace these players with others who were able to fill the shoes of the older generation of Yankee regulars. The Yankees' relationship with the Kansas City A's throughout the '50s was perhaps the most glaring example of the ease in which the Yankees were able to find suitable replacement parts for their dynasty (players such as Roger Maris, Ralph Terry, Bobby Shantz, Ryne Duren, and Clete Boyer were just a few of the dozens they easily acquired from their compliant "rivals"),[49] but practically every other MLB team likewise had a hand in the Yankees' perpetual dominance. Johnny Mize, Bob Turley, Hector Lopez, Johnny Sain, Enos Slaughter, and Don Larsen were only a few of the horde of players acquired by the Yankees from their rivals in either flat-out purchases or thinly veiled one-sided trades with teams looking to dump salary and balance their ledgers at the end of a season.[50]

Now, in this newly cutthroat environment, the Yankees found fewer trading partners than ever before. If an aging, yet expensive star was one of the few reasons for fans to remain interested in an otherwise losing local baseball team, that star had value to the organization and could not simply be unloaded without the team receiving something that it could at least market to its fans as equally enticing. All of this further frayed the once cohesive unit that was MLB ownership. Without the Yankees as strong leaders, they were no longer able to sway their brethren to take action "for the good of the game" (that is, the Yankees). Instead, each club was increasingly out for itself as it calculated how any particular decision affected its standing vis-à-vis the local football, basketball, and hockey teams.

Television also managed to end the subservience of the rest of MLB to the Yankees in that it put enough money in the owners' pockets to grant them their independence. Now, not only did these owners no longer want to sell their most popular players to the Yankees for competitive reasons, they no longer had to because they could now balance their books without help from the paternalistic Yankees. This allowed them to hold on to talent both on their rosters and in their farm systems and build from year to year.[51] The days of teams such as the Phillies of the 1930s and '40s who routinely sold off any player of value and remade themselves from year to year (and put a faceless team on the field to boot) were finally over. Television revenue increased rapidly through the '60s and then exploded in the '70s; by 1980, it had increased 355 percent in the previous ten years alone.[52] All of this money meant that club owners no longer had to pull together in one direction to survive. They were finally free to choose their own path. The lifeline that was the Yankees was no longer needed. As it went unused from one year to the next, the Yankees crumbled, unity within the owners' camp dissolved, and competitive balance finally came to MLB as it fought for the spotlight.

By the dawn of the '70s, every club put substantial effort into the product it put on the field.[53] Clubs poured money into their farm systems, player development, and with the birth of free agency in 1976, player procurement. For the first time, true competitive balance was finally achieved: all twelve National League clubs finished first in their division at least once during the 1980s, as did eleven of the fourteen American League clubs. And, despite the efforts to improve the product on the field, if a competitive team was nevertheless still not imminent, there would at least be none of the organizational indifference that fogged the game of previous generations; public relations at last became a powerful arm of almost every club. Colorful mascots, animated scoreboards, giveaways, promotions, and any and all sort of "fun" was packaged and presented to the sporting public in most baseball cities.[54] Bill Veeck was derided by his fellow owners when he tried to bring entertainment to the ballpark in the '40s and '50s. Bill Giles was hailed as a marketing genius by his peers for doing many of the same things with the Phillies in the '70s and '80s.[55] In twenty years' time, the mindset of club owners had shifted 180 degrees.

Although the full effects of television would not be felt until the 1980s, it had already succeeded in pitting the owners against each other by the mid-1960s. Television, combined with the corporate revolution and the obvious dilution of power that came with significant expansion, left the owners in a curious position: individually they were stronger, richer than ever. Collectively, they had never before been so fractured and weak. When Marvin Miller arrived on the scene in 1966 the owners were easy prey. America's game, "their" game, was to be theirs no more in a very short time. For this, they and much of the media blamed Miller and his Players Association. However, upon closer inspection, societal changes affecting corporate America were the more likely culprit, changes that had nothing to do with the Players Association and which predated Miller's arrival by several years.

Miller and the Players Association are not wholly irrelevant to this story, however. For MLB did not simply cease to be an owners' game; it became very much the players' game instead. The players' ascension as the new collective face of baseball was not a mere, inescapable consequence of the owners' weakening power; rather it was likewise the result of a concerted effort of the Players Association, itself driven by societal forces that caused its members to reassess their place not only in the game but in American society as well. Contrary to the yelps of the owners and many in the media, the players' uprising was not the result of their having been brainwashed by Marvin Miller; it was the obvious extension of their bearing witness to a unique moment in American history—a moment where privileged people just like they were rose up and demanded an end to the paternalism that had presided over them for decades. The players could not help but be influenced by what they saw going on around them. Inevitably, they saw a lot of themselves in these other uprisings and became motivated to instigate one in their game as well. Black players such as Curt Flood had even more of a reason to do so. In all of this, Marvin Miller was the facilitator. But he was hardly the cause.

THE RISE OF THE PLAYERS

It was Aristotle, not Marvin Miller, who first recognized that, in any society, authority is always in danger of degenerating into a manipulative power struggle whenever "persons of great ability, and second to none in their merits, are treated dishonorably by those who enjoy the highest honors."[56] Aristotle may have never met Del Webb, Walter O'Malley, and their cohorts, but it was as if he had them in mind. For decades it seemed as if it was club management's primary responsibility to degrade and denigrate its players whenever and however possible. It only took the players to recognize their own worth for the owners' already tenuous grip on the game to unravel for good.

Dating back to the birth of the National League, club owners always considered it of utmost importance to beat into their players that despite their talents on the field, it was the owners who constituted the essence of the game. Although much of this was in furtherance of the owners' pursuit of status, there were obvious financial benefits to this tactic as well. If the players could be convinced that they were fortunate to be playing ball for a living and that they could easily be replaced at any moment, salary negotiations would be a breeze in most cases. Much of ownership's treatment of players served to confirm this supposition and bludgeon the players into a subservient role. For decades, players were paid only during the season; during the winters they were on their own.[57] This was consistent with the notion that professional ball playing was a privilege: when the privilege ended every October, so did the paychecks.[58] What the players did for rent and food money during the off-season could not be the owners' concern. Until "Murphy money" came along in the late 1940s and relieved them of the burden (the result of the near-unionization of the Pirates in 1946 by labor lawyer Robert Murphy), players were responsible for their own spring training expenses even though they were required to attend.[59] They were also expected to purchase their own gloves and shoes.[60] Travel was brutal, with road trips *averaging* between twenty-one and thirty days at a clip, thereby putting tremendous emotional strain on young families, leading to the dissolution of many marriages and families.[61] All of this for the privilege of playing Major League baseball. Although life in the minors was far worse in some respects, occasionally a promotion to the majors represented a step down for a player: after starring for Baltimore of the International League in 1949, pitcher Al Widmar's 1950 contract was purchased by the St. Louis Browns—complete with a $2,000 pay cut.[62] Widmar's situation was hardly unique. When players finally made it to the big leagues, they were immediately disabused of any notion that they had achieved any sort of stature within the game.

And then came the yearly contract negotiations. Regardless of the season a player had just completed, the message was the same: just be glad you are still on the roster. Browns' owner William O. DeWitt could seemingly never be impressed; his team finished in the basement regardless of the performance of any one player. From his perspective, no individual player could have any particular worth to him at all and he was not shy in informing them of this. Players requesting a salary boost on the basis of recent performance were quickly set straight: DeWitt would find a way to disparage their talents anyway. And if he could not, he fell back on the old reliable: the perceived sorry financial state of the Browns that, he claimed, made significant raises impossible.[63] DeWitt's strategy was a familiar one, as most clubs tried similar tricks. The underlying goal was always the same: to convince the player that regardless of his salary, he was overpaid. Branch Rickey was a master at the art of contract negotiation, going so far as to preen that actual negotiations were occurring despite the presence of the reserve clause that left players ultimately with no option other than to accept whatever their club offered. One witness to Rickey's act considered him nothing less than an "ethical fraud" come contract time.[64] Even players on the few teams making healthy profits were abused at the so-called bargaining table. After winning the 1956 Triple Crown, Mickey Mantle approached Yankee GM George Weiss seeking a significant raise. Weiss replied that Mantle ought to keep his mouth shut and threatened that if he did not accept the team's offer, Weiss would have no choice but to turn over to Mantle's wife the findings of the private detective Weiss had hired to follow Mantle and teammate Billy Martin.[65] Whether a player suited up for the woeful Browns or the majestic Yankees, the message was unchanged: the owners deserved their positions within the game, the players did not. The concept of privilege was constantly drummed into their heads.

It was true that, despite the harsh realities of professional ball playing in the 1940s, '50s, and '60s, the life of a Major League baseball player could be a comfortable one, relatively speaking. Even though they were squeezed during contract time and unpaid during the off-season, at least the established veteran players were relatively well-off compared with society overall (although the hordes earning salaries at or near the Major League minimum were not). In 1950 the average Major League salary was $11,000; U.S. senators earned $12,500, physicians earned on the average $12,324, attorneys $8,349, dentists $7,436, and schoolteachers $2,794.[66] However, with farm systems now so large and so many minor-league players seemingly ready to take their place (26.7 for every Major League position as compared with only 5.9 in 1990),[67] players had no job security and hence, no rights. Soon, the mere privilege of playing Major League ball for a living was no longer enough.

There had always been sporadic player uprisings, dating back to the nineteenth century with the formation of John Montgomery Ward's Brotherhood of Professional Base Ball Players and the creation of the Players League in 1890 (formed as a rebellion against the oppressive National League). However, none of these earlier movements could be sustained over the long haul; eventually the aggrieved players would come back into the fold and the business of Major League Baseball would continue as it always had. By the 1940s, a more sustained movement began to take root, although it seemed toothless and harmless for many years.

The near-unionization of the Pirates in 1946 was an early example of the awakening of the players, and although the movement failed, albeit barely, the rumbles of discontent began to brew. The owners realized that they needed to pass at least superficial reforms to quell the murmurs of discontent, so in 1946, along with the Murphy money, they created a pension plan for the players, complete with player representatives on the pension committee.[68] Their input was consistently ignored, however. After requesting modest increases to the pension plan and being turned down flat, player representatives Ralph Kiner and Allie Reynolds decided to hire a lawyer, J. Norman Lewis, and bring him to the December 1953 winter meetings.[69] The owners then agreed to meet with the players but instructed them to leave Lewis out in the hotel's foyer.[70] The frustrated player representatives then met with each other and agreed to form what was to be known as the Major League Baseball Players Association when it became operational on July 12, 1954.[71]

Although the received wisdom holds that the Players Association was an impotent body prior to the arrival of Marvin Miller, it was successful in laying the foundation necessary for Miller to succeed. From the outset, the Players Association was effective, at least occasionally, as an information-gathering and dissemination body. This was crucial in enlightening the players on the realities of their situation. In 1958 the law firm retained by the Players Association (the retention of a law firm being, by itself, a monumental step by the players) released its "Salary Report for Major League Baseball Players," which was distributed to the representative of each team.[72] Although its conclusion—that the players were underpaid—was hardly surprising, its significance lay in the methods used to demonstrate precisely why and how this was so. By showing the players how they were being taken advantage of rather than merely telling them what they already knew, the report empowered the players to speak with authority and specificity on the financial side of the game rather than in the general platitudes (for example, "I was ripped off") common to earlier eras that were easy to brush aside. For instance, the report discussed relative cost of living standards as a means to comparing salaries across eras. By doing this, it was able to clearly convey just why it was that although the minimum salary had recently been raised from $6,000 to $7,000, this nevertheless left the players in worse financial shape than they had been in just a few years earlier. It also pointed out that, in 1929, team salaries accounted for 35.3 percent of Major League expenses, whereas by 1956 that percentage had dropped to 12.9. The implications of this were clear: the owners were making more money than ever before but were pocketing all of the profits. As it was, the players *were* being ripped off; only now they knew the particulars of the theft. As the saying goes, with knowledge comes power, and the "Salary Report" provided the theoretical foundation for what was to come later. If the presence of the farm system and reserve clause thwarted the players from acting individually, they finally were coming to the realization that they would have to band together and attack the problem as a collective. That they began to see the solution of their problems in terms of collective action during the 1950s was not merely a function of the "Salary Report," however; it was in keeping with, and most likely driven by, the times.

With the postwar economic boom, combined with the recent horrors of fascism and the ever-present threat of looming communism, capitalism thrived throughout America during this era as it never had before.[73] The old radical left of the '30s, which used Marxist or quasi-Marxist doctrine to call for fundamental changes to the nature of American life—the end of capitalism, the promotion of socialism—was effectively marginalized. The American system was triumphant in the worldwide ideological battle and few were willing to lend any credence to dissidence questioning the fundamental soundness of its political philosophy. Of course, a left remained but this transfigured left was far different than the old left; to them, private enterprise seemed a safer alternative than Stalinism or fascism, so whereas their predecessors railed against capitalism, the new left embraced it. Their goal, therefore, was not to convince everyone to opt out of the American economy but to find ways for more people to opt in. Rather than calling for the overthrow of the system, they focused instead on using the law to help influence and regulate market outcomes to generate greater equality within the existing structure. In this respect, the left of the '50s and '60s would be far more mainstream than the left of a generation earlier.

In short, by now practically everybody wanted in on the American capitalistic system. However, not everyone had the ability to take full advantage of it on their own. As a result, individualism took a backseat to collective approaches as the left now applied increasing pressure to ensure that as many people as possible were benefiting. They increasingly looked to the government and labor unions to provide a "safety net" for those who were disadvantaged in the free-market system, with the idea being that every American, not merely those in the most advantageous positions, was entitled to enjoy its benefits.[74] The economic boom meant that a measure of affluence was increasingly becoming the accepted standard of living. With the rapid transformation of postwar American society from one of "poverty and modest means" to one of relative opulence, fewer and fewer groups were content to take less then what they considered their fair share.[75] It was not surprising, therefore, that organization and labor movements thrived.

Of course, the labor movement had been around for decades by then, slowly gaining power as checks against the increasingly ominous monopolists and industrialists who had toppled the WASP elites in the latter half of the nineteenth century. Although the labor movement began with the populists (with populist presidential candidate James Weaver declaring in

1892 that "[i]t is a fight between labor and capital, and labor is in the vast majority"[76]), it soon expanded into larger American society. In the 1890s, as the popular outcry over the trusts grew louder, professionals joined the more radical left and began to rail against those who had seemingly surpassed them in both wealth and status.[77] Likewise, more and more members of the clergy (victims of the status revolution themselves as their positions as rural and small-town moral and intellectual leaders diminished in an increasingly urban, increasingly secular society) joined forces with the populists and the professionals. In contrast with their earlier views, now more clergymen were supportive of strikes and other action taken by labor in its attempt to repel the perceived overreaching of the industrialists.[78] In addition, and consistent with his vision of a relatively impotent Sherman Act, "trust buster" Theodore Roosevelt likewise urged workers to protect themselves against the monopolists through unionization instead.[79] Within this atmosphere, the newly formed American Federation of Labor was able to grow rapidly: by 1911, trade union membership had risen fivefold from what it had been in 1897.[80] Strikes abounded, and although many were crushed, gains were made as well: an 1894 Pullman strike led to the empowerment of workers nationwide as President Cleveland's commission appointed to investigate it concluded that workers could not be denied their right to organize and bargain collectively.[81]

These gains were met with predictable resistance. Many courts, fearful of what they interpreted as social revolution and protective of big business, issued rulings designed to thwart the labor movement.[82] Some social Darwinist thinking was likewise hostile to organized labor and the strikes that followed, theorizing that group action diminished the self-reliance needed to succeed in modern society and was, therefore, unmanly.[83] Other social Darwinists were more amenable, however. Although labor unions themselves disturbed him, William Graham Sumner came by the 1890s to believe in the necessity of what he termed *antagonistic cooperation*. "The struggle to maintain existence [is] carried on, not individually but in groups," he wrote, expressing his belief that, irrespective of the notion of survival of the fittest, cooperation likewise was an unavoidable reality both in nature as well as society.[84] Soon, many neo-Darwinists came to believe in not merely perpetual struggle but struggle that took place between groups rather than between individuals.[85]

Out of this evolving mindset came the notion that labor rights were both natural and civil rights.[86] In 1935 Congress passed the Wagner Act, which effectively limited private-sector management's ability to impede the organization of its workers and compelled it to bargain collectively with recognized unions. On a larger scale, the New Deal cemented the emerging concept of labor's patriotic purpose. As labor historian David Brody observed, the New Deal "attach[ed] labor's interest to unimpeachable national economic goals."[87] By stressing the need to protect workers through the Wagner Act as a means to reviving the economy and battling the Great Depression, Roosevelt equated labor's interests with capitalistic ones. Not surprisingly, union membership mushroomed in this era; no matter how strong the corporation, it seemed it could not avoid the onrushing national urge to organize and unionize.[88] Even those workers who did not unionize themselves received the attention of the labor movement: in 1932 the American Federation of Labor pushed for public unemployment insurance, shorter work hours, and increased wages for everyone, irrespective of their union affiliation. In the words of labor leader John L. Lewis in 1935, the AFL was out to "befriend the cause of humanity and champion human rights."[89] This national "safety net" would be, when viewed through the prism of the New Deal, consistent with nationalistic and capitalistic ideals.

The concepts of unionism and collectivism flourished up to and through the war. Union membership approached fourteen million workers during this time, with the president of the probusiness U.S. Chamber of Commerce commenting in 1944 that "labor is a power in our land."[90] And with this power came the inevitable strikes that regularly resulted in gains for workers in all fields. Both during the war and afterward, frequent and successful labor agitation ratcheted up the national standard of living, "convincing other groups that the 'union ethic' was a sure way to affluence."[91] Despite the more publicized blind patriotism of the era, the labor movement thrived during the height of World War II not only in sheer numbers but in the level of its agitation as well, with more than fourteen thousand strikes involving nearly seven million workers—a greater number that at any other time theretofore in American history.[92] After the war, labor strikes actually intensified—three million workers were on strike in the first half of 1946 alone.[93] The success of this movement resulted in increased affluence nationwide and led to an ironic result: greater faith in the collective as a means to achieve the full benefits of the capitalistic system. As Brody further observed, the Wagner Act appeared, at least for a time, to solve "the riddle of freedom and solidarity." Despite their collective action, unionized workers (which by the mid-1950s now encompassed one-third of the American labor force) considered themselves nonetheless free, "but they would express that freedom collectively and reap the benefits of 'actual freedom of contract.'"[94] The nascent Players Association surely was not ignorant of the world outside baseball. It, like so many others within the American labor force, heeded the words of contemporary sociologist Robert S. Lynd: "We live in an era in which only organization counts; values and causes with unorganized or only vaguely organized backing were never so impotent."[95] The Players Association of the '50s was simply coming to the same conclusion as many of its fellow laborers in other fields.

As it would turn out, the players not only had compatriots in the workforce but, as the '60s unfolded, found them on college campuses as well. In fact, many of the postwar movements—labor, civil rights, student, and the Players Association—had one thing in common: the goal of further participation in the American democratic and capitalistic system. They were hardly the "radical" movements they were portrayed as being.

Perhaps surprisingly, the 1960s student "movement" was particularly instructive to the players in that, underneath their obvious differences, the players and student protesters shared many commonalties, not only in what they sought but how they were perceived by outsiders. The success of the student movement served as crucial inspiration for the players and their own burgeoning movement. The labor movement itself could only serve as inspiration to the players to a limited extent. For, despite Lester Rodney's pioneering coverage of player holdouts within the *Daily Worker* and his attempts to equate their causes with the labor movement as a whole,[96] the players never considered themselves "labor" per se. Rather, it had been drummed into them for so long that they were privileged Americans that it took agitation by another group of privileged Americans—college students—for the players (along with many other groups of seemingly privileged citizens) to finally feel comfortable stepping out of their subservient roles and asserting their rights.

The student movement began in earnest in late 1961 with a document entitled "The Port Huron Statement."[97] Authored by the Students for a Democratic Society (SDS), the manifesto took note of racial bigotry and the pockets of poverty that still dotted the country despite the exploding economy of the '50s, as well as the "powerlessness of ordinary people." It declared that society, rather than the "power elites," should be involved in the political and economic decisions that affected their lives and called for a "revitalized labor movement" along with a "participatory democracy" "in which all Americans would decide national issues in a public forum and in which opposing views would illuminate diversity and choices in the Republic." Although it was derided as a radical manifesto by the power elites it challenged, the statement was, in fact, a very traditional reform document given that it drew as its inspiration participatory reform movements from the nation's past that were hardly radical. Its backers were in many ways no different than the Jacksonian democrats, populists, progressives, and new dealers that came before them in that they argued for greater inclusion in the system rather than the destruction of it.[98] In fact, the document represented a clear break from the more radical politics of the old left in that the issue of communism versus capitalism was no longer one for vigorous debate. The document included a statement that "private enterprise is not inherently immoral or undemocratic," with the hope of quelling fears that the New Left intended to travel down the worn out path of the old.[99]

One of the early student leaders, Mario Savio, made an explicit connection between the traditionally perceived downtrodden and those of more privileged status when he said in 1964, "Last summer I went to Mississippi to join the struggle there for civil rights. This fall I am engaged in another phase of the same struggle, this time in Berkeley. In Mississippi an autocratic and powerful minority rules, through organized violence, to suppress the vast, virtually powerless majority. In California, the privileged minority manipulates the university bureaucracy to suppress the students' political expression."[100] Although it may have initially been difficult for Major League players to see anything of themselves in the faces of Mississippi sharecroppers, they had far less trouble seeing the connection between themselves and the students. As society changed, as authority was challenged in other areas of American life, the players could not help but take notice. Like an increasing number of Americans, baseball players as well were becoming more skeptical of the traditional order of things. The "Depression-era mindset" of the players, where they were happy just to be in the big leagues, was disappearing. Red Sox owner Tom Yawkey once boasted, "[t]o me the greatest example of American democracy is the right a player has to sit down with a general manager and negotiate his contract." By the '60s, Yawkey's fiction had been exposed in the many different movements then taking place within American society. The "rugged individualism" of earlier eras had been replaced by a group ethos forged first by the New Deal mindset and now the New Left, with both preaching that collective action was not only patriotic and capitalistic but led to tangible results. The paternalism of earlier eras, where workers, students, and players sat back and blindly trusted that their superiors would act in their best interests, was finally being challenged.

In fact, it was paternalism, in the form of the *in loco parentis* powers of their university administrators, that really irked the majority of the students involved in the "movement" of the '60s.[101] These powers, in place ever since Harvard College first enacted them in the 1640s, essentially permitted university deans to treat students like children, denying them many of the rights ordinary citizens enjoyed outside the university setting.[102] By the mid-1960s student protestors began to ask: "Are students full citizens, ones protected by the Constitution?"[103] Many of the issues raised by the students were ones that would easily resonate with the Major League players of the era: they had no say in an environment that would not exist without them; they were repeatedly told to keep quiet and be happy that they enjoyed the privilege of attending their elite institution; they were often treated like cattle, with little thought paid to their personal well-being and wishes. In short, the students brought to the American consciousness the concept that relative privilege was not, in and of itself, enough.

The fact that the students were, by and large, products of privileged backgrounds further explained the relatively conservative nature of their rebellion, which was crucial in ultimately helping them forge a deeper connection with both mainstream America as well as the Major League players. Unlike the radical youths of the 1930s, who often came from minority (typically Jewish) backgrounds, the beatniks of the '50s and the student protestors of the '60s were in many cases children of the establishment.[104]

Many of the beatniks came from WASP households; many protestors likewise grew up in relative privilege. They had already developed a taste for the good life; they simply wanted more of it and on their terms. As such, their fight was for status (something else the players could relate to) more than anything else.[105] And in their actions, the benefits of sticking together were once again on display. Activists began calling each other "brother" or "friend," drawing even further attention to the notion that cohesiveness brought results.[106] By the mid-'60s, they were starting to see significant gains. Slowly but surely, more and more universities began withdrawing from their *in loco parentis* roles. In so doing, these universities were granting their students the heightened status—that of independent adult rather than of naive child—they so badly craved.

The student movement was an inspiration to many groups of Americans, not just baseball players. People from all walks of life, privileged and otherwise, began seeking out others like themselves in the hope of achieving results through collective action. By the late '60s, the formality of the labor movement of the '50s was joined by countless informal movements across the nation, demanding their rights in all sorts of areas. These "backyard rebellions" took the forms of neighborhood associations, seniors' rights groups, historic preservation movements, street art movements, and so on.[107] Within this atmosphere, the amped-up players' movement was hardly out of step with the national character. In fact, a couple of players engaged in a "backyard rebellion" of their own before Marvin Miller ever had the opportunity to stir things up on a larger scale. During spring training 1966, two of the game's greatest pitchers, Dodger teammates Don Drysdale and Sandy Koufax, staged a joint holdout, figuring that while management might conclude that the team could get along without one of them, it could not reach the same conclusion if both went missing for an extended period of time. Dodger management was livid but eventually was forced to concede, giving Koufax a $40,000 raise from his $85,000 1965 salary and Drysdale a $35,000 raise from his $80,000 1965 salary.[108]

That same spring, Marvin Miller was appointed executive director of the Players Association. He toured spring training camps and was educated as to the players' developing mindset.[109] Because they did not consider themselves labor per se, they did not want the Players Association to negotiate their contracts for them as would a traditional trade union.

However, on issues regarding the minimum player salary in the game and the pension fund, they were more willing to band together. Miller took his cues from the players rather than vice versa, and decided to initially focus on these areas. By concentrating his efforts on those issues that already rankled a significant pool of players, he was well on his way toward gaining their confidence in that he showed that he was responsive to their concerns. Regardless, the owners and many within the media repeatedly attempted to paint him as a "Svengali" "mesmerizing unsophisticated players into following his lead for his own aggrandizement."[110] One of his most vocal critics was Dick Young of the *New York Daily News*, who alleged that Miller "brainwashed" his players with his "steel trap mind wrapped in a butter melting voice. . . . With few exceptions, they follow him blindly, like Zombies."[111] Young may have chirped the loudest but the overwhelming majority of sportswriters harbored similar thoughts, and voiced them frequently in their columns throughout the '60s, '70s, and '80s. Young found a willing ally in Hall of Famer Ted Williams, who by the late '60s was on the side of management rather than the players. He branded Miller's union a "radical Players Association"[112] although in actuality it was something else entirely.

The players were hardly zombies. Through the years, Miller encouraged them to attend bargaining sessions with the owners so they could see for themselves what they were up against.[113] Very quickly they became extremely well informed. They witnessed firsthand the stonewalling and evasive tactics used by the same owners who had always told the players to trust them because they had the players' best interests in mind. A few minutes in a bargaining session disabused them of that belief. They saw how the owners were willing to use any weapon available to them against the players, no matter how trivial the point at issue. The unreasonableness of the owners was perhaps never so clearly demonstrated than in the reaction of Giants general manager Chub Feeney to an offhand remark made by pitcher Jim Bouton. When Bouton suggested, facetiously, at a bargaining session that a player be granted free agency at age sixty-five, Feeney growled in response, "No, because that would get you a foot in the door."[114]

In one sense, Feeney's reaction was to be expected. For what was being contested during these bargaining sessions was the point made by the owners for decades: that they, not the players, constituted the essence of the game. This mindset was behind much of what Commissioner Bowie Kuhn imparted to the media throughout the turbulent bargaining sessions that defined his tenure (1969–84). "I will say," he remarked in a typical comment uttered in 1980, "that the greatest long term interest in the game is held by the club people. Their financial interest is longest and deepest. They'll still be around as the generations of players pass."[115] The stability of the owners was a theme repeatedly hammered home by Kuhn even as the turnover in ownership continued to increase at an unprecedented rate. Cincinnati Reds general manager Bob Howsam sounded a similar theme in 1973 when he not only pitted the players against management but against America in general. In his view, management protected the game and its American ideals, whereas the players wanted to destroy "the institution that reflects all that is America . . . the freedoms we cherish and the liberties we defend."[116]

Miller saw things differently. Through time he was able to convince the players that it was they, not the owners, who defined the game of baseball. Soon, the players were issuing statements of their own, challenging the owners' worldview. In 1967, Mets pitcher Jack Fisher addressed his fellow players as well as the owners present at a bargaining session: "It's a matter of taking pride in your profession. . . . We don't think we[are] fighting for ourselves. We[are] fighting for baseball."[117] As this mindset took hold among the players, they began speaking of their baseball careers as professions that came with rights and not merely privileges. This theme particularly hit home with Curt Flood and other black players given the civil rights and black power movements that provided the backdrop to the era.

In his December 24, 1969, letter to Kuhn requesting free agency, Flood turned the owners' arguments on their heads, implying that when it came to the doling out of rights and privileges, the owners had things backward. "After 12 years in the major leagues," he wrote, "I do not feel that I am a piece of property to be bought and sold irrespective of my wishes. I believe that any system that produces that result violates my basic rights as a citizen and is inconsistent with the laws of the United States and the several states."[118] According to Flood, if anything, it was the owners who should have considered themselves privileged simply to maintain an association with the national pastime; all that was required of them was a sufficiently fat wallet. The players, on the other hand, owing to their unique skills, were entitled to their presence in the game on merit alone. For that reason, a fair share of the profits derived from the game was likewise rightfully theirs. Flood continued to hammer away at the owners throughout his battle. The following year in an interview, he remarked: "They say baseball is the all-American sport. When you think of all-American, you would think of something democratic, something free."[119] The decades of blather by the owners about baseball as America had finally come back to bite them. If they were serious about the connection, they would have to set the players free. As players such as Flood pointed out, any other result would be absurd.

Predictably, the reaction to Flood's cause and outspokenness was overwhelmingly hostile. As one baseball historian noted, if Flood's comments on freedom and his right to participate in America's free enterprise system had been uttered instead by Walter O'Malley as justification for relocating his Brooklyn Dodgers to Los Angeles, they would hardly have registered much reaction at all. But because they were uttered by a player, and a black player at that, they were taken as outrageous and dangerously radical.[120] Most of the mainstream press ridiculed Flood. In reaction to his statement that "a well-paid slave is still a slave," many sportswriters asked, "How can there be such a thing as 'a ninety-thousand-dollar-a-year slave?'" Dick Moss, the Players Association's attorney, recognized the racial and social commentary that was on display in the reaction to Flood. To Moss, the reaction was "violent in nature and racist in quality. It is a reaction, I believe, of white America to a black man who has been permitted to 'make it' and then turned on his benefactors."[121] In this respect, the Flood saga was representative of the larger players' movement but in even starker terms. It was a more pronounced, clearer symbol of the overall upheaval of the era and, therefore, subject to the most violent reaction nationwide.

The reaction of the black press to Flood was far different. There, Flood found great support for his cause, with many writers labeling him a "racial pioneer." Within the pages of black newspapers, the mainstream sportswriters' puzzlement over Flood's "well-paid slave" comment was answered: "a man who makes $20,000 a year is entitled to no less constitutional protection than a man who makes $5,000."[122] More urgently, Flood's comment illustrated the gravity of the situation—if a black man making $90,000 could be treated as poorly as Flood, what did that say about the treatment of those making far less than Flood, out of the public eye?

As a result of the civil rights and student movements (on many campuses that were experiencing their first significant era of integration),
black and white youths intermingled like never before. The cultural mix was
empowering, as many middle- and upper-class whites learned firsthand
of true oppression while blacks saw up close the middle-class lifestyles
they aspired to.[123] Through this cultural exchange, both groups emerged
stronger. In baseball, the modicum of integration that had occurred in the
two decades or so since the debut of Jackie Robinson presented the players
at last with leaders like Flood who through their words, actions, and mere
presence gave confidence to other players, black and white, to stand up for
themselves. In his stand, Flood convinced many players who previously
were on the fence with regard to the Players Association that their cause
was just. Through Flood, they were able to see that their demands were not
selfish; they were representative of something bigger than simply wanting
a larger slice of the financial pie. It was this mindset that led to successive
collective bargaining agreements that steadily ratcheted minimum player
salaries up to acceptable levels after decades of stagnation. Although the
extra income realized through these agreements was welcome, the collective bargaining agreements were ultimately not just about money. They
were also about power. They were about rights and privileges and who,
between the players and the owners, most appropriately lined up on which
side of the ledger.

Throughout the 1970s, the Players Association gained strength until
it finally toppled the owners for good. In 1975, when arbitrator Peter Seitz
freed Dodgers pitcher Andy Messersmith and Expos pitcher Dave McNally
from their contracts, ruling that the owners' hallowed reserve clause permitted them merely a single year of absolute, despotic power over their
players beyond the end of their contractual term (the owners had always
held that the clause permitted them to unilaterally renew players' contracts
interminably, thus binding their players to them forever), the reserve clause
was effectively killed.[124] The collective bargaining agreement negotiated the
following year officially buried it when it allowed for free agency after six
years of Major League service. Thus, in a few short years, the entire structure of the game had been overhauled. It was now a players' game, not an
owners' game. By the time negotiations had begun on the 1980 collective
bargaining agreement, the players were firmly in control. With salaries

soaring and baseball booming as it never had before, now it was the players who spoke of "protect[ing] the game and ensur[ing] its prosperity."[125] Tearing a page out of the owners' playbook, it was now the players who claimed to be the true protectors of baseball—against the selfish owners who were merely out for themselves to the detriment of the game.

The owners countered with statements and positions rooted firmly in the past. They clamored throughout 1980 for "equity," claiming that clubs deserved some sort of compensation when they "lost" a player to free agency. But "equity" assumed that a free agent was still somehow property of the club he was leaving, and that his "loss" created a hardship for the club. The reality was different, however, as the rules now in force contemplated limited, short-term contracts that, when completed, left both the player and the club free to go their separate ways. There could be no "equity" because there had been no "loss" suffered by the club.[126] It had paid the player, received performance in exchange, and that was as far as the relationship went. The players now controlled their destinies. The owners were reduced to fighting among themselves for the privilege of convincing the best ones to play for them. It was tough medicine to swallow and many owners could never bring themselves to come to grips with the new landscape of the game.

The owners had been soundly defeated by the players but they came to battle mortally wounded. Up against a collection of players strengthened from within by leaders such as Curt Flood and others, and empowered by the social milieu of the era, they would have had a difficult battle in any event. That they were already weak doomed them from the outset. Although the struggle between the players and the owners was portrayed by people such as Ted Williams and many within the media as a classic clash between conservatives and radicals, it was conservative and traditional capitalistic values that both weakened and transformed the owners and emboldened and strengthened the players. Despite the owners' bleats to the contrary, it was the core beliefs they always espoused—pure capitalism and traditional values—that wound up being responsible for taking away from them the game that had defined them for so long.

"WAIT 'TIL NEXT YEAR" AND THE DENIAL OF HISTORY

The collective ethos represented by groups such as the Players Association, among others, may have been gaining popular support by the mid to late 1960s but it was threatened from the outset by another American ethos, one that had more deeply entrenched roots dating back well into the nineteenth century, that itself felt threatened by the collective movement. This ethos—the individualistic, "positive thinking" movement—rejected out of hand the critical, often grim portrait of America drawn by the collectivists and chose instead, as it had for decades, to embrace an unadulterated optimistic worldview that depended upon the willful ignorance of the types of inconvenient facts often highlighted by the collectivists in their quest to bring about social change. The clash of these competing visions of American life would result in the culture wars that have dominated the national landscape ever since and led a majority of Americans to turn against the civil rights, student, and Players Association movements to embrace the sunnier outlook of the positive thinkers, siding instead with people and views that were otherwise in many ways contrary and detrimental to their own self-interests. In the end, the pull of the well-entrenched "positive thinking" ethos was so strong and well-embedded in the American consciousness that the natural alliances between most Americans and groups such as the Players Association became lost in the haze of "pro-American" rhetoric, causing the Players Association to lose in the court of public opinion despite winning at the bargaining table.

THE AMERICAN UNDERDOG DELUSION

The positive thinking movement reveals itself most tellingly in the causes underlying the nature of American support for the underdog, which is nowhere embedded more deeply than in our national pastime.

There is perhaps nothing more American than rooting for the underdog. As much as any other single trait, it defines us as a nation. And we know we root for underdogs because we keep saying that we do. As sociologist Edward Sagarin observed: "Historians and social commentators repeat it, and then one goes to the sports arena and hears the cheering of the tumultuous crowd, as the brave and small Battling Joe, with the odds three to one against him and no takers in sight, comes from behind, and begins to knock the champ right out of the ring. The pandemonium is contagious, and everyone joins in the enthusiastic encouragement . . ."[1] In such an environment, there are hardly any in the crowd who "cannot help but express their admiration for the man who came from behind."[2] As for why Americans identify so heavily with the underdog, psychologists have surmised that rooting for the underdog correlates with the American values of hard work, struggle, risk taking, and courage. In the words of one, "to overcome odds is the great American dream."[3]

Of course, being our national pastime, it was only natural that baseball embraced this value, which it has, practically from its inception. Indeed, much of the rhetoric of the baseball creed is directed toward societal underdogs—the disadvantaged, dispossessed strivers (such as those late-nineteenth-century immigrants) hoping to one day knock out the champ themselves. In his satiric ode to the concept of baseball as America, *The Great American Novel,* Philip Roth captured the nation's underdog spirit in a scene where one of his characters attempts to lift the mood of members of the sad-sack Ruppert Mundy's baseball team, who felt shafted after being informed that, owing to a series of events beyond their control, their home field would be unavailable to them all season and they would therefore be condemned to play their entire schedule on the road: "Well, like Ulysses S. told you boys, that's *good* for you that it ain't fair. That's gonna make champs out of you, if not in this here season, then in the next. Wait'll next year, boys! . . . You want me to tell you boys somethin'? This bein' homeless is just about the best thing that has ever happened to you, if you only had the sense to know it."[4] The inverse of the nation's underdog obsession was expressed in Ernest Thayer's "Casey At the Bat" wherein the obvious favorite, mighty Casey, struck out. It is likely the poem would not have become as ingrained in the national consciousness had he homered, as he was expected to do. As both Roth and Thayer understood, in both American letters as well as American life, it is often preferable to be the underdog. There is just something more "American" about it. In this sense, it is not so much a human trait, we have come to believe, as a national one.[5]

From this perspective, to be the favorite is to be, in a sense, the oppressor, and as anyone who survived elementary school history understands, America stands up to oppressors and defeats them. Stalin, Hitler, Mussolini, Khrushchev,[6] and, most recently, Saddam Hussein all fit this mold. America's international involvement throughout the twentieth century confirmed the righteousness of this position; not only did America make a practice of defeating tyrants, it emerged from its greatest battle against oppression—World War II—unbelievably healthy, wealthy, and powerful.[7] Given our good fortune as a result of our good deeds, it was hard not to believe that this was more than mere economics at play. Rather, it was a form of cosmic justification of America's role.[8] "[I]n a world of good and evil our totalitarian enemies represented evil, and we exemplified good."[9] The American perspective, informed by unique American values, made the world a better place. As Americans, all we had to do was work hard and we could not lose, no matter the odds.[10]

That some values are quintessentially "American" has been suggested empirically.[11] As it turns out, as far as American sports fans go, those who typically root for favorites exhibit traits that many would consider "un-American." Such fans are more likely to score high in measures of right-wing authoritarianism, conformity, and a belief in a just world—that is, that people, namely the downtrodden and less fortunate, get what they deserve.[12] Not surprisingly, all of these traits are ones typically associated with oppressors such as Hitler, Stalin, and the like. Conversely, fans more likely to root for the proclaimed underdog generally score higher in traits that seem more "American"—empathy, individualism, and a belief in social equality.[13] As such, it is no surprise that sitting in the Wrigley Field bleachers and rooting for the perennially hapless Cubs can feel like the embodiment of the American experience. There is a sense of nobility, of righteousness, of patriotism to it, one that is felt as well by Pirates fans, Reds fans, or supporters of virtually any team except the Yankees (which, despite their name, feel somehow un-American to most baseball fans—"the evil empire" moniker was not coined to inspire nationalistic feelings in the club). Like Philip Roth wrote, supporting these perennial underachievers is perhaps the best thing that ever happened to us as sports fans. It is what makes us Americans.

Through the Cubs and Red Sox most notably, but to no lesser degree to fans in other cities, baseball has embraced the romance of the underdog like no other sport. Given the underdog's connection with perceived American values, it is no wonder that baseball is considered our national pastime, the ratings of NFL broadcasts notwithstanding. In *True Believers*, Joe Queenan's literary quest to better understand just why it is that American sports fans torture themselves by rooting for teams that have no realistic hopes for success, Queenan found a nation of optimistic souls on a "semipermanent high," reality be damned.[14] Inevitably, his journey led him finally to Wrigley Field, where he came upon a seventy-five-year-old fan soaking in his Cubs. After remarking how this man had not seen his Cubs play in the World Series since the Truman administration nor win it in his lifetime (their last title came in 1908), Queenan asked him what it was like to spend his entire life rooting for such a team. The old man "smiled, and spoke with the peerless eloquence of the common man. 'Well, they've been playing pretty well lately,' he said."[15]

As far as it goes in the stands at Wrigley Field, it is perhaps an innocent enough sentiment. After all, there is no readily apparent harm in rooting for a perennial loser, particularly if doing so is nevertheless fulfilling. But within a larger context, this Cub fan's statement speaks volumes. For the reasons why he and so many others continue to believe, despite hard evidence to the contrary, reveals what it really means when Americans root for the underdog and uncovers yet another American story—one that becomes relevant and informative when considering the curious public reaction to the players movement as well as to the myriad other collective social movements from the 1960s onward. Supporting the underdog may be a well-known American trait. But what is less well known is how Americans define the term and what that definition says about what American values are in practice, opposed to what we claim them to be.

Contrary to popular American sentiment, support for the underdog turns out to be a well-ingrained trait in many cultures across the globe. Therefore, it is more of a human trait than simply an American one after all. This is not to say, however, that there is nothing unique about Americans and our feelings toward underdogs. For while other cultures likewise support them, their definition of the term is typically somewhat different than the American one. And it is this difference that sets Americans, baseball fans and otherwise, apart.

In Australia, for example, there is a strong historical penchant for supporting the underdog, with the rationale being, at least according to some, that these sympathies are rooted in Australia's origin as a convict society.[16] According to this theory, rooting for a doomed participant with no hope of success harks back to the days when the country was overrun with felons and societal outcasts. As a society, they were up against an all-powerful bureaucratic system designed to subjugate them—one in which they had no possibility of overcoming. Within this environment, the admired trait was standing up to it anyway and never surrendering, despite the foregone certainty of the ultimate outcome that did, in the end, come to pass despite heroic resistance. In this vein, one of the great Australian national folk heroes was Ned Kelly, a nineteenth-century bushranger and outlaw who, with his gang, futilely attempted to take on the British Empire.[17] In a hail of bullets (twenty-eight of which hit him, as the story goes), he stood up to police in his fabled last stand, continuing to advance on them until his legs were literally shot out from under him. In death he became a national icon, recognized as one who never lost his fighting spirit despite the absence of hope that he could somehow overcome the overwhelming forces against him. "As game as Kelly" remains a popular Australian saying, with the intent being that the object of the saying nobly persevered. Overcoming the odds plays no role in this term of affection.

This definition of an underdog—one who loses in the end—is the traditional (and dictionary) definition of the term and one that likewise held sway in America until the late nineteenth century. In its early usage in America, the term applied to "a person in a position of inferiority, esp[ecially] a victim of misfortune or injustice."[18] In fact, when not used to describe combatants in a dog fight, the term mostly applied to slaves or former slaves—individuals who were in inferior positions but who were not expected to succeed.[19] And, in post-Reconstruction America, there was hardly an overwhelming clamor of sympathy for them; very few Americans using that term to describe them likewise rooted for them to ultimately triumph or thought that they would. By the early twentieth century, however—not coincidentally, at precisely the same time the baseball creed gained a foothold—the popular American definition of the term changed; now the "underdog" was thought to be not merely one in an inferior position but one who ultimately overcomes this disadvantage to emerge victorious.[20] And with this new definition came sympathy for one in the inferior position. Now, the American definition of the term implied ultimate success despite overwhelming odds. To root for the underdog in America came to be synonymous with somehow casting one's lot with the ultimate victor—a concept that is the antithesis of the Australian definition of the term. Within a relatively short period of time, the American definition underwent a metamorphosis to the point where the combatant in the inferior position was believed to have an equal, if not better, chance of ultimate success. Rooting for the underdog became little different than rooting for the favorite—both supporters believed their side to have the advantage.

Again, recent empirical evidence suggests this revised American mindset.[21] As Americans, we somehow associate the "underdog" *both* with an inferior initial position as well as the concept of "looming success," that is, that ultimately, despite its initial disadvantage the underdog would emerge victorious.[22] Although at first glance these two associations appear to be contradictory, they in fact are not, as we seem to consider an underdog to be an entity in flux; in the process of transforming itself from a loser into a winner.[23] Returning to the perceived "American" or "un-American" values associated with underdogs discussed earlier, it turns out that the "American" values of empathy and social equality may be little more than a delusional linguistic construct—associations that make us feel better and allow us to assert a moral superiority but that actually explain very little when it comes to separating true (as opposed to perceived) "American" values from those of people we as Americans generally find repugnant. For when put to the test and challenged on the steadfastness of our stated beliefs, we tend to support much more enthusiastically participants labeled as "underdogs" than participants labeled as "disadvantaged."[24] In other words, as Americans we may say we value empathy and social equality but this appears to be the case only in those circumstances where we believe that those who initially find themselves in an inferior position will eventually pull themselves up by their bootstraps and emerge triumphant, without any help from us. When we do not believe that a participant can overcome the odds—when confronted with a participant who is truly "disadvantaged" and who requires our assistance to succeed—we do not seem to have much empathy for him or her. Rather than trigger our supposed desire for social justice, these victims of inequality often lead us to withhold our support rather than give it. In short, when our values are put to the test, we are more likely to turn away, not unlike those we consider to hold un-American beliefs.[25]

Despite reality, which necessarily must conclude that underdogs have a less than equal chance of emerging victorious (if they did not, they would be favorites), many Americans somehow believe otherwise.[26] This delusion allows us to preach high-mindedly but to remain disengaged from the struggle—for in our minds the downtrodden will emerge victorious on their own, without the need of aid. This mindset is consistent with American actions, as opposed to the verbal gymnastics used to nevertheless equate "American" values with support for the truly disadvantaged. In sports, the American penchant of rooting for the underdog really has more to do with rooting for the favorite in the mind's eye—reality be damned. In life, traditional American attitudes toward disadvantaged groups (ones defined by an absence of the type of "looming success" that pervades the American definition of "underdog") show little sympathy or empathy for actual victims of social injustice—Native and African Americans, immigrants, and women, to name but a few such groups.[27] All of the perceived "American" values somehow fall by the wayside in the face of true disadvantage. It is therefore not surprising that the American definition of "underdog" does not extend far beyond the sports arena.[28] In an athletic contest, we can sit passively in the stands holding firm to our stated beliefs without concern that we will be called upon to act on them. Once the game ends, however, and our beliefs have consequences, we are more likely to shy away from them.

In the end, it is not the underdog after all that Americans cherish. It is instead the optimism to believe that the underdog will win despite reasonable, concrete evidence to the contrary. Returning to the Australians for a moment, it becomes clear that besides a shared attraction to the term, Americans and Australians actually have very little in common when it comes to the national ethos supporting underdogs. Perhaps Americans are unique when it comes to our support for underdogs, but not in the way we normally assume. What may be unique about us (or at least unusual) is not our affection for the term but our delusion fueled by unwarranted optimism that underdogs will emerge victorious more often than not, even though by definition, they will not. It is this unwarranted optimism that, as it turns out, opens the door for what we would otherwise conclude are some very "un-American" behaviors by those claiming precisely the opposite allegiance.

For more than a century, unwarranted, irrational optimism has been seen by some of its critics and most ardent supporters alike as a diversionary device used to great effect to preserve the status quo and fend off change: the heroic stories of underdogs (from Horatio Alger's tales onward) being fodder used to present the facade of overcoming even the most dire of situations, which in the process diverts attention from the world as it actually exists.[29] With each underdog that emerges victorious, the focus remains on the extraordinary individual who accomplished the feat rather than on the situation that created the imbalance that necessitated the superhuman acts to surmount it. The psychologist and philosopher William James, although considered a "hero" of what would come to be known as the "positive thinking movement,"[30] recognized as much a century ago when he noted that unfettered optimism and happiness presented potential dangers, given that they require "blindness and insensibility to opposing facts." Although James did not conclude that such happiness was itself a sickness (indeed he believed it to be the socially desired state), the historian Donald Meyer noted that it led to a vulnerability to sickness if the achievement of a state of perpetual bliss became one's overarching priority.[31] In this way, the shutting out of opposing information and facts was, in James's view, under certain conditions "quasi-pathological"—although in his view this was not necessarily a bad thing. Several decades later Roth, a critic of the movement, would sound a similar, although more desolate, theme in *The Great American Novel* when his protagonist considered the magical pull of the word "America" and all it connotes: "America? . . . [W]hat's America to you? Or to me? Or to those tens of thousands up in the stands? It's just a word they use to keep your nose to the grindstone and your toes to the line. America is the opiate of the people . . ."[32]

Sports, particularly baseball as well as the popular depiction of baseball as America, have helped to grease the wheels of the status quo through tales of triumphant underdogs to the point where that seventy-five-year-old Cubs fan could believe from the stands at Wrigley that this, irrespective of the last hundred, was the year his Cubbies were finally going to put it all together. This mindset, "quasi-pathological" at a minimum, is at its essence quintessentially American. Although the unquestioning devotion, the "blindness and insensibility to opposing facts," ironically increases the likelihood of this fan's perpetual misery (after all, there is little incentive for real change to occur if hope and optimism remain regardless of results), he is supportive nevertheless, for to abandon hope is contrary to the national character.

As it turns out, it is by design that this fan, along with countless others, feels this way and continues to look for roses—at the ballpark and, more importantly and with greater consequences, elsewhere—where there are only thorns. For as Americans we are the product of decades' worth of rhetoric aimed directly at us with the goal of encouraging us to resign ourselves to the status quo and ignore our feelings of unease over our own place within the existing social structure; to give in and accept our fate rather than challenge a social and economic hierarchy where the overwhelming majority of wealth, power, and benefits reside with an ever-shrinking few. This rhetoric is evidenced within the baseball creed and has its roots in the societal upheaval caused by the rapid industrialization of America during the last half of the nineteenth century. The positive thinking movement would find a natural ally in baseball very early on as it attempted to calm the fears of those who had the means, numbers, and ability to overthrow the status quo if something was not done quickly.

THE POSITIVE THINKING MOVEMENT

Positive thinking has been woven into the fabric of baseball practically from its inception. In its earliest days, the "patience of hope" allowed even the most dismal teams to reassure themselves that, despite a 106–10 drubbing, "with a little more work they would have every chance to win."[33] This mindset provided them with the faith to believe that, all evidence to the contrary, success was within their grasp if only they worked a bit harder and believed just a bit more.[34] These beliefs did not come by way of accident, for it was the very people who gravitated toward baseball—the middle-class strivers shut out of the WASP cricket clubs—who were also the target of a large-scale movement aimed at promoting this very type of optimism as a means of social control.

America was not always the optimistic country it considers itself today. Indeed, the traditional definition of "underdog" is testament to this; despite the "rags to riches" Horatio Alger tales (which were at least initially directed toward a limited demographic—the Protestant establishment—that itself was hardly on the bottom rung of society) the downtrodden were expected to stay down. As American society evolved and grew throughout the nineteenth century, this distressing mindset caused tension and anxiety in those who were the backbone of the emerging industrial society and whose full-scale energies were required in order to run it.[35] In 1881, as immigrants poured into the country and as America developed into an industrial giant, a New York neurologist, George Beard, diagnosed this emerging national malady. In his book, *American Nervousness,* Beard concluded that "nervousness" was becoming a widespread ailment.[36] Moreover, he contended that this condition was specific to the America of the moment: one that was undergoing a metamorphosis that, in his opinion, was the cause of the condition. As for why America was the cause of such a malady, Beard reasoned that one only had to look around for the answer: what had once been a disparate nation focused on local centers of trade, production, finance, and communication had, in remarkably short order, reinvented itself as a centralized power with a national economy, where increasingly more localities were becoming linked through an improved communications network.[37] What had been local and personal had become national and overwhelming seemingly overnight. In short, American had become a "system" with each individual reduced to a mere function and a part. The concept of the "man-machine" complex portended grave and dehumanizing possibilities as it increasingly became the model for the economy at large. Viewed through this lens, nervousness was practically a foregone conclusion.[38]

According to Beard, everything that defined the reinvented America—"noise, railway travel, buying on margin, liberty, rapid turnover of ideas, climactic variations"—was responsible for a nationwide crisis of nervousness.[39] In his mind, the connections were obvious: because America was the most modern country in the world, it was likewise the most nervous. Within America, because the North and East were more modern than the South and West, Americans living in these areas were the most nervous of all. "In short, nervousness beset the most advanced people, the successful people, the people who most fully indulged modern civilization."[40] Beard was hardly the first or only one to make this assessment of the national character. Walt Whitman had made many of the same points earlier; Stendhal took note of the American temperament several decades prior when he wrote that Americans "are just and they are rational, but they are not happy";[41] and the evangelical Josiah Strong took note of the nation's heavy drinking to allege that the culprit was its location within a climactic "nervous belt."[42] Beard, however, couched his opinion in medical terms[43] and, by doing so, rendered a sobering national diagnosis that felt more scientific and tangible than any that came before: it was modernism that was the cause of a debilitating national disease. Soon, others echoed his stark assessment, finding not blissful, contented Americans at peace with the comforts provided by the tools of modernity but angry and frightened ones, confronted by a chaos and cacophony that permanently unsettled them. The successful ones, the strivers—the very class of people hoping to advance from the middle to the upper class who were drawn to baseball in this pursuit—were apparently victims of their own success. They were sick and America was to blame.

As discussed in chapter 1, depending on where an individual found himself on the social scale in the latter half of the nineteenth century, baseball promised a cure. For those looking for club membership as a social marker but kept out of the WASP cricket clubs, baseball provided an avenue for such an affiliation. For immigrants or the sons of immigrants looking to assimilate, the baseball creed offered both guidance and hope. And for anyone stricken with the "physical as well as spiritual degradation" believed by people such as Beard and others to be caused by their role as a mere cog in the newly industrialized nation, the open spaces of the ball field combined with the promise of honest competition offered respite.[44] The nineteenth-century journalist Henry Chadwick, the so-called "father of baseball," was a firm believer in this ideology and was influential in promoting it (he too preceded Beard in his diagnosis). To him, baseball was "a moral recreation" that merited "the endorsement of every clergy-man in the country . . . [as] a remedy for the many evils resulting from the immoral associations [that] boys and young men of our cities are apt to become connected with." In its rules and mores, which Chadwick was then in the process of helping to create and promote, baseball provided an order and discipline missing in the newly industrialized society.[45] There was, in Chadwick's eyes, a higher, moral purpose to baseball. In many ways it was an antidote to the ills of modernity identified by Beard and others.

Chadwick's beliefs notwithstanding, baseball could do only so much. The physical release offered by the game may have relieved some tension, but the feelings of confusion and hopelessness caused by the man-machine complex would not simply dissipate forever through a ball game. Something more was needed—a cure. Given Beard's belief that it was the imbalance between individual thoughts and modern civilization that caused the malady, he concluded that the imbalance could be righted by focusing on either side of the equation. However, considering that he believed it was too late to turn back the clock and somehow cure the ills of modern civilization, the focus of any cure must be on the individual.[46] Thus, because it was too much to expect civilization to bend to meet the expectations of the individual, Beard leaned heavily upon the individual to bend to meet the expectations of civilization. With this in mind, Beard then focused his cure on the most grievously ill—the rising middle class, the ones who had achieved a level of success and believed their success entitled them to happiness but were nervous and anxious instead—and developed a therapy that gave them what they were seeking: instant bliss.

As his prescription, Beard advised his patients to, in essence, think God's thoughts; to take it upon themselves to seize the power he believed to be inherent within to control the external world and its effect upon the individual. Armed with this power to control one's thoughts and fates, happiness was a foregone conclusion. For if one had the power of a God, one could simply wish for a more pleasing altered reality and it would suddenly come to pass. And happiness was the ultimate goal in Beard's social construct. By defining nervousness as sickness and health as happiness, Beard redefined what it meant to be healthy: no longer was health a means toward other things; now it was the end in and of itself. To be cured of nervousness was, to Beard, to be healthy—to live a life free of affliction. If one could successfully remove all impediments toward happiness, one could be healthy—cured of the ills caused by American modernism.

In fact, Beard was drawing on an already well-established American ethos for his prescription, one that likewise focused on the power of the individual spirit and was embodied in the aforementioned Horatio Alger tales of the mid-nineteenth century. In those tales, the will and determination (along with copious amounts of blind luck) of even the most hopeless yokel invariably led to success despite all odds.[47] However, although both Alger and Beard were addressing Americans of native stock, Beard's approach differed in a significant way. Whereas the heroes of Alger's tales were typically rural or small-town souls invoking the virtue and purity of the village, Beard, and others like him, spoke primarily to the mushrooming urban population.[48] As such, he did not preach a return to rural, simpler ways; instead he offered his followers a tonic for their ills that in no way disrupted modern society.

Conveniently (and crucial to Beard's prescription), the tools required to reach this desired state of bliss were already hardwired within every individual, so although one may not be able to control the cacophonous, rapidly changed world, he could control his mind and how it processed this information—what it let in and what it shut out. This theory, as it grew in influence and popularity, came to be known as the "mind cure." Pursuant to this theology, no matter the question, there was always an answer available internally; knowledge on demand was its touchstone. Regardless of the dehumanization of the industrial system, a proponent of mind cure could never go wanting, because "it offered a total sufficiency of the present." All one had to do was know how to ask. Significantly, the answers were always available internally, not by looking to society for assistance. According to Ralph Waldo Trine, one of the propagators of what came to be known as the "New Thought movement" that grew out of Beard's philosophy: "He who lives in the realization of his oneness with this Infinite Power becomes a magnet to attract to himself a continual supply of whatsoever things he desires."[49] The power to deny nonwishful reality was really all that mattered. If sickness was the undesired state, simply projecting health would provide the cure; if poverty was the ailment, projecting wealth would be the treatment. Negative thoughts lead to negative realities; positive thoughts lead to positive ones. "If only 'you really want him to,' God will give you anything. God obeys man."[50]

On the surface, the New Thought movement appeared to be a repudiation of the social Darwinism of the era, which many interpreted to preach a grim, eternal struggle for survival of the fittest.[51] In New Thought, the converse was proposed: good thoughts leading directly to blissful realities. Whereas Darwinism, and its sociological outgrowth social Darwinism, focused on struggle and failure, New Thought focused on belief and success.[52] The sheer negativity of Darwinism led to the inevitable backlash of those who proclaimed that, contrary to Darwin, heredity did not invariably rule each individual life.[53] Instead, the individual had control, if he only understood how to exercise it. Very quickly, positivism—the belief in the scientific method and the requirement of scientific proof as a necessary prerequisite for belief—found itself in the crosshairs of the New Thought movement. "Where faith in a fact can help create the fact," said William James in 1896, "that would be an insane logic which should say that faith running ahead of scientific evidence is the 'lowest kind of immorality' into which a thinking being can fall!"[54] The power of self-direction and control, not unlike that expressed in the earlier Alger stories, provided the foundation for the New Thought movement.[55] Reality was a consequence of, not a precursor to, one's ideas. To the New Thought movement, the positivists had things backward.[56]

At its core, however, New Thought was a natural extension of social Darwinism that was itself neither Darwinism nor positivism but rather pseudoscience—status justification masquerading as evolutionary biology. New Thought was in many ways a worthy successor to this in that it too focused on status, but here, status was defined by desired states of mind rather than the character traits and lineage that defined the champions of social Darwinism, the WASP elites.[57] In this way, New Thought appealed to a wider swath of the public—the native-born masses trapped in cities and in jobs they did not understand who may not have had the lineage of the WASP elites but were similarly wary of both the wealthy industrialists above them and the immigrant tide below.[58] Not unlike Dewey's evolutionary environmentalism, it was a malleable social theory that could include anyone who thought "positively." In this respect it broke from social Darwinism, because whereas the social Darwinists trumpeted that only the "fittest" survived, the New Thought disciples contended that survival, and success, was available to all.[59] Perceiving this threat, many social Darwinists rejected the concepts of New Thought—Herbert Spencer himself dismissed an early incarnation of it as "semi-scientific sentimentalities"[60]—but at its core, social Darwinism itself was little more.

Very quickly, variations on New Thought and the mind cure spread throughout the nation and seeped into many different disciplines, offering the promise of control and happiness to its anxious, middle-class audience. Novelist Theodore Dreiser was a believer and wrote of the power of the creative mind to construct its own reality.[61] Beyond the worlds of literature and theology, it soon became an accepted branch of political science. Laissez-faire economics was justified by these proponents as "a repression of politics, analogous to the repression of negative thoughts and ideas of sickness."[62] Thus, in a free market, prosperity thrives. In 1907, New Thought practitioner Frank Haddock published *The Power of Will*, part of his growing "Power Book Library," which preached financial success through the endless repetition of drills in which positive thoughts were repeated throughout the day.[63] By the early part of the twentieth century, the mind cure philosophy was gaining a significant foothold. Dozens of mind cure magazines sprouted and, although most of them came and went, a few prospered and eventually were bought out by larger magazines with greater circulation, thereby spreading mind cure values across the nation.[64] By the 1920s, many mainstream, middle-class magazines extolled the virtues, running stories of business leaders who attained their positions seemingly through little more than sheer perseverance and a positive outlook. The message of these sketches was difficult to miss: "Insofar as every man could control his own thoughts, every man could succeed by thinking right."[65] Out of this outlook grew a new form of what turned out to be overwhelmingly popular writing: tracts by medical and business professionals offering advice on how to live a successful life.[66] Books by psychologists, psychiatrists, business executives, economists, and others sprang up—many of them selling very well—and all offering similar advice: think positively and anything is within your grasp. The world is there for the taking. All that was needed was the ability to grab it.

One of the most successful writers in this genre was Napoleon Hill, whose 1937 book, *Think and Grow Rich,* remains in print today and has sold more than thirty million copies to date.[67] His philosophy of "what the mind of man can conceive and believe, it can achieve"[68] won him many influential followers, including President Franklin Roosevelt, who brought him on staff as an advisor for a time. He also counted as a faithful devotee Cubs owner William Wrigley Jr. who, along with others such as Woodrow Wilson (who also employed him as an advisor) and Herbert Spencer's American champion Andrew Carnegie, sang his praises and testified on his behalf as to the soundness of his philosophy.[69] For men such as Wrigley and his fellow MLB owners, the positive thinking movement was in many ways a godsend; despite the absence of any true competition throughout the pre-expansion era, the positive thinkers would summon hope anyhow, thus allowing Wrigley and his cohorts to continue to ignore the competitive deficiencies of their clubs while enjoying the benefits of membership in their exclusive social society. With a fan base increasingly sold on the concept of shutting out the negative and thinking only positive thoughts, Wrigley and others felt reduced external pressure to deliver anything over and above the bare minimum to their customers.

Of course, fans would complain from time to time, they would boo, they would become disenchanted with a particular manager or player, but they rarely if ever would challenge the structure of an industry that seemingly was perpetually out of balance. To do so would be to think negatively and to think negatively was a sickness. There had to be something wrong with someone—something un-American—to think that way. A true American, a healthy American, always believes in his team, no matter what. In the words of Dr. William Sadler, a proponent of faith for faith's sake: "All faith tendencies are toward mental happiness and physical health. All people, good or bad, get the physical rewards of faith, regardless of whether the objects of their faith and belief are true or false."[70] Thus belief, in and of itself, was its own reward.

Cultivated ignorance of inconvenient realities was the touchtone of the positive thinking movement. By instructing followers to ignore potentially messy factors such as the economy, personal existence, desires, and impulses, they "could not be in tension with the system."[71] By making personal happiness the goal of highest order, the positive thinking movement effectively stifled any potential disharmony with the system by counseling followers to simply ignore contrary information. In this way, the principles of conformity and unwavering submission to right-wing authority crept into the American value system despite our avowed aversion to such traits.

This trend only intensified post–World War II. By this point, positive thinking and its mind cure ethos had seeped into the established churches, with even the most conservative Protestant churches embracing it.[72] Personal growth through therapeutic psychology became a more frequent topic of Sunday sermons, as now even old denominations were offering cures for the anxieties of modernity. All of this was premised on the unspoken idea that the weak and unempowered could nevertheless feel strong while remaining weak and unempowered.[73] Perhaps the external world could not be changed, but by thinking right at least some form of action was taken in response, and this brought a measure of relief. In the process, a withdrawal from the world as it actually exists took place as the positive thinkers took solace in the idea that they were improving their health—and improving themselves—by avoiding the modern incantation of Beard's "nervousness."

In 1952, the positive thinking movement dominated the national conversation when Norman Vincent Peale's *The Power of Positive Thinking* was published.[74] It quickly rose to the top of the best-seller lists and remained there for two years. By 1955 Peale had sold two million copies of his book, which was outsold during this era only by the *Revised Standard Version of the Bible*.[75] Peale himself became a national celebrity as a result, as well as the nation's de facto cultural guru, appearing, through the auspices of the National Council of Churches, on radio or television on an almost daily basis, offering advice on a wide range of topics from manners to morals.[76] Peale himself was a right-wing extremist: he believed FDR to be a dictator, supported Douglas MacArthur for president in 1948, and opposed taxes, minimum wages, maximum hours, pensions, unions, and anything else that he believed stood in the way of unfettered laissez faire capitalism.[77] In an effort to reach a mass audience, he soon began censoring his own political views and preaching positive thinking only. "As he thinketh in

his heart, so is he. . . . Religion teaches us to allow only good and beautiful thoughts to enter the unconscious because of the obvious fact often
demonstrated that the unconscious can only send back what was first sent
down."[78] The basic tenet of Peale's philosophy was thus, if you think it, it
must exist. Necessarily, then, if you ignore it, it does not.

Peale's cause was later taken up by the evangelists, who pounced upon
the anxiety and despair felt by many throughout the 1960s and '70s to offer
a similar cure. Assuming the role of modern-day George Beards, they took
it upon themselves to diagnose a new form of "nervousness" and prescribe
a cure of blissful avoidance. When during the Nixon administration the
FCC rescinded its ban on stations selling airtime to religious programs,
evangelicals took over the airways, multiplying from twenty-five television
ministries in the late '70s to more than 330 a few years later.[79] Several of
them became, like Peale, celebrities who counseled their flocks on morals,
manners, and how to achieve a state of happiness and material wealth
through positive thinking. One of the early celebrity televangelists was
Reverend Ike, who became the first black man in America to preach the
power of positive thinking to the black masses. "The way to prosper and
be well," Reverend Ike preached, "was to forget about pie in the sky by
and by and look instead within oneself for divine power."[80] By the mid-
1970s he was preaching on more than 1,770 radio stations, on television in
major markets, and through his magazine, which reached more than one
million readers. His cohorts preached similar ideas. Televangelists such
as Kenneth Copeland and others grew their audiences steadily over time
until the largest, such as that of Copeland's, reached overseas with profits
in the multimillions. Copeland's broadcasts eventually beamed into 134
countries, with an annual resulting income of roughly $100 million.[81] And,
just like Beard's, their audiences were largely comprised of working- and
middle-class strivers.[82]

By the second half of the twentieth century, the ethos of positive thinking and willful blindness toward uncomfortable facts was all-encompassing.[83] On the secular level, this was evident in the backlash against multi-
culturalism with books such as Allan Bloom's *The Closing of the American
Mind* on the forefront, railing against the discordant portrait of America
painted by groups that gained their voices through the civil rights and
student movements. Responding to those who drew attention to some

uncomfortable truths of American history, Bloom wrote, "America tells one story: the unbroken, ineluctable progress of freedom and equality. From its first settlers and its political foundings on, there has been no dispute that freedom and equality are the essence of justice for us."[84] For the positive thinkers, anything that challenged their worldview had to be erased, for these discordant thoughts were roadblocks on their path to happiness.[85]

As Bloom's screed illustrated, the positive thinkers were oftentimes quite hostile. When challenged, they frequently became irritable and angry, uncomfortable in the face of the negative thoughts they had worked so hard to eradicate from their minds. Positive thinkers such as William F. Buckley Jr., Billy Graham, Pat Robertson, and Jerry Falwell thus adopted a double-fisted approach in their missions: the preaching of optimistic ethical absolutes "and a rejection of the 'relativism' which had allegedly corroded Western values and produced an intolerable vacuum that was filled by demonic ideologies."[86] Any thought or idea that clashed with the vision of America created through these optimistic ethical absolutes was rejected outright and demonized as a way of permanently marginalizing it and removing it from consideration.

Given the heft of the positive thinking movement by the second half of the twentieth century, it was no wonder that when the players and other social groups banded together in the 1950s and '60s, the backlash was both forceful and ugly. After all, by this point many Americans had come to believe that they controlled their own realities and had the ability to influence them merely through their desired perceptions. To them, external thoughts, facts, and ideas that conflicted with or challenged this reality were not merely wrong but evidence of sickness and depravity; healthy people simply did not think that way. It followed that anything that challenged accepted notions of America was evil and the product of sick minds—people trying to undermine the American way of life. It was not such a large leap, therefore, for the positive thinkers to conclude that any negative connotation of America or American life was necessarily the product of the perceived greatest threat to the nation throughout much of the twentieth century—communism. Viewed in this light, any uprising or concerted movement for change was not simply a response to an injustice inherent within the American system but rather a "communist-inspired" threat to the tenets of democracy and the American way of life.[87]

Soon, anyone or any institution challenging the prefabricated, sunny American outlook was fingered as communist inspired, with national leaders urging vigilance against the perceived spread of anti-American, communist thoughts and ideas. "The communists cannot defeat America," President Nixon once said, "only Americans can do that."[88] Institutions such as Hollywood and universities, which traditionally offered alternative perspectives on America and encouraged the discussion of ideas that challenged their audiences to critically analyze society and their place within it, were targeted and branded as dangerously, hopelessly, infiltrated with communists.[89] When alternative ideas came to more traditional institutions such as baseball, the outrage was even more intense. Decades before the arrival of Marvin Miller, accusations of communist plots were hurled freely at any suggestion that the traditional portrait of baseball as America was somehow flawed. In response to Danny Gardella's lawsuit arising from the Mexican League affair, Branch Rickey charged that the only people who could possibly oppose baseball's reserve clause were persons of "avowed Communist tendencies who deeply resent the continuance of our national pastime."[90] Commissioner Chandler insinuated that those who had fled to Mexico in search of higher wages were disloyal and subversive; instead, he urged all Americans "to stand by the flag of Organized Baseball."[91] Fearful of being tarred as subversive communists, Gardella's fellow players abandoned him and his cause.[92] Later, when Miller arrived on the scene and the players movement picked up steam, journalists labeled him "Comrade Miller," or "Marvin Millerinski."[93]

Because the positive thinking movement stressed the power of internal thoughts and a disengagement from society, any sort of collective action was seen through this prism as "communist" and an indication of depravity—the result of those with sick minds. After all, if everything that was needed to improve one's lot in life was contained within the mind, then there was no need to call on others for assistance. In baseball, this mindset was predominant, at least to the extent that it benefitted those in power. When, in 1951, Cardinals owner Fred Saigh suggested that visiting teams share in the profits from home television agreements, Dodgers owner Walter O'Malley (who stood to lose the most from this arrangement, given his own lucrative agreement) replied that this suggestion was "socialistic." "Why doesn't he continue the thought," O'Malley went on, "and call for an equalization of players' salaries, no matter where they play? To be logical, why does he not demand a common treasury, with all clubs share and share alike?"[94] His patriotism challenged, Saigh dropped the matter before being impugned further.

Confronted with the counter-movement of collectivism and the unprecedented number of union strikes both during World War II and afterward, the positive thinkers struck back, with tomes such as Peale's as ammunition. Drawing on the ethos of individualism inherent in the New Thought movement and mind cure philosophy, many positive thinking publications attacked the modern union man as one afraid to dare, afraid to go it alone; one who cowardly opted for security, pensions, and higher salaries (all of the benefits that accrued from union membership) rather than the important things in life.[95] In 1951 Fortune magazine, "the evangelical voice of big business,"[96] began running a series entitled, "Short Stories of Enterprise," which attempted to correct the perceived problem.[97] In them, tales of moderately successful entrepreneurs were told; stories of men (and some women) who passed on the security offered by union membership to achieve more profound (if less remunerative) success on their own. Because unions were achieving so much for their members at the time, these stories deemphasized the financial aspect of entrepreneurship, stressing instead the reward of independence. "This job is more fun than making money," one small business owner crowed.[98] That he likely would have earned more and received better benefits had he been a union employee was beside the point. He had his independence and that, according to the tales, was something money could not buy.

Baseball management, aided by the media, hammered home similar points over the next several decades. In 1967, after Miller ascended to his position as the head of the Players Association, Atlanta Journal baseball writer Furman Bisher made no effort to hide his disgust of the union ethic: "I cannot see the major league baseball player demeaning himself to the status of a unionized laborer."[99] Perhaps unwittingly drawing upon the values stressed in publications such as Fortune, Bisher continued: ". . . they should have enough pride in their job to realize they should not associate with unions." Baseball executives likewise took whatever opportunity available to them to demonize unions. In 1958, Cleveland Indians general manager Frank Lane warned his players of the evils of unions by reminding them of the "ghost towns" in New England that he asserted were created by union greed, cautioning that similar results could very well come about in baseball if the union influence seeped in there as well. Of course, he failed to draw the players' attention to two baseball "ghost towns" created just a few months earlier in the neighborhoods surrounding the Polo Grounds and Ebbets Field that were the byproduct of management's greed in an environment of free enterprise.[100] He pleaded for his players' trust, assuring them that he was "your general manager, as well as the club's. You have to have confidence in me."[101]

Lane's plea was a critical component of management's strategy toward the players in that the clubs realized it was imperative that the players trusted management to do right by them and protect their interests; without such trust, the clubs feared that the players may very well run toward the security and benefits of union membership that was by that point, in their eyes at least, overtaking the nation. Thus, benevolent paternalism was often preached to the players, as it was to the American public throughout the era. Indeed, from the very beginning of the corporate era, business leaders recognized the necessity of forging this trust if they were going to maintain the level of power they desired. Frank Munsey, the director of U.S. Steel, was speaking for many of his colleagues when he confided in Theodore Roosevelt in 1912 that the nation needed to move toward a more "parental guardianship of the people."[102] To achieve this, the frequently repeated tales of large industrialists such as Henry Ford, Andrew Carnegie, and others were often told with an undercurrent of benevolent paternalism. Left to their own devices and free of interference, these real-world magnates were portrayed not only as symbols of what could be achieved within the American capitalistic system but as examples of how those in charge take care of their employees and society in general. Through their tales the message was clear: labor laws and unions were unnecessary; these right-thinking American industrialists did not merely look out for themselves but for all who came under their control. When this message was received by a positive thinking nation, many happily submitted to powerful authority. They were content to cede power to a strong centralized authority which was, in Munsey's words, doing its job "to think for the people and plan for the people."[103] In the process, the concept of labor rights as civil rights fell by the wayside. Instead, labor's cause became a marginalized special interest, and one contrary to national interests at that.[104]

In baseball, the tradition of benevolent paternalism ran particularly deep. Owners had acted as manor lords for generations, doling out privileges to "their" players on their whim, and withholding them likewise. Gussie Busch of the Cardinals was perhaps one of the more notable in this regard, but he was not much different from the majority of his brethren, offering perks to his favored players such as a restaurant for Stan Musial, a beer distributorship for Roger Maris, and a yacht for Lou Brock.[105] To him, patronage and paternalism were the defining characteristics of his job description. Most players, whether they played for Busch's Cardinals or elsewhere, were lulled into complacency for decades by management's oft-repeated phrase, "we'll take care of you."[106] And sometimes, as in the cases of Musial, Maris, and Brock, they did. But many other times they did not. Longtime Dodgers general manager Buzzi Bavasi often talked publicly of "his" boys, but come contract time, they became unknowing stooges in his financial shell game. In fact, in a series of 1967 *Sports Illustrated* articles, he even boasted of his ability to take advantage of the trust he worked so hard to engender come contract time. He bragged of his trick of pulling out fake contracts misrepresenting the salaries of other players in his attempt to convince the player in his office to accept his lowball offer.[107] "[S]ome ball players just don't understand money at all," he said, "or they don't stop to figure things out . . . you could take advantage of them something frightful. . . . [I've] pulled that phony contract stunt a dozen times, and I'll do it every chance I get, because this war of negotiations has no rules . . . the easiest players to deal with are the ones who leave it all up to you. They have enough faith in me to know that they are going to be paid what they're worth."[108]

The players were not the only ones to fall under management's spell. Most baseball writers likewise preached deference to the owners' sensibilities, concluding that, as the obvious guardians of the game, they would take care of everyone within their orbit. When it came to labor issues, there was no issue to many of them; the owners would naturally take care of "their boys."[109] As a result of this mindset, even before the Marvin Miller era, whenever a player engaged in a salary dispute, sympathy from most writers, and consequently most fans, lay with the owners.[110] Even after Miller took charge and began to make the case for the players, pointing out one indignity (such as Bavasi's shell game) after another, most writers and fans nevertheless sided with the owners.[111] No matter how much contrary information came to the public's attention, by the mid to late '60s the positive thinking American public had become so adept at blocking out the negative and putting their faith in powerful authority figures and institutions that the force of this new information was muted. On an intellectual level, many of Miller's arguments were irrefutable, but because the positive thinking movement effectively demonized critical thinking, the logic of his points only further demonstrated his anti-American ideology, to many of his detractors.

By virtue of necessity, one of the hallmarks of the positive thinking ethos has always been its anti-intellectualism. Because critical thinking hampers unrealistic positive thoughts, the mind cure philosophy necessarily dictates that it must be the product of disturbed minds. In this sense, virtually from the turn of the twentieth century the predominant American ideology has held that intellectuals betray capitalism and the American spirit, while those who blindly place their faith in powerful institutions embody it.[112] In 1906, mind cure enthusiast Orestes Swett-Marden warned of the perils of knowledge when he wrote that mental auto-manipulation could be imperiled by "overculture and wider outlook." "The weakening self-confidence, the development of timidity, is often the result of a liberal education . . . [The] brain powers [of the ignorant man] have not been weakened by theories or by the knowledge of how much he does not know."[113] Later, Peale was proudly anti-intellectual in extolling the virtues of the "plain folk."[114] For decades, the message has been the same: in America it is the critical thinkers—the "elites"—who are the enemy.[115] Anyone who questioned received wisdom must be un-American, possibly a communist, and a person whose beliefs indicated that there was something fundamentally wrong with him or her. Interestingly, in this construct it was those who possessed knowledge rather than money who were pejoratively classified as "elites"; for they possessed something far more powerful and potentially destructive than mere wealth. Because many union, civil rights, and student activists were highly educated critical thinkers, they were demonized from the outset.[116] In this environment, Miller's revelations only further alienated him and his cause from much of mainstream America.

THE PLAYERS ASSOCIATION AND
THE CHALLENGE TO POSITIVE THINKING

In an America where negative thoughts and ideas were repressed and positive ones repeated over and over like a mantra, with the belief that if this was done often enough the good thoughts would turn into good things, the arrival of Miller and the tactics of the Players Association were a splash of cold water in the nation's face. Miller did not care one whit for positive thinking. Instead he focused solely on the tangible issues affecting the players; namely, getting them a fair deal with management, on providing them with some dignity in a relationship where they had none.[117] To achieve his goals, he believed it necessary to smash the romantic myth of baseball as America. If the owners' rhetoric was consistent with the American tradition of positive thinking, Miller's goal was to be the antithesis of that: to point out to the American public that all of the rhetoric was just that, nothing more. Contrary to the approach of the positive thinkers as descended from George Beard, Miller believed that it was not only possible but necessary to alter the system; therefore, he focused on external change rather than on the internal rationalizations that had sustained the status quo for generations. However, he was preaching to a public that had long since learned how to either tune out arguments such as his or, worse, turn on them.

The narrative Miller put before the American public was hardly the romantic one of baseball and American history. Rather it was a brutal "slave narrative" where the allegedly privileged players were not granted even the most basic rights afforded to ordinary citizens.[118] He, and later other player spokesmen as well, "employed the language of labor—scabs, work stoppages, picket lines"[119]—to align the players with the powerful labor movement of the era, and he chose his words carefully, with the intent of provoking the owners as well as the public to acknowledge a reality of baseball's management-labor relationship that had been up to then blissfully ignored in favor of the more optimistic, reassuring myth of the baseball creed. At one point in 1973, Miller invoked the sting of baseball's segregationist past by remarking that any gains made by the Players Association could easily be thwarted by a "gentlemen's agreement" between the owners, a statement that recalled the so-called "gentlemen's agreement" that kept black players out of the game for decades.[120] Miller's choice of the phrase was intentional: there existed beneath the veneer of our national pastime something unsavory and cruel about the business of baseball, and Miller wanted everyone to be cognizant of it. In his words and actions, Miller attempted to demonstrate that the owners were not to be trusted, that they were merely presenting a facade of themselves as romantic baseball men "using tradition to mask self-interest."[121] They were hardly the gentlemen they portrayed themselves to be.

In essence, Miller was on a crusade to show that the concept of benevolent paternalism simply did not exist within the game of baseball. This was bound to be received with hostility by a positive thinking public that considered it to be a foundational belief, not merely within baseball but in American life. To make his point, he had to break the stereotype of the "aw shucks, gee whiz, I'm so glad to be a major leaguer that I would pay to put on the uniform" player of romantic myth.[122] Although the realities of Major League baseball never aligned with this myth, it nevertheless served the owners well for decades, permitting them free rein to pay the players less than their true value, withholding benefits from them, and ensuring that no player could speak up without fear of public censure. By breaking the chains of this myth and allowing the players a voice in their profession, Miller angered many fans and sportswriters who preferred to believe that life as a Major League player had always been idyllic; that the owners had created an Eden and were vigilant in protecting all who were blessed enough to walk through it.

If the purpose of the mind cure was to reassure the people that everything was fine, Miller's was to jar them out of this complacency. For this he was vilified and his allegiances regularly called into question. Beyond the snarky communist-baiting mocking of his name in newspapers across the nation, he was identified as a threat to the American way of life by Commissioner Bowie Kuhn, who believed Miller to harbor "a deep hatred and suspicion of the American right and American capitalism."[123] Critics disparaged him for having a "narrow mind,"[124] and in many ways they were correct: Miller refused to look beyond the concrete issues before him in an effort to mythologize the game. He refused to block out the negative and focus only on an idealized positive. He refused to use the rhetoric associated with baseball to justify the fundamental inequalities and subjugation that existed within it.

For sure, Miller saw no obvious connections between baseball and larger American life, at least none within the romantic realm. He saw only the labor issues that confronted his clients and considered it his job to address them. In the process, he perhaps unwittingly drew a distinctly different portrait of both baseball and America than the one most Americans had grown up with through the baseball creed. In Miller's world, the game, as well as life, was harsh, cold, and unforgiving. Although he rarely encouraged the connection between baseball and America, it was inevitable that the public would make one, given that the relationship between the two had been forged through nearly a century of association by the owners as well as the media. As such, Miller's take on baseball's labor issues was received by a public who saw it as a critique on a grander scale. And because it was critical, Miller himself was maligned as a sick soul. Given the choice between the romantic story of baseball or the unsympathetic one, most people chose to believe the romantic one, siding with the owners and vilifying Miller. To take the side of the players, one would have to confront and accept an unflattering portrait of reality. This necessity, in itself, doomed Miller and the Players Association in the court of public opinion from the outset.

The divergent portraits of baseball were never more clearly on display than in the Supreme Court's 1972 opinion in *Flood v. Kuhn*.[125] In the majority opinion upholding baseball's antitrust exemption and thwarting Curt Flood's quest for free agency, Justice Harry Blackmun's syrupy opinion (as discussed in chapter 2) announced himself as firmly within the camp of the romantics.[126] In that case, the justices were required to not merely resolve the legal dispute but to announce their preferred vision of the game: the romantic one offered by the owners or the brutal slave narrative propounded by Miller. If they chose the former, deference to the benevolent protectors of the game would be an acceptable result. If they chose the latter, a ruling placing the fate of players such as Flood in the hands of these self-serving manor lords could only be absurd. In the end, the majority sided with the owners, choosing romance over reality. As such, even though the Court retreated from its position in *Federal Baseball* that baseball was not engaged in interstate commerce, it held that ultimately, this fundamental shift in perspective was not dispositive. Instead, it held that the Sherman Act was nevertheless inapplicable to Major League Baseball, concluding simply that its decision in both that case and *Tooslon* were "aberrations confined to baseball."[127] Quoting the trial court, Blackmun affirmed that:

> Baseball has been the national pastime for over one hundred years and enjoys a unique place in our American heritage. Major league professional baseball is avidly followed by millions of fans, looked upon with fervor and pride and provides a special source of inspiration and competitive team spirit especially from the young.
>
> Baseball's status in the life of the nation is so pervasive that it would not strain credulity to say the Court can take judicial notice that baseball is everybody's business. To put it mildly and with restraint, it would be unfortunate indeed if a fine sport and profession, which brings surcease from daily travail and an escape from the ordinary to most inhabitants of this land, were to suffer in the least because of undue concentration by any one or any group on commercial and profit considerations. The game is on higher ground; it behooves every one to keep it there.[128]

Accordingly, the technical merits of Flood's case were beside the point. In fact, following this twisted logic, it was baseball that needed protection from the likes of Flood.

In dissent, Justice William O. Douglas adopted Miller's worldview. In a direct rebuke of Blackmun and the romantics, Douglas remarked that *Federal Baseball* was "a derelict in the stream of the law that we, its creator, should remove. Only a romantic view of a rather dismal business account over the last 50 years would keep that derelict in midstream."[129] Taking note of the modern realities of Major League Baseball (those realities ignored by the owners and hammered upon time and again by Miller), Douglas wrote: "Baseball is today big business that is packaged with beer, with broadcasting, and with other industries. The beneficiaries of the *Federal Baseball Club* decision are not the Babe Ruths, Ty Cobbs, and Lou Gehrigs. The owners, whose records many say reveal a proclivity for predatory practices, do not come to us with equities. The equities are with the victims of the reserve clause. I use the word 'victims' in the Sherman Act sense, since a contract which forbids anyone to practice his calling is commonly called an unreasonable restraint of trade."[130] To Douglas, underneath the patriotic rhetoric lay a "dismal business" ruled by men who routinely took advantage of their position to the great detriment of those within their employ. If there was anything "inspiring" about the relationship between the owners and the players, anything that necessitated it being elevated to the "higher ground" Blackmun spoke of, Douglas did not see it. But he was only able to convince two of his colleagues to see things his way.

On the few occasions when Miller did make an attempt to equate the players' cause with American values, he wound up on the wrong side of public sentiment here as well. At one point during negotiations for the 1970 collective bargaining agreement, Miller made what seemed to him an innocuous comment, stating that what he was attempting to gain for the players—freedom of contract—was an American ideal. Very quickly his assertion was challenged by the owners' lawyers and dismissed out of hand.[131] Perhaps unwittingly, Miller touched a nerve by focusing his cause on individual freedom; to many conservatives, liberalism's greatest sin was its focus on individual rights and liberty.[132] Consistent with the mind cure ethos, the conservative movement was premised on the belief that a society's ultimate goal should be virtue, not freedom—by thinking only good thoughts, virtue could be attained, conveniently without any disruption to big business and the status quo. The conservative revolt of the 1960s (which sparked the ascendency of Barry Goldwater and Ronald Reagan, among others) was, at its core, a reaction to the collective movement and its incessant harping on freedom; the civil rights, student, and players movements all centered on the issue of individual liberty. All of these groups painted an unflattering portrait of a supposedly pristine America and were duly demonized consistent with positive thinking philosophy. "America," wrote a student protestor, "Listen to it. *America*. I love the sound. I love what it could mean. I hate what it is."[133] There simply was no room for such sentiments in the minds of the philosophical descendants of George Beard. They needed to be washed away before they irrevocably thwarted the mind cure.

Because thoughts were all-important to the positive thinkers, the disconnect between words and actions became increasingly irrelevant as the twentieth century progressed. Hypocrisy became meaningless in a world where thoughts were paramount and reality merely a malleable concept, open to interpretation or avoidance if necessary. The mind cure was based on the divergence of attention from the world as it existed to an internal one where anything was possible—where even the most hopeless underdog could emerge victorious. In such a world, the collective movement was stripped of its greatest weapon: the highlighting of insincerity and duplicity on behalf of the nation's most formidable positive thinking cheerleaders. As a result, the owners, among others, were armed with a ready-made shield providing them with the ability to fend off even the most spirited attacks of their adversaries. Public opinion would always be on their side, no matter the allegation or their own actions that seemingly undermined their positions.

To their followers, televangelists such as Jerry Falwell, Jim Bakker, Jimmy Swaggart, Pat Robertson, and others remained influential voices preaching the spirit of positive thinking despite the scandals, investigations, and occasional criminal proceedings that revealed a divide between their sermons on the pulpit and their actions off it.[134] In 1980, Ronald Reagan became the positive thinker in chief when, in the grip of a crippling recession, the Iranian hostage crisis, the second oil crisis in six years, and the aftermath of Vietnam and Watergate, he nevertheless successfully preached his fawningly optimistic message to a nation desperate for good news and tired of the perceived pessimism of Jimmy Carter.[135] During his 1984 reelection campaign, after a first term that saw the nation's economy descend even further, he announced that, irrespective of reality, it was "morning in America," invigorating an electorate that was more than willing to exchange the nation as it was for the nation as Reagan claimed it to be.[136] In so doing, his supporters overlooked the discrepancy between the idea of Reagan and the reality of the man. They were in thrall with his incessant preaching of the twin values of God and family, despite the fact that he was not particularly religious himself and not merely the nation's first divorced president, but a father who was estranged from some of his children and grandchildren.[137] To them the facts did not matter. Thoughts were paramount, everything else was secondary.

The collective movement was the antithesis of this in that, by design, it attempted to draw the nation's attention to the very inconsistencies the positive thinkers disregarded. To the extent the leaders of the collective movement hoped that this tactic would draw converts from the positive thinkers, they were sorely mistaken; if the positive thinkers did not simply ignore the allegations hurled their way, they would use them as fuel for their own movement, pointing out that such thoughts were the product of the sick minds of the collectivists. In baseball, the overwhelming appeal and power of positive thinking became even more apparent during the 1994 work stoppage, which resulted in the cancellation of the World Series. In the battle to win the public's hearts and minds, the denial of history and embrace of romantic myth soothed a nation of disgruntled baseball fans and doomed the Players Association once again.

Despite the two decades of free agency and three decades of collective bargaining that preceded the stoppage, the owners quickly discarded the protracted labor issues that led to the current stoppage as irrelevant and not worth discussing, and encouraged the nation instead to focus its attention on baseball's romantic past, contending simplistically that everything in baseball was fine until the Players Association came along.[138] In so doing, they dismissed the more recent past as having any measure of validity. For fans in search of positive thoughts, the denial of the messy realities of the labor struggles in favor of the pristine images of baseball lore proved attractive. Thus, while the Players Association spent its time trying to draw attention to the issues that led to the stoppage, the owners invited the public to ignore all of that and focus instead on more pleasant thoughts. It was not surprising that the overwhelming majority of fans sided with the owners, given that choice.

As the stoppage wore on, many fans began to alter their definition of baseball itself rather than confront the unpleasant realities of the labor situation at the heart of the matter. Whereas for generations the game was defined through players such as Ruth, Mantle, Mays, and Clemente, with "baseball" and "Major League Baseball" being synonymous, now "baseball" was something else altogether, something divorced, severed from its professional incarnation. As Robert Lipsyte wrote on the day after the season was cancelled: "Baseball has less to do than one might think with the major league season. Baseball is about the family farm, which few of us grew up on, and it is about railroad trains keening in the night on the prairies, which few of us have ever heard. It is about daydreaming of drinking the same beer with your dad as he drank with his dad, of screaming at your son's little league coach in the same obnoxious way your father screamed at your coach."[139] By magical transformation, necessitated by the ugliness of the work stoppage, baseball was once again something pure and beautiful. Now, rather than being about labor, management, salaries, and pensions, it was about mythical (as Lipsyte plainly acknowledged it to be) prairies, trains, farms, and fathers. Once again it was about America; only now it had been remade because the old definition now longer fit the desired outlook. Because the fiction was more appealing than the reality, many people chose the fantasy in the hope that, if they believed in it deeply enough, it would eventually become the new reality.

Critics of Ken Burns's *Baseball* documentary, released during the stoppage and which focused on the off-field struggles along with the on-field glories of the game, harbored similar sentiments. One reviewer, in condemning Burns's focus on the game's racial and labor issues as "politically correct baseball," contrasted the modern game with the "simpler" game he knew as a child, where the mythical image of baseball as America as trumpeted by the owners and the media reigned supreme: "No one knows just how much damage this season's strike, and the cancellation of the World Series for the first time since 1904, has done to fan loyalty . . . the major-league game has been corrupted over the last twenty years, on the field and in the stands, in ways that threaten baseball's continuity with its past."[140] The unanswered question in his review, however, was which past he was referring to: the actual one where the unpleasant realties existed or the romanticized one where they did not.

National leaders also weighed in on the stoppage, offering the mind cure as a remedy. Newt Gingrich, the driving force behind Congress' 1994 "Contract with America," suggested that if the owners and players would only sit down together to watch *Field of Dreams,* play would resume at once.[141] (This was consistent with Gingrich's prescriptions for many of society's ills; he also believed that Spencer Tracy's *Boys Town* could be instrumental in solving the problem of teen pregnancy.)[142] Gingrich's remedy of *Field of Dreams* was telling in that the film offered up mythology as history, something Gingrich himself endorsed. Such mythology was in evidence in one of the film's signature lines, uttered by James Earl Jones: "The one constant through all the years, Ray, has been baseball. America has rolled by like an army of steamrollers. It's been erased like a blackboard, rebuilt, and erased again. But baseball has marked the time. This field, this game—it's a part of our past, Ray. It reminds us of all that once was good and could be again."[143] In suggesting that the game serves as a cultural reminder of "all that once was good and could be again," the film appeared untroubled by the incongruity of such a line being uttered by a black man who would not have been able to step on his own field of dreams prior to 1947, and who would have been subjected to various quotas and humiliations for decades thereafter as a consequence of the color of his skin.[144] In its attempt to posit that baseball connects Americans with their past, the film conveniently ignored the very real past of baseball itself and chose instead a sanitized, romantic one where inequality and subjugation were nonexistent. All of this was of little matter, however, to Gingrich and his fellow positive thinkers.

To Gingrich, the facts were often irrelevant, a point he liked to make clear to his students in his "Renewing American Civilization" course at Reinhardt College: "So, I don't really care what history you read. If you want to get rich, then read the histories, the biographies of people who got rich. If you want to be a famous entertainer, then read biographies of people who became famous entertainers . . ."[145] The veracity of the history his students read was of little concern to Gingrich; not unlike Jones's *Field of Dreams* speech, what mattered most was merely the ideas they generated. Belief makes it so. Anything was possible for those who filled their minds with positive thoughts. Just as William Sadler taught that faith was its own reward, Gingrich believed that faith was an educational tool as well. Intellectual rigor and analysis of the realities of a given situation was not required. In the 2000s, Commissioner Bud Selig likewise endorsed this worldview when he repeatedly stated that, all evidence to the contrary, he believed in the long-discredited myth that Abner Doubleday invented baseball.[146] As the French philosopher Bernard-Henri Lévy observed, by connecting baseball with both Doubleday as well as his bucolic home of Cooperstown, Selig, not unlike so many before him, "joined in a celebration that had the twofold merit of associating the national pastime with the traditional rural values that Fenimore Cooper's town embodies and also with the patriotic grandeur that the name Doubleday bears."[147] The only problem, however, was that as Lévy likewise observed, "this history is a myth, and every year millions of men and women come . . . to visit a town devoted entirely to the celebration of a myth."[148] To the positive thinkers, however, this was beside the point.

What lay underneath Gingrich's prescriptions for both baseball, through *Field of Dreams*, and America, through his "Contract with America," which preached a return to supposed "traditional" American values, was the belief that everything that happened as a result of the civil rights, student, and players movements from the mid-sixties forward could simply be ignored, and that in so doing, baseball and America could return to the perceived "simpler" time before the collectivists drew the nation's attention to the disconnect between the ideal and the reality. Gingrich offered a return to a romanticized, idealized past that existed only in fantasy. Through the mind cure, however, the fantasy becomes truth simply because it is more palatable. To those within the nation who felt discomfort when prodded into questioning the tenets of their beliefs by the collective movement, the option of wiping away these negative thoughts was appealing. So many of them did, choosing to retreat to the false history of both baseball and America as viewed through a more reassuring, rose-colored lens. In the classic, positive thinking tradition, the false history became reality and the more recent events non-history simply because they challenged accepted beliefs rather than confirmed them.[149]

Although baseball and America had been intertwined for decades, it was not until the rise of the Players Association that a fuller nexus of the two was formed. Through the public response to the Players Association, baseball finally offered a glimpse of more than simplistic patriotic rhetoric. Now, depending upon the perspective, baseball portrayed both the romantic myth of America as well as the disdain for those groups seeking to challenge it and force the nation to live up to its stated ideals.

THE STORYTELLERS

The stories of baseball would, of course, not amount to much if not for the storytellers. Through them, the baseball creed, the elevated national status of baseball, the tale of Branch Rickey and the desegregation of the game, the power and benevolence of the owners, and the uniquely American glory of the underdog all received confirmation as the unquestionable righteousness of these tales was dispersed throughout the country, seeping into the national consciousness. Not surprisingly, given the power of these stories, they have been zealously promoted and protected practically since the game's inception. For more than a century baseball has been sold to the American public as much more than simply an athletic contest; its enduring popularity stems, at least in part, from the reality that many people do in fact see it as more than merely a game. For this, MLB and the media that have covered it for more than a century, from Henry Chadwick to the present, deserve much of the credit; together they have spun tales of baseball as America that are believable not so much because they are true but because they are reaffirming. These stories, devoid of critical analysis as well as anything else that muddies them and renders the intended message anything less than crystal clear, have been the default narrative for decades—told and spun by one generation of storytellers after another.

One day, however, another storyteller came upon the scene—an outsider, unaffiliated with either Major League Baseball or the traditional media—one who had a different story to tell. In so doing, Bill James cast doubt upon many of the game's assumptions and tenets and begged America to see the game through a different lens. From that moment, the tight control over the stories of baseball began to loosen and, through the subsequent explosion of the seemingly uncontrollable storytelling devices of fantasy baseball and Internet blogs, fans were finally free to frame the game through their own eyes rather than through the filter of the game's protectors. All of this has begun to reshape the nation's portrait of the game into something else, something other than simply a blind metaphor for patriotic America. But the traditional storytellers are not wholly without power in this new age, not by a long shot. They have fought legal battles as well as ideological ones with these outsiders, and have engaged in a pitched struggle to determine who ultimately will define how the game is to be seen from here on.

HENRY CHADWICK AND HIS PROGENY

All of the game's storytellers can trace their lineage back to one man: Henry Chadwick. Considered "the father of baseball," he was the game's first influential writer (although he was not technically its first—William Cauldwell of the *Sunday Mercury,* as well as perhaps numerous others, beat him to the punch[1]); it was through his influence that sports, most notably baseball, came to be perceived as news and not simply leisure activities.[2] Within a decade of his first writings on the game in the 1850s, newspapers were covering sporting events and, by the 1880s, the concept of the sports page was developed.[3] In 1895, the first sports section was launched, as America by now was devouring sports news of all kinds.[4] Chadwick's impact on how America viewed baseball was profound in that not only was he among the core group of individuals who were instrumental in setting down many of the technical ground rules that provided the foundation for modern baseball, but his broader, overarching vision of the game, and its place within American society, colored practically everything he did.

Notably, Chadwick was not born in the United States. He spent the first thirteen years of his life in his native England, where he developed an affection for that country's national game, cricket.[5] Once in America, he set out to tie baseball to the American fabric much the same way cricket was interlocked with national character in his home country, and as it was in the many other current or former British colonies. His love of both sports and newspaper writing put him in an optimal position to achieve his goal in mid-nineteenth-century America.

Newspapers in the 1850s were in many ways similar to television a century later: an exciting new medium that fascinated the populace.[6] In this atmosphere, the potential for a journalist to impact the games he covered was significant. However, in his early days, Chadwick's writing was limited to cricket; he was a cricket journalist for the *New York Times,* the *Long Island Star,*[7] and other papers, and honed his skills within the boundaries of that sport.[8] In his writing, he brought to his readers the English notion of sports as a morality tool, the idea that inherent in cricket were all the utensils necessary to make it a socializing and civilizing agent.[9] Through the game (or at least Chadwick's idealized portrait of it—he ignored its rougher aspects and focused instead on the game's alleged "gentlemanly" qualities[10]), one could become not merely a successful competitor but, more important, a better citizen. Indeed, much of his early cricket writing contains the bones of what later became the baseball creed: he regularly referred to the "manly" abilities inherent in the game, the "scientific" skills required to master it, and the quality of person who could be expected to excel. To Chadwick, the game was for sophisticates only, as it "forms no debasing habits . . . it is suited to the softer feelings of a refined age."[11] Through all of this came the message that cricket was far from simply a game. Rather, it was vital to the training of future aristocrats or national leaders. It spoke to the nation on a larger scale; naturally, those who listened, those who appreciated it, were most likely to be adept in other important societal roles.

Chadwick was also influenced by his father, James, who was a fervent believer in Enlightenment concepts and the moral philosophies that emanated from them. James ingrained within Henry a belief in the hard and social sciences and saw to it that his son became educated in these disciplines.[12] Henry would draw from them his entire life and reference them in his future writings on baseball. His older half-brother Edwin was another major influence, and it was Edwin's belief in sanitary reform and his reliance upon statistics to demonstrate the righteousness of his positions that led Henry similarly to rely upon the use of statistics to prove his theories.[13] Through the influence of both his father and half-brother, Henry developed his philosophy of attempting to cleanse America through baseball and his strategy of using statistics to support his conclusions.

Once he shifted his attention from cricket to the burgeoning game of baseball, Chadwick quickly saw within the new American game the potential for many of the same social reform and morality lessons as those offered through the native game of his childhood. Much as he did in his cricket reporting, he chose to paint a portrait of a gentlemanly game to his readers, focusing his attention on the genteel game as played by the Knickerbockers and their cohorts rather than the more brutish variations of baseball as played in Massachusetts and elsewhere.[14] This provided him with the ideal vehicle to preach the tonic of baseball for self-improvement as well as national betterment.[15] For practically everything that seemingly ailed America—the side effects of industrialization, urbanization, and the development of a national economy (many of the same ills soon to be identified by George Beard and the positive thinking movement)—Chadwick believed that baseball offered a cure. This philosophy expressed itself in how he viewed the game and how he sought to promote it. Aspects of the game he considered to be curative he promoted; those he considered to be destructive to the national character he attempted to either eliminate or punish through his chosen methods of statistical analysis. In short, how America came to understand the game emanated in large degree from Henry Chadwick's personal beliefs of right and wrong, not merely on the ball field but within society.[16]

That he believed it to be his right to exert such influence stemmed from the philosophy that dominated American life in the mid-nineteenth century. As social Darwinism dominated the conversation within the upper classes of American society (prior to the emergence of the new social science), Chadwick preached a baseball philosophy that was evocative of its accepted tenets. He believed that the game was in the process of evolving from a lower form to a higher one and felt it to be his responsibility, as the foremost baseball journalist of his era, to mold it, tweak it, alter it until the public saw a game that conformed to what he believed to be the best aspects of American society, and that spoke to those classes that either saw or strove to see themselves as societal leaders.[17] Within this framework, baseball's rules were malleable because his goal was not so much to see to it that the players conformed to the rules as were then understood but, rather, to mold the rules until eventually, they demonstrated "what the game was capable of under a more perfect code."[18] Thus, he tinkered and fussed with the game until he developed one that served as an exemplar of larger American life. In many ways, Chadwick was a bridge between the old social science and the new—his feet were planted firmly in the old world but, contrary to the social Darwinists, he believed in evolutionary environmentalism. Eventually, the early baseball "magnates" would build upon his beliefs and the baseball creed took hold.

Chadwick had plenty of opportunities to create a game that conformed to his idealized image of baseball. In 1857 he was an integral member of a convention of New York clubs that gathered for the express purpose of establishing a permanent set of rules for the game. At that convention it was agreed, among other things, that the bases were to be set at ninety feet apart and that a winner was to be determined after the completion of nine innings.[19] A decade later, in 1867, he became a member of the Committee of Rules and Regulations of the National Association—the only nonplayer invited to join. Although technically an "outsider," he was by that time the game's staunchest promoter, hyping the game through his newspaper columns as well as his other baseball publications (he was the only one publishing baseball journals at this time). Even though he lived his life outside the white lines, the players recognized him as "clearly, the voice of the game." More significant, given his penchant for linking baseball and society as well as his detailed analyses of the social benefits of his proposed modifications of the game, he was likewise considered the game's moral conscience. For instance, in the late 1880s, Chadwick advocated for an alteration of the number of balls and strikes permitted a batter. Four strikes and five balls, he argued, would achieve the socially desirable goal of encouraging the skill of both the batter and pitcher and reduce the instances of "the wild speed previously in vogue" with pitchers, encouraging them to learn control instead. Skill, as measured through patience and control, was to be valued over speed and power, which he argued were more brutish, ungentlemanly, qualities. Thus, he believed that any rule changes should necessarily encourage the former and discourage the latter.

In 1860 he published *Beadle's Dime Base Ball Player*, the first magazine devoted exclusively to baseball and, in the process, jump-started an entire industry of annual or recurring baseball publications devoted to promotion of the game as well as giving fans new ways of following, understanding, and appreciating it. The 1861 edition was particularly groundbreaking in that it was the first one that contained what was to become Chadwick's legacy—statistics. In it, he created a scoring system that allowed fans to follow the game and track the progression of events even if they had not seen them in person. He also created a box score (fashioned from cricket) so that fans could, in his words "obtain an accurate estimate of a player's skill . . ." Later, he revised and simplified the box score to make it easier for fans to use. However, underlying this seemingly neutral statistical compilation was Chadwick's moral philosophy: the choices of what to include and what to omit reflected his beliefs as to what skills most benefitted the game and, in a larger context, society. Without their even realizing it, baseball fans were coming to learn and appreciate the game through Chadwick's eyes, seeing the game as he did, unconsciously making the same moral choices he did.

One of the most obvious examples of this comes through Chadwick's beliefs concerning the base on balls. To him, there was no value in the walk; it was not a true test of a batter's skill. Rather, it was merely a case of bad pitching. Therefore, his early box score counted walks as errors on the pitcher. Through this form of social engineering, Chadwick was hoping to encourage pitchers to improve their control (by providing batters with better pitches to hit) and encourage batters to swing rather than be selective at the plate.[20] He later developed and relied upon a host of other statistics as a means of both understanding the game as well as viewing the game through the "proper" lens. Drawing on his half-brother's work on sanitary reform, Chadwick realized that baseball gave its fans many meaningful things to count and, because they could count them, the resulting statistics were necessarily important and telling and could provide irrefutable proof of proposed beliefs.[21] In fact, ever since the Enlightenment, people such as his half-brother Edwin had come to rely on statistics as "authentic facts" that they believed ended debates rather than started them.[22] By creating a box score and counting certain activities that occurred during a game and, later, through the course of a season, Henry Chadwick believed that he could tell the truth of a player's ability.[23] And to unearth those statistics that told the truth, one had to focus on those that measured preferred skills. None of this was neutral; all of this was based upon Chadwick's belief regarding which statistics told the truth as he saw it, and which ones did not.

Although he did not create the batting average (Chadwick credited H. A. Dobson with that invention), he fervently promoted it because he believed it to be an accurate representation of the skills required for the improvement of the game and the social betterment of the nation.[24] Chadwick was drawn to the batting average because it highlighted the skill he valued above all else: the clean base hit. In that act, good hitting as well as good pitching were both on display. Despite the fact that a batter likewise reached base on a walk and had as much of a chance to score that way, walks were not factored into the compilation of the batting average. Even more to his liking, errors, regardless of the fact that they too resulted in the batter reaching base, actually reduced a batter's average. The moral decisions involved in the creation and promotion of the batting average as a valuable statistical tool were many. On the page, however, they were buried underneath the simplicity of the resulting numbers. Although they most likely never realized it, fans were becoming inculcated into Chadwick's moral and social philosophies every time they opened their sports pages.

In the 1880s, his quest to encourage individual sacrifice and team play led Chadwick to once again seek out the necessary statistical incentive. Eventually, he developed the Run Batted In (RBI) which, by 1891, became an official element of the box score.[25] To Chadwick, the RBI represented an act that brought out the best in man: taking action for the betterment of others (in this case, enabling one's teammates to score runs). Viewed in this light, it was a singular act of achievement that spoke volumes of the individual who successfully accomplished it. As such, it quickly became one of the most important statistical measures in the game. That the RBI involves skill but also copious amounts of luck (after all, without men on base, the batter cannot drive in a run in any way other than through a home run—a selfish and brutish act in Chadwick's eyes), was not contemplated by Chadwick—he had no room for luck in his statistics.[26] Instead, they were accurate, foolproof "truth tellers." They were designed to hold players accountable for their actions on the ball field. For if every act was deliberate and luck taken out of the equation, developing a workable incentive system was possible.[27] Through his statistics, Chadwick spent the latter half of the nineteenth century working through just such a system in his quest to present to the American public a game that mirrored what he believed to be the favored qualities of the nation.

Chadwick also used nonstatistical means within his columns to hammer home his philosophies. As a sportswriter he often focused on the skills of certain players he found to be admirable or wanting. In an 1861 column in the *New York Clipper*, he attempted to define the characteristics of what he believed to be the model player. Tellingly, none of the attributes that drew his attention were directly relevant to success on the field. Rather, to him, the successful player "[comports] himself like a gentleman" and possessed other gentlemanly qualities that may have laid the foundation for a model citizen but were extraneous to the actual playing of the game.[28] In addition to his columns and statistical work, by 1892 Chadwick had ascended to the position of editor of *Spalding's Official Base Ball Guide*, the preeminent guide within the professional game. If there was ever any question before, by this time Chadwick was clearly the game's mouthpiece. It was not long before the self-declared baseball "magnates" recognized just how much of an ally a powerful and influential man such as Chadwick could be to them in their quest to climb the societal ladder.

Very quickly, in fact, National League team owners looked to journalists such as Chadwick and his progeny to help them promote the game and, in the process, the owners themselves. To aid them in their quest, they began to facilitate access to favored journalists and made sure they accompanied their teams to important games and influential tours. Without the journalists, the owners would have had a far tougher time convincing the nation that not only was baseball an important pastime but that it was the owners who made it all happen. As Chadwick and others published column after column on not merely the games themselves but baseball as a tool for social betterment, the owners basked in the reflected glow as their social status increased as well. By the late nineteenth century, there was no shortage of journalists willing to do the owners' bidding—Chadwick was not merely the father of baseball, he was the father of the baseball writing profession. Scores of writers followed in his footsteps across the country. Not all wrote in the same style as Chadwick but nearly all wanted to promote the game in much the same way he had. By the 1880s there were more baseball writers than ever and, owing to new technology that made newspapers easier and cheaper to mass produce, baseball became a greater part of working-class culture because there were now exponentially more people who could afford to buy a daily paper. Now, through the writing of Chadwick and others, a broader swath of fans could read about the game and "understand" it in much the same way Chadwick did. Although these fans read the columns with their own eyes, when they looked up from their papers and saw the game on the field, they were viewing it largely through Chadwick's. That he encouraged fawning journalism rather than a critical examination of the game was appropriately summed up in a eulogy to him upon his death in 1908: "There never was a word in all the miles of copy Henry Chadwick has written that was not penned for the betterment of the game as he saw it."[29] Examining his life's work as a whole, Chadwick's eulogist had, perhaps unwittingly, hit upon an essential truth: at his core, Chadwick was not merely a baseball writer, he was a promoter. And he succeeded wildly.

Chadwick's penchant for promotion fit neatly within his era and the realities of the newly expanded America. As noted in chapter 1, booster-ism was rampant as newspapermen sought to promote their teams and towns as a means of self-preservation. Sportswriters often held the local team close to their chests and considered it their job to give voice to the feelings of the club and its supporters, rather than objectively analyze the game from afar.[30] So, for example, ran this hyperbolic account in a Chicago newspaper after the local White Stockings were defeated by the St. Louis Brown Stockings in an 1875 game: "a deep gloom settled over the city. Friends refused to recognize friends, lovers became estranged, and business was suspended. All Chicago went to a funeral, and the time, since then, has dragged wearily along, as though it were no object to live longer in this world."[31] Because of the realities of the times, sportswriters quickly became comfortable with reporting stories as opposed to the facts. To them, economics and social conditions mandated such an approach.

In the early decades of the twentieth century, the atmosphere of boost-erism and promotion continued to predominate. By this point, promotion of the game above all else had become the accepted, unchallenged approach to baseball writing and reporting. By the 1920s, sports sections were manned by baseball "experts" such as Grantland Rice, Ring Lardner, Damon Runyon, Arch Ward, and others who were, in essence, storytellers rather than reporters.[32] Educated in the "Gee Whiz" school of journalism, they were "optimists, mythmakers, and sentimentalists."[33] As a group, they were interested in narrative, in drama, in the glory of the game, and were interested in facts only to the extent that they added to their stories. When the facts clashed with the portraits they were painting, they were swept to the side. The media's coddling of the biggest star of the era, Babe Ruth, was perhaps the most blatant example of this phenomenon.[34] To the writers who covered him, it was not enough that Ruth was merely the greatest hitter in the game. Instead, he was portrayed, as per his wishes, as the prototypical American success story. Although the truth of his difficult childhood would most likely have been material enough for this narrative, the media went further and repeated the story that Ruth was an orphan—a tale Ruth himself conjured up to burnish his story and one in which there was no basis in fact.[35] As a professional, Ruth encountered numerous difficulties that were known to many within the media and would have tarnished his legend—he was sued by several women for paternity and child support, he was suspended by the Yankees five times in 1922 alone—but these were never reported.[36]

As new media crept into the game, they quickly took their reportage cues from the sportswriters. Like the scribes, newsreels and radio also sought to not merely cover the games on the field but to promote the nexus between baseball and America. In the process, players such as Ruth were treated as unadulterated heroes, with their foibles either ignored (such as Ruth's paternity suits) or treated in humorous ways (such as attributing Ruth's absences on the field to excessive hot dog consumption) that only furthered endeared them to the public. Very quickly sports, and particularly baseball, assumed a significant role in these emerging technologies: sports coverage accounted for 25 percent of all newsreel coverage during the '20s, and commercial photography likewise boomed at this time, with flattering shots of Ruth—at orphanages, posing with children, celebrities, and chimpanzees—plastered seemingly all over the tabloid newspapers and magazines of the day.[37] All of this was in furtherance of the story of baseball. Not even baseball's most notorious scandal—the fixing of the

1919 World Series—was considered appropriate subject matter by the media because it clashed with the scripted image of the game. Hence, it languished in obscurity until Hugh Fullerton dragged it, amid significant resistance, into the public eye. Even before the fateful World Series, the media following the White Sox were aware of the groundswell of disgust with owner Charles Comiskey within the team locker room.[38] Regardless, they continually hailed him as an enlightened business genius, benign and benevolent, despite persistent player complaints that Comiskey routinely had them play in dirty uniforms so he could save money, which he would then use to lavish upon the writers in the form of a generous buffet during White Sox home games.[39] In this instance it was literally a case of the media refusing to act for fear of biting the hand that fed them.

The conspiracy of silence with regard to negative or contrary information perpetuated for decades, with the media often and unabashedly crossing the journalistic line between writing about the players and writing for them. Between 1921 and 1937 sportswriter Christy Walsh led a syndicate of thirty-four baseball writers who acted as ghostwriters for popular players of the time, promoting them, encouraging the tall tales that grew around them, all in an effort to encourage a scripted vision of the game—one populated with larger than life yet symbolically all-American heroes.[40] In St. Louis, Roy Stockton of the *St. Louis Post-Dispatch* had no qualms about covering Gas House Gang stars Dizzy and Paul Dean for his paper while simultaneously serving as a willing conduit of their fabrications, both within his own paper and, later, in the pages of the *Saturday Evening Post*.[41] His lack of ambivalence was typical: the *New York World-Telegram* likewise ran an invented conversation between the brothers, complete with humorous and endearing malapropisms, documenting their discovery of the big city—New York—in an attempt to burnish their image as lovable rubes.[42] In New York, the legend of Joe DiMaggio was forged in large part by influential *New York Post* writer Jimmy Cannon, who saw to it that the slugger's star was burnished and never tarnished.[43]

Of course, not all players were accorded such deferential treatment. In Boston, Ted Williams had few allies in the media and, as a result of his icy relationship with those who covered the Red Sox, was often portrayed as the contrast to the all-American hero that was DiMaggio.[44] The distinctions that were routinely drawn between Williams and DiMaggio often had little to do with their abilities or even their temperaments (which were remarkably similar—driven, moody at times, uncommunicative at others) and much to do with their personal relationships with those whose job it was to cover them. At one point in 1950, Williams was able to convince Red Sox management to ban writers from the locker room until thirty minutes after the game, turning an already frosty relationship with the Boston media downright frigid.[45] The denial of access struck some writers as treasonous, believing as they did that there existed an unspoken alliance between those who played the game and those who covered it. Having broken that bond, Williams was never forgiven. Thereafter he became a convenient measuring stick by which DiMaggio's greatness could be appreciated and applauded. Together they were used to promote a chosen image of the game, with the darkness of Williams used to further illuminate the brightness of DiMaggio. Through this combined portrait, a distinct and unmistakable vision of the game blossomed.

The emergence of radio in the 1920s only enhanced the storytelling abilities of the media. Although many newspapermen felt threatened by the new media and some sparring between the old media and the new occurred, the message that reached fans via radio did not differ much in substance from that which newspapers had delivered for the previous half century. If anything, the story only became tighter and better focused than ever before. Because local broadcasters were typically employed directly by the clubs, it was clear that they were not going to delve into the realm of critical analysis as far as their employers were concerned. Instead, just like their newspaper counterparts, they were well-versed in the "Gee Whiz" style that, in the words of baseball historian Ben Rader, "sometimes elevated ordinary play into the realm of the immortal."[46] Not all were so effusive (Red Barber of the Dodgers famously was not), but many were, with the result being that what fans heard on the radio was little more than an audio account of what they had become accustomed to reading in their daily sports pages. Promotion through storytelling and a patriotic vision of the game predominated in most markets. Dizzy Dean once remarked that it was not until he heard one of the game's pioneering broadcasters, Graham McNamee, broadcasting the 1925 World Series that he understood that baseball was not merely a game but the great American pastime.[47]

One facet of early radio broadcasts that enhanced broadcasters' storytelling abilities, necessitated by the limited technology of the time, was that most games were re-creations rather than live, on-the-scene broadcasts. Because they were a re-creation of reality rather than reality itself, the freedom of early broadcasters (which included future president and positive thinker Ronald Reagan) to mold a game to fit their idea of how it should play out was nearly boundless.[48] Most fans were not aware of the fact that they were listening to fiction rather than fact, much as they were unaware that the game accounts and player profiles they were accustomed to reading in newspapers and magazines were similarly oftentimes the product of fanciful imagination.[49] These re-creations set expectations as to what baseball broadcasts were supposed to sound like (most broadcasters made ample use of sound effects), how the game was to be paced, and how the drama was to unfold.[50] The role of an underdog team or player could be highlighted throughout the contest, thereby building suspense; heroes and villains could be created and sharply defined, the ambiguities and nuances that complicate reality brushed to the side. In these re-creations the most important role was played by the broadcaster—the players were merely the raw material at his disposal that could be used to develop the story he wanted to tell. Although the raw data of the actual games being played on the field was conveyed to listeners (the winning and losing teams and pitchers, key hits, and so forth), the overall portrait of the game was colored by the broadcaster who chose what to highlight, what to ignore, when to stretch the truth, and when to simply make something up to add interest or drama to his tale.

Re-creations continued into the 1950s and were particularly popular during World War II when the exaggerated drama and patriotic themes were beamed to military personnel overseas, who unwittingly received a dose of nationalistic inspiration along with their baseball fix.[51] One of the last masters of the re-created game was Gordon McLendon, the "Old Scotsman," who, through the Liberty Broadcast System, broadcast the "Game of the Day" on 430 radio stations by 1952.[52] By this time, live, on-the-scene broadcasts were becoming more of a regular occurrence but, even so, many fans preferred McLendon's re-creations to the live broadcasts.[53] In this transitional era, when fans in many markets were given a choice between the story of baseball and something that more closely resembled the reality of it, many opted for the story: road games, which were often re-creations, were typically more popular than home games, which were increasingly live broadcasts. To many fans, the road games conveyed something that the home games could not. The grass seemed greener, the ballparks quainter, the action crisper, the good guys and bad guys more cleanly defined.[54] It was this vividness, available on demand in re-creations but more elusive in live broadcasts, that resonated with the many fans who looked back upon "the golden era" of baseball with nostalgic longing. As the re-creations made clear, it was, as it always had been and in the tradition of Chadwick, the exaltation of the game that mattered most. In Chadwick's image, sports-writers and later radio broadcasters embellished game accounts, massaged facts, and managed truth to produce a glorious portrait of the game. The resulting stories of baseball resonated through the emotional pull of these fictions; the untethering of the game from reality.

THE LIKE-MINDEDNESS AND
RIGHT-MINDEDNESS OF THE PRESS

Beyond the factors specific to sportswriting and broadcasting, the sporting media was and is not immune to the same sorts of constraints that hinder the impartiality of mainstream journalists in any field. Although it is a generally accepted tenet that the media is independent and committed to reporting truth as opposed to stories, journalists cannot escape the inevitable gloss on the facts that comes with the determination of how to choose among all of the available facts, how to organize the ones they have chosen, and how to present them to their readers. In the process, what is offered up to the public is, best intentions notwithstanding, a story anyway, one that discourages critical questioning given that it comes complete with a certified journalistic stamp of approval.[55] Contrary to the cries of conspiracy theorists, this occurs in the absence of any sort of overt systematic attempt to deliver a prepackaged message. Rather, it is the process of the free market that produces the complicity of the media, in the form of each individual media outlet's selection of "right minded" people to gather and deliver the news, who then proceed to each do what they think is best.[56] Any form of censorship—the omission of inconvenient facts that blur the preferred story—is overwhelmingly self-censorship by reporters and commentators who have internalized the necessary con-straints and who use them to determine what to report, what to omit, and how to shape the resulting story.[57]

In the world of baseball journalism this is particularly true. For most baseball writers and commentators, their unabashed love of all aspects of the game as they understood it as children—the game on the field as well as the romance that surrounds it: the stories, the myths, the legends— was what drew many of them to it professionally. Naturally, they would be hostile to anyone or anything that attempted to cast a shadow upon any of this. As such, it is not difficult to understand why so many baseball writers were antagonistic toward the Players Association despite the fact that many were union members themselves. Irrespective of the union connection, these writers largely became frustrated and angry when the off-field events of the 1970s and '80s compelled them to write about the mundane problems of everyday life rather than the glorious stories of baseball that enthralled them.[58]

Because of this, the owners were able to use the writers and many within the media as a battering ram against the players in labor negotiations.[59] They knew that the media would more often than not see the issues through their eyes because they (the owners) were selling the romantic story of the game that appealed to the media and was responsive to why they entered the profession in the first place, whereas the Players Association was challenging all of this. In the aftermath of the work stoppage of 1972, many within the media (with the notable exceptions of writers such as Red Smith, Leonard Koppett, and a few others) were particularly hard on the player representatives they blamed for disrupting the game while overwhelmingly supporting the owners.[60] During the 1981 strike, the media's disparate treatment of the players and owners was much the same, with some members of the media so agitated that they could not even bear to write about the labor issues at all. The *New York Daily News*'s three baseball writers refused to cover it; a labor writer had to be called in to provide coverage of what was unquestionably the largest baseball story of the year, if not the decade.[61]

Outside the labor arena, members of the baseball media have been similarly hesitant to cover anything that challenged the accepted stories of baseball. As noted in chapter 2, steroid and drug use within team locker rooms was an issue broached by some writers on occasion throughout the 1980s and '90s (enough to seemingly draw the attention of Selig and MLB, although, as highlighted within the Mitchell Report, to no apparent effect), but most steered clear of it, preferring to strap the blinders on and ignore all sorts of information that challenged the image of the Major League player as hero. And even those few who did raise the issue proceeded with extreme caution, concerned as they were over how their stories would impact the game's image. Likewise, the media's portrayal of the "baseball academies" that have sprouted up in Latin America over the past few decades has, overall, been supportive at best and neutral at worst even though the basic facts seemingly scream for widespread exposure. Despite the reality that the academies, as run by Major League baseball clubs, traffic in children and in some instances subject them to living conditions compared with "concentration camps"[62] and "Vietnam"[63] by some players and critics, many within the baseball media have nevertheless overlooked these realities.[64] Instead, they focused on the Horatio Algeresque aspect of these academies—the "rags to riches" tales of impoverished boys succeeding beyond all expectations. In so doing, they shifted the spotlight on the academies from one of exploitation to one of opportunity—and protected the game's image in the process.[65]

Beyond the baseball academies, the baseball media's approach to Latin ballplayers in general has similarly treaded in the shallows of easily told, culturally affirming Alger tales that promote the game as well as America rather than in ways that present more complex issues. Players such as Fernando Valenzuela and Sammy Sosa have been packaged and sold to the American public as Algeresque figures who came from abject poverty (much was made of the fact that Valenzuela's hometown—Etchohuaquila, Mexico—did not have electricity until 1970,[66] and that Sosa shined shoes and sold oranges as a youth in the Dominican Republic to help his widowed mother make ends meet[67]) only to succeed beyond their wildest imaginations in the United States. Earlier Latin players such as Roberto Clemente and Orlando Cepeda were often portrayed as classic Alger rubes, with their attempts to speak a second language—English—mocked in an effort to accentuate their perceived unrefined characteristics and burnish the "rags to riches" angle that some sportswriters insisted on stressing in their reporting. Clemente in particular was occasionally quoted phonetically in ways that embarrassed him: "I no play so gut yet. Me like hot weather, veree hot."[68] Clemente later responded angrily to these portrayals: "I never talk like that; they just want to sell newspapers. Anytime a fellow comes from Puerto Rico, they want to create an image. They say 'Hey, he talks funny!' But they go to Puerto Rico and they don't talk like us. I don't have a master's degree, but I'm not a dumb-head and I don't want no bullshit from anyone."[69] In addition, few sportswriters make mention of the fact that, as a rule, Latin players receive meager if any signing bonuses and thereafter are paid on the whole far less than white-skinned, American-born players. As the Cuban-born shortstop Zoilo Versalles once remarked: "Bonus? Sure, we all get bonus. You know the bonus we get? Carfare, that's the bonus. . . . Latin boys never get no bonus."[70] In the end, despite their journalistic credentials, many media members were and are unashamed fans of the game and have simply been unwilling to present a more complex, perhaps less zealously patriotic, image of something they had looked up to all of their lives.[71] Of course, not everyone with an interest in baseball saw the game similarly. For those who did not, however—those who would have written a different story of baseball—there were few outlets available to them throughout most of the twentieth century.

One of the largest barriers to the achievement of a legitimate diversity of opinion within the media is the cost of membership into the media fraternity itself. It is not enough to have a perspective; one has to have the ability to disseminate it efficiently. Unfortunately, it has always been an expensive proposition to produce even a small daily newspaper with the capability of reaching a significant audience.[72] This difficulty is only compounded when another barrier is added to the mix—advertising.[73] By necessity, given the cost of producing a daily newspaper or buying airtime on television or radio, content providers are obliged to advertisers who essentially underwrite the resulting product in whole or in part. Within this framework, the news—be it local, national, global, or sports—must be presented in a way that is friendly, or at least not overly antagonistic, toward those who are paying the bills. As a result, contrary information, regardless of whether it constitutes actual news, can become filtered out and left on the newsroom floor. Hence, when in 1937 Joe DiMaggio answered a reporter's question by stating that the best pitcher he had ever faced was the Negro League star Satchel Paige, his answer appeared only within the pages of the *Daily Worker*, which was not beholden to advertisers.[74] As Lester Rodney once replied to a fellow sportswriter: "I can do things a lot of you guys can't. I can belt big advertisers, automobile manufacturers, or tobacco companies. . . . You guys can't write anything about the ban against Negro players. I can do that."[75] Without advertising, the cost of a newspaper becomes wholly borne by its readers. This inevitably results in higher-priced papers (indeed, readers wishing to follow Lester Rodney's campaign to end segregation in the Major Leagues had to pony up for the privilege: the *Daily Worker* cost 60 percent more than the *New York Times*).[76] Competing against advertiser-supported newspapers, which have the ability to lower their prices below the cost of the production of the paper itself,[77] these reader-supported papers and the disparate voices within become marginalized until they disappear—victims of the competitive marketplace.[78]

Public relations represents yet another obstacle to journalistic diversity. The public relations industry was developed as a vehicle to make things easy for the media; to provide them with facilities, orchestrated press conferences, and advance copies of speeches and news releases to facilitate the transfer of preferred information from the makers of the news to the disseminators of it.[79] Consequently, these (largely) corporate-sponsored tools subsidize the media not unlike advertising by reducing the costs of acquiring and disseminating information. Presented with such easily obtainable facts and sound bites, journalists simply have less incentive to undertake independent investigations and develop their own perspective on the news. The baseball world has been a mirror of society in this regard, with public relations becoming an ever-increasing presence, offering the baseball media the carrot of spoon-fed information at the price of depth and journalistic independence. By regularly holding controlled media events (run by their PR staffs), and creating the concept of the "media room," clubs have encouraged a pack mentality among the media, where everyone moves as a herd chasing the same story at the same time, with the result being that the same information—the information offered up at these quasi-official media events—gets disseminated and reported, regardless of the media outlet.[80] Although on the surface, such conceits as the daily postgame press conference in the stadium's designated media room appear to be examples of an unprecedented granting of access (earlier generations of media personnel never had so much alleged information made available to them so effortlessly), they actually reduce it in practice because they encourage reliance on these club-sponsored events. By offering reporters a constant stream of effortlessly available information, club management can effectively control the flow of information out of the locker room and into the daily papers. For at these press conferences, journalists often assume the passive role of stenographers, copying down what is said rather than actively probing their own angles, digging behind the scenes, searching for the story that perhaps is not the one presented to them but the one that lies behind it.[81] The genius of the press conference has always been that it creates the illusion of access while limiting it in practice. As club owners became more conscious of the value of public relations, they gravitated toward this vehicle in their continual quest to get their preferred message across to the American public.

On top of everything else comes the invisible albatross of access. In defining their journalistic worth by their ability to gain access to the players they cover (as limited and orchestrated as that may be), traditional journalists have in many instances become beholden to them, ever vigilant to protect them and their image for fear of losing these sources of information in the future. Requests from players and club officials not to cover particular stories—ones that would challenge accepted beliefs and assumptions—have always been the norm and are routinely honored.[82] By partnering with their subject-matters, journalists have allowed them to have significant input into the determination of what gets printed and what does not. In the end, when everything is taken into account—the pressures and constraints applied by access, economics, advertisers, and public relations—combined with the time and space constraints imposed by the traditional media, it is simply easier to write or present a conventional story that conforms to traditional beliefs than one that challenges them. As media critic Noam Chomsky observed, "[t]he technical structure of the media virtually compels adherence to conventional thoughts; nothing else can be expressed between two commercials, or in 700 words, without the appearance of absurdity that is difficult to avoid when one is challenging familiar doctrine, with no opportunity to develop facts or argument."[83] The imposed hurdles are simply too great and/or enticing for all but the most inspired and dogged journalists. The conventional story—the preferred story—is sitting right there, prepackaged and ready to go. Only the few have the means and fortitude to ignore it.

Of course, there are always those few, the ones who refuse to move in lockstep with their cohorts and who are most certainly not "right minded."

Despite all the obstacles, they have always existed (witness Hugh Fullerton and his dogged pursuit of the 1919 World Series fix, Red Smith and Leonard Koppett throughout the mid- and late twentieth century, and Steve Fainaru in his more recent reporting of the Latin American baseball academies) and always will, and at some of the largest news organizations, both on the local and national level. Though these voices are heard and do have a measure of influence, ultimately they often ironically serve as credibility enhancers for the preferred stories they are challenging. For they serve as illustrations of the proposition that the media is not monolithic, that debate and dissent are permitted, and that the majority opinion is one that has been freely reached and not compromised.[84] By the late 1950s, in fact, the baseball media was developing a reputation for nonconformity on a large scale that was crucial in cementing their credibility for decades to come. The era of the overtly fawning journalist had come to a close, and the transformation in tone that occurred gave credence to the idea that the baseball media was not beholden to those within the game. Underneath the hype, however, the substance of what was reported did not change much.

The transformation dates roughly to 1958, when a fight on the Yankees' team train between reliever Ryne Duren and coach Ralph Houk went unreported by the beat reporters, as per the expected journalistic etiquette of the day.[85] When *New York Post* reporter Leonard Schecter was scolded by his editor for missing a different, unrelated story, he offered up his account of the Duren-Houk tussle as a substitute. The story was published a few days later (without a byline), leading to a debate within the New York sports pages on the merits of the "conspiracy of silence" between the media and their subjects that dated back to Chadwick's time. Soon, the trust between players and beat writers evaporated as more off-field events found their way into print and "the race for the salacious was on."[86] From this a new breed of baseball journalists was spawned, "chipmunks" as they were called, who as a group were more interested in backstories and personal information than their predecessors. They asked personal questions of the players, infused the offbeat into their reporting, and generally wrote with much less overt reverence than their journalistic forefathers.[87] Still, despite their reputation, the chipmunks did not write everything, or even nearly everything, they knew. They too defined themselves through access, touting their bona fides as insiders and, as a result, had sources to protect. In addition, they were the product of the same selection process as their predecessors and felt the same pressures from editors and advertisers. In any event, the era of the chipmunk as rabble-rouser was short-lived—by the 1970s, the majority of them had become established writers firmly on the side of ownership in the ensuing labor wars, repeating the same conventional wisdom as their predecessors. With limited exceptions, most journalists, chipmunk or otherwise, were still more interested in promoting the culturally affirming, patriotic story of baseball rather than delving deeply underneath the hype. After all, the chipmunks were fans too.

ENTER THE OUTSIDER: BILL JAMES

If the "inside" nature of journalism was the problem, then only an outsider could present a solution. Living in Kansas, unaffiliated with professional baseball or the media that covered it in any way, Bill James was perhaps as far outside the game as one could get. Rather than consider this an impediment, he recognized the advantages of his position. Through the late 1970s, '80s, and '90s he capitalized on his advantage and revolutionized how fans thought about baseball, paving the way for millions of other outsiders to take control of the stories of baseball, mold them to suit their personal tastes and perspectives, and free them from the grips of the owners and traditional media. To a point.

Although James has come to be known, sometimes pejoratively, as the Guru of Stats, he was but the latest in a long line of people who embraced statistics in the hope of better understanding the game. After Henry Chadwick, statistics remained an integral part of baseball as both the game and its attendant statistics evolved throughout the twentieth century. This was consistent with the increased emphasis on statistics in American society overall during the late nineteenth and early twentieth centuries. If the Enlightenment sparked an interest in statistics as "authentic facts," the Progressive Era saw that interest explode as more and more people were discovering just how many different "facts" statistics could explain, depending on how one counted.[88] In 1913, the Elias Sports Bureau was founded and soon convinced the National League to designate it as the league's official statistical organization (the Howe News Bureau soon took control of the American League). With statistics in each league now centralized and therefore more accessible to the media, their usage became more common. Throughout the golden age of the 1930s, writers began to bring them into more frequent practice, sprinkling them into their narratives and columns.[89] Many writers kept their American League *Red Book* and National League *Green Book*—the official statistical compendiums for both leagues—on hand for quick and easy reference, with the belief that somewhere within their pages existed an interesting or illuminative statistic—an "authentic fact"—that would enliven their prose or help them make their point.[90] Eventually, Elias assumed control of both major leagues, and the accessibility of statistics increased once again. In the late '50s Seymour Siwoff joined Elias and helped to heighten the awareness of statistics, and Elias, even more; he was particularly fond of using statistics to compare players of different eras.[91] Through Siwoff and Elias, fans were able to understand the game better than they had before. But with Elias inexorably tied to MLB, they were still seeing it through the eyes of insiders subject to the inherent bounds and constraints of an industry seeking to further the accepted, traditional stories of baseball.

Bill James was different. Raised a Kansas City Athletics fan, he became orphaned in a rooting sense when the A's packed up after the 1968 season and took off for Oakland. Left without a team to develop his affections, he transferred his interest in baseball from a particular team to the sport as a whole.[92] This revolutionized his outlook and, eventually, the game itself. Separated from the emotional attachment to the game, and no longer bound by adherence to the traditional stories of baseball as told through local allegiances and heroes, James embarked on a broader analysis of the game, taking his cues on how to understand the game not from sportswriters but from academia. James, much like Chadwick a century earlier, was fascinated by the social sciences and often found within them explanations for things he was seeing on the diamond. In this way, James was very much Chadwick's intellectual heir. Also like Chadwick, James too was, at heart, a promoter, although while Chadwick sought to promote a connection between baseball and mythology, James sought to promote a separation of the two—of looking at baseball as baseball rather than baseball as metaphor.

In November 1975 James introduced himself to the nation through an article in *Baseball Digest* entitled, "A New Way to Rate Baseball Excellence," in which he in essence challenged Siwoff by postulating that because Major League statistical levels vary so greatly from decade to decade, it was impossible to compare players of different eras simply by comparing their statistics. A better way to do it, he claimed, was to compare league leaders in a given season against the runner-up. In this way, true dominance, across eras, could be analyzed. In 1977 he self-published his hucksterishly titled *1977 Baseball Abstract: Featuring 18 Categories of Statistical Information That You Just Can't Find Anywhere Else.* To promote it he placed an ad in the classified section of the *Sporting News* and found a few curiosity-seekers willing to pay $3.50 to find out what this was all about. When their copy arrived, they found an entirely new way of looking at a game they thought they had already understood. He analyzed players' and teams' monthly progression throughout a season, showing how the year-end records and averages that had become sacrosanct hardly told the whole story or even served as accurate gauges of ability; he studied the records of rookies, showing how it was possible to actually "see" a young player learning to hit at the Major League level simply by looking at the proper set of statistics; he presented a game that before then had never been seen. The next year his *Baseball Abstract* nearly doubled in size as he provided detailed analysis of every team. Once again he challenged traditional assumptions by concluding that, for example, Roger Maris's single-season home run record of sixty-one would have been broken by George Foster of the Reds in 1977 (who hit fifty-two) if Foster had played in a "neutral" park rather than the "pitchers" park that was Cincinnati's Riverfront Stadium. (James concluded that Foster would have hit sixty-five.) He also demonstrated that the allegedly big-hitting Red Sox were merely the product of playing one-half of their games in hitter-friendly Fenway Park; in actuality, they were a better pitching team than they were given credit for but a pedestrian offensive one.

He also, both directly and indirectly, challenged the baseball creed. Attitude, leadership, and desire were irrelevant to the game of baseball, he concluded: ". . . if you don't turn them into results . . . they're meaningless words. . . . If you lose a ballgame on the field you cannot win it back in the clubhouse, and anybody who thinks you can is a loser." A recurring refrain in his *Abstracts* through the years was this plea to look on the field for the clues to success, not anywhere else. Morality, sportsmanship, temperament did not win ballgames; there was no higher moral purpose of the game and there could be none because the game existed only on the field.

Societal values (preferred or otherwise) did not translate into results; they had no place in either the game itself or the understanding of it. The creed, so far as it was used to determine success, was nothing more than a collection of those "meaningless words," carelessly tossed around in the blind supposition that they explained anything having to do with baseball. It was shots across the bow like this one—challenging and dismissing a century of baseball beliefs—that led James's biographer to conclude that "his place in baseball tradition is as a questioner of the status quo."

James also challenged the notion that one needed to be an insider to understand the game from the inside. His 1984 *Abstract* made clear his disdain for "inside baseball" as popularized by the chipmunks as well as their forbears: "Inside looks, inside glimpses, inside locker rooms, and inside blimpses; within months we shall have seen the inside of every-thing that one can get inside of without a doctor's help. . . . This is *outside* baseball. This is a book about what baseball looks like if you step back from it and study it intensely and minutely, but from a distance." A year earlier, in his '83 *Abstract*, he wrote that his was "a book for those who abandon themselves to the game, for those to whom the hurried and casual summaries of journalism are a daily affront." The problem with sportswriters, he believed, was that they had an overwhelming urge to simplify everything, to search for the "master switch" that explained ev-erything in the game in one fell swoop: "Baseball is 90 percent pitching, sportswriters argue, not because this makes any sense or because there is any evidence to support it, but because it reduces the terrifying complex-ity of the game to a single switch." As James highlighted again and again, despite their access, or perhaps because of it, the traditional media were not portraying a true picture of the game to the public. Instead, they were telling stories—fanciful ones, convenient ones, ones based on untested assumptions and misplaced morality tales. Stories, all of them.

By the time of his first *Abstract*, many fans believed that they knew all there was to be known about baseball. They had internalized Chadwick's box score as well as the statistics that followed from it and as developed by Elias. They knew, from reading their sports pages and listening to their local broadcasters, what a .300 hitter was and how that differed from a .220 hitter. And they assumed that this was the end of it. What James did was to inform them that what they saw when they read a box score was merely the tip of the iceberg; that lying underneath it was an entirely new way of understanding the game that theretofore had remained untouched. The concept of the batting average was one such example. Ever since Chadwick's era it had been seen as an end unto itself (players with high batting averages were de facto believed to be more valuable than players with lower batting averages). James reasoned that because the point of baseball was not to hit for a high average but to score runs, the batting average might be an incomplete statistical measure—if a player with a lower batting average was nevertheless responsible for creating more runs (as, he showed, was often the case, even between players with as much as an eighty-point disparity in batting average), he would be more valuable than his higher-averaged cohort. In this sense, he urged that it was necessary to look beyond the traditional box score, to look within the numbers we all thought we knew and try to understand not merely what they said but, more important, what they meant. Those who refused to do this, who instead protested "that they are suspicious of statistical analysis are simply not thinking about what they are saying." James continued, alleging that "people who don't study the records become prisoners of them."

Despite his reputation, James's analysis was not solely grounded within the world of statistics. In fact, in his 1982 *Abstract* he railed against "statistical idiocy"—"the assertion that nothing is real except that which is measured in statistics." He, like Chadwick, often wrote narrative pieces on players that drew upon the social sciences and the humanities. Regardless of the form of his critiques, they routinely challenged the long-held tenets of the system that had become "baseball" as an iconic culture. Not surprisingly, the system fought back. Traditionally, those within MLB and the media have always been suspicious of outsiders, particularly ones such as James, who they saw as someone with a slide rule and a spreadsheet pretending to know more than they did. What made James particularly dangerous to them was how quickly and deeply his influence ran. Through his *Abstracts* and myriad other publications he demonstrated time and again that it was not necessary to have access to players in the locker room to understand the game. Anyone with an analytical mind and/or a computer and a desire to become intricately involved in the game could theoretically know as much, if not more than, the most well-connected general manager.[93]

In true MLB tradition, the innovations James was offering were resisted in much the same way baseball had resisted television and other technological advances generations earlier. Many general managers and other "baseball men" ignored James as well as the computer that offered up endless quick and simple ways to analyze performance like never before. As late as 1983, no team utilized the computer in any meaningful way and by 1987 only one-quarter of them even owned one.[94] Part of the hesitation was probably the result of simple fear of new technology, but some of it was most likely grounded in the democratic prospects of the computer: if everyone had equal access to information, then the "baseball men" could not possibly know more than their fans. At his core, James was promoting, in the words of baseball historian Jules Tygiel, populist baseball—a game owned and controlled by fans who were no longer dependent upon insiders for their enjoyment of the game.[95] This message of empowerment also meant a loss of control for those who for decades presided over an unchallenged monopoly on baseball's nuances. They were the anointed storytellers of the game. James and the computer threatened to end all of that. So they brushed off the computer as irrelevant and fought James at every turn.

The biggest battle between baseball and Bill James came over the right to information controlled by Elias. James realized that the data existed to solve all kinds of baseball questions but, owing to Elias's refusal to release its official scoresheets to the public at anything less than a prohibitive cost, these questions would remain unsolved.[96] He briefly considered a legal challenge but his distaste of litigation steered him in another direction. Nevertheless, James argued that Elias's hording of statistical information was improper and possibly illegal. As he contended, Elias's insistence that it had a proprietary right to the information was wrong because "[t]he entire basis of professional sports is the public's interest in what is going on. To deny the public access to information that it cares about is the logical equivalent of locking the stadiums and playing the games in private so that no one will find out what is happening."[97] Instead of suing, James decided to beat Elias at its own game—to compile scoresheets that not merely replicated the ones hoarded by Elias but were superior. He kicked off this initiative in 1984 with a nonprofit venture he termed "Project Scoresheet," where he and his cohorts set off to create and make available for public consumption scoresheets of all games going forward.[98] Just like that, there was no longer any need for Elias in this regard. Later, another venture, "Retrosheet," sprung up to tackle the historical record, undertaking to recreate scoresheets of all MLB games prior to 1984.[99]

James's battles with Elias did not end there. In 1987 he published an essay entitled "Wake-Up Call" wherein he expressed his concern over Elias's assumption of responsibility for compiling and issuing the American League *Red Book*.[100] After being assured by the league office that no information would be excised from the book, he found that, in fact, thousands of pieces of information had been eliminated. Once again he railed against Elias's claim that game accounts were somehow private property. With Elias asserting itself as the owner and protector of the vital information of the game, fans increasingly turned to people like James and others such as SABR (the Society for American Baseball Research) who created their own statistics and player profiles and analysis without access or the apparent desire for it.

Eventually, the insiders began to soften their stance against the onrushing outsiders. Throughout the '90s and early 2000s computers became standard issue in most organizations, and people with less traditional baseball pedigrees, such as Theo Epstein of the Red Sox, worked their way into at least some front offices. In 2002, the Red Sox hired James as a senior consultant and, in a triumph of Jamesian analysis (otherwise known as "sabermetrics" after the statistics-based approach of some SABR members) the Baseball Writers Association of America awarded the 2009 American and National League Cy Young Awards to Kansas City's Zack Greinke and San Francisco's Tim Lincecum after overlooking the traditional standard-bearer of the award—wins—and focusing instead on the newer metrics James and others had promulgated and promoted over the past few decades.[101] Upon the hiring of James, Red Sox owner John Henry wondered aloud why it had taken so long for him to find a job within MLB.[102] He need not have looked further than the issue of control. James threatened the assumptions and existence of everyone on the inside. Gradually, the insiders began to realize that it was easier to bring the outsiders in than to fight to keep them out forever. Perhaps they figured they could regain control of the game's narrative by doing so. By this point, however, it was too little too late.

FANTASY BASEBALL AND THE DEEPENING LOSS OF CONTROL

Although MLB and its attendant media dominated the narrative for decades, there have almost always been others out there, even before James, intent on creating their own stories of baseball. Thanks to James and his compatriots they have moved from the background to the foreground and have nearly overtaken those traditional storytellers in influence. This is particularly the case with regard to fantasy baseball.

At its core, fantasy baseball is baseball as defined by those playing it rather than by how MLB or its attendant sportswriters see it. It is overwhelmingly popular today but has been around, in one form or another, for decades. Jack Kerouac—a writer best known for his own take on the American dream—played a precursor of it as far back as 1933.[103] By 1936 he was playing a game that involved hitting a marble with a toothpick and by 1938 he had developed one that, much like the fantasy game that exists today, mirrored MLB in many ways except that he controlled the story, not MLB. He developed his own team names (he was fond of names based on automobiles, hence the "Boston Fords," "St. Louis LaSalles," and so forth), drew up imaginary rosters (from names culled from the Lowell, Massachusetts, telephone directory), and created player profiles complete with statistics.[104] Kerouac even wrote mock sports columns using the breathless, inflated prose that was the style of the gushing baseball journalism of the era.[105] He also presaged the modern fantasy game by imagining himself as a general manager and, in fictitious letters to real-life owners such as Tom Yawkey of the Red Sox and others, proposing trades of real players in his attempt to create his own "fantasy" team.[106] As late as 1958 the thirty-six-year-old Kerouac was still playing a version of his fantasy game, complete with a forty to fifty game season, an All-Star game and a World Series, demonstrating that even before the modern incarnation of the hobby, fantasy sports were hardly restricted to the domain of childhood.[107]

In the spring of 1960 the modern fantasy game was born when sociologist William Gamson introduced his new game to a few of his colleagues at the Harvard School of Public Health. He called it the "Baseball Seminar" and explained that participants were to act as if they were general managers, bidding on the rights to actual Major League players in an auction, and then playing games using these players' actual game statistics.[108] The general manager whose team's players performed the best by the conclusion of the actual Major League season would be crowned the Baseball Seminar's league champion. Later, Gamson relocated to the University of Michigan and brought the game with him, introducing it to his new colleagues. The game was wildly popular as the sociologists quickly recruited their friends to join either Gamson's league or a variation of it. Eventually, Tigers broadcaster Ernie Harwell was a participant. He enjoyed it so much that he recruited writer Roger Angell. In 1979, an outgrowth of the Baseball Seminar was created by writer and editor Daniel Okrent and friends at La Rôtisserie Française restaurant in New York. Okrent called his game, aptly enough, Rotisserie League Baseball and acknowledged that it was the Baseball Seminar that influenced him to create his own game.[109] From this, fantasy baseball mushroomed in popularity across the nation throughout the 1980s and '90s.

Although a seemingly harmless diversion, fantasy baseball in fact challenged the very structure of Major League Baseball as it offered an alternative to how the game had been traditionally understood and appreciated. With its focus on players rather than teams, and with each fantasy owner able to mix and match players from different teams, rooting allegiances shifted and eventually became, to many of its participants, less relevant—at one moment a fantasy owner might be a Dodgers fan, the next a Giants fan, all depending on which of "his" players was at bat or on the mound. Fantasy baseball offered a deconstructed game to its participants—one that discouraged traditional loyalties and "reconstitut[ed] it on an individual statistical basis."[110] This was the antithesis of the game Chadwick had imagined and that was grounded in the concept of the team and those selfless skills and behaviors that ultimately served as a metaphor for his vision of America. In this way, fantasy baseball represented its own challenge to the baseball creed as it required its participants to see the game as a function of its component parts rather than as a complete whole. In the process, the grandeur of baseball Chadwick promoted so fervently was diminished as the game became simply that—a game. Viewed in this light, baseball became little more than an amalgam of hits, walks, saves, and runs rather than a unified entity that spoke to morality and American values.

As fantasy baseball developed, participants inevitably yearned for a greater breakdown of the game—more statistics, different statistics—that would help them measure performance of "their" players. They demanded new ways of looking at the game that responded to how they saw it; they were not content to rely on the pro forma statistics that had been handed down to them for generations by Elias and their local sportswriters. All of this was in furtherance of their attempt to make the game something they considered to be their own. As Okrent explained to his fellow Rotisserie colleagues: "It wasn't enough to watch baseball, or to study it in the box scores and leaders list. We all [wish] in some way to possess it, to control it."[111] By the turn of the twenty-first century, fantasy baseball was big business. In 2006 there were, by one estimate, sixteen million fantasy baseball players and the economic impact of the hobby had exceeded $1 billion.[112]

The alliance between fantasy baseball and Bill James was a natural one. Consistent with James's interest, fantasy baseball was both a search for new ways of understanding the game and a decoupling of the game from the constraints imposed by MLB and its attendant media. Freed from the romantic allegiances to a particular team, fantasy baseball likewise offered its participants an opportunity to step back and examine the game from a less emotional place. From this, a new breed of fan emerged; one similar to James in that he or she was very much a baseball fan but much less a fan of any one team. These new-age fans would be much less susceptible to the sway of the baseball creed in that they were interested in the game for other, more pragmatic, reasons. It did not take long for these new fans to call on James for his assistance in helping them manage their teams. Because the number of his Lawrence, Kansas, office was listed, he received calls at all hours of the day and night from fantasy players asking whether to pick up this player or cut that one.[113] Eventually he published his Player Ratings Books designed specifically for fantasy players in the mid '90s.[114]

Inevitably, MLB sensed the loss of control that fantasy baseball represented and, just as it fought James, engaged it as well. The ensuing legal battle was one that cut to the essence of the game and required the courts to determine the most basic question of all (and one that James himself posed over a decade earlier): who, if anyone, owns the statistics that emanate from the game? The litigants were Major League Baseball Advanced Media (MLB AM), an entity created by MLB to control the Internet and interactive media aspect of MLB, and C.B.C. Distributing and Marketing, Inc., a corporation that provided a variety of products, including the statistics, that facilitated fantasy baseball games over the Internet.[115] MLB AM signed a five-year $50 million deal with the Players Association in 2005 to acquire what it believed to be the exclusive rights to players' names and statistics for use in fantasy baseball as well as other forms of online content.[116] To protect what it considered its property right, MLB AM charged a licensing fee to online companies involved in fantasy baseball and issued cease and desist letters to those companies that refused to pay up. C.B.C. balked at the fee, contending that, because the statistics were within the public domain—available to anyone who picked up a newspaper or purchased one of James's books—it had a First Amendment right to use the statistics.[117] MLB AM disagreed, stating that it had purchased exclusive rights to them—even the ones created by James and the sabermetricians that MLB otherwise spent so much time disparaging—and was entitled to enforce those rights.[118]

Although significant dollars were at stake in the ensuing litigation, a more fundamental question was involved, namely, the one that asked who controlled the story of baseball: was it in the public domain, as C.B.C. contended, or was it within the exclusive control of MLB, who could then distribute or withhold the necessary facts that supported the story as it pleased in an effort to create and mold the story pursuant to its wishes? At both the trial and appellate level, the courts held in favor of C.B.C. and endorsed its public domain argument, holding that irrespective of whether the players themselves had a right of publicity that attached to their statistics (the district court held that they did not, the Eighth Circuit on appeal held that they did), this was trumped by the First Amendment.[119] In reaching its decision, the Eighth Circuit in effect endorsed the argument made by James more than a decade earlier in his battle against Elias, holding that because baseball is the national pastime, the "recitation and discussion of factual data concerning the athletic performance of [players on Major League Baseball's Web site] command a substantial public interest, and therefore, is a form of expression due substantial constitutional protection."[120] Just as James contended, it was baseball's status that heightened the public interest in the players' names and statistics and rendered them unobtainable as a private property right.

The rulings, by both the district court and the Eighth Circuit, were likewise affirmations of the courts' continuing deference to the sovereign nation of baseball, albeit this time with a twist. Once again, the courts justified the suspension of the normal rules of law that would otherwise have dictated the outcome and held that baseball's elevated status necessitated a different result, in the interest of protecting this national asset.

Here, it was the players' rights of publicity that were pushed aside in the courts' zeal to protect the game above all else—the district court held that the players did not have such rights here, while the Eighth Circuit went further by holding that even though they did, this was ultimately irrelevant. However this time, the courts' holdings in favor of "baseball" led them to rule *against* MLB rather than for it. For decades, as courts and legislatures bent over backward in deference to the game, there was an implicit assumption that a ruling for MLB was necessarily a ruling for baseball—after so many years of MLB holding itself out as the natural guardian of the game, MLB and the concept of "baseball" as the national pastime had become inexorably intertwined. Now, however, perhaps owing to the changes in the nature of team ownership as a result of the corporate takeover from the '60s going forward, along with many fans' redefinition of the game as a consequence of the 1994 work stoppage, combined with continuing national animosity toward the Players Association as fueled by the positive thinking movement, baseball and MLB were no longer synonymous. For the first time, the judiciary recognized that the sovereign nation of baseball truly was sovereign, not even answerable to MLB itself. It would have been unfathomable just a couple of decades earlier to even consider that a court would issue a ruling protecting baseball that did not also rule in favor of the self-designated custodian of the game. Now, after the C.B.C. ruling, baseball and MLB were distinct entities at last.

Beyond the specifics of the decisions, the C.B.C. litigation illustrated just how much MLB's grip on the game had loosened. In so many ways, it could no longer control the story of baseball. The emergence of Internet blogs would further drive this point home. However, never content to surrender, MLB and its attendant media have demonstrated that they are not completely without bullets in this battle.

BLOGS—THE FINAL FRONTIER

Not surprisingly, blogs have been derided by the traditional media from the outset as self-indulgent and worthless, diverting readers from real news to the news they prefer to read. One *New York Times* columnist termed the democratization of news via the Internet as a search for "The Daily Me" where readers troll the Web for "information that confirms our prejudices."[121] "When we go online, each of us is our own editor," he wrote, "our own gatekeeper. We select the kind of news and opinions we care most about." From this perspective, the increase in choices offered by the Internet leads, ironically, to a homogenization of the news, where rather than a "clash of opinions," what emerges is an "echo chamber" where our own perspectives are merely reflected back at us. Blogs do not add to the national conversation, the critique goes, they mute it.

This sort of criticism is not unique to Internet blogs, however. In fact, it is a tradition that stretches back decades, if not longer, and has been directed toward all forms of media at one time or another, depending on what constituted the established media and who the perceived interlopers were. Baseball, being particularly conservative by nature, has its own tradition in this regard. It and its attendant media have always voiced their suspicion of new entries in the field, perceiving threat whenever something or someone new arrived on the scene, concerned as they were over these challenges to their ability to control the story of the game. Before Chadwick convinced them otherwise, many clubs were wary of the ability of sportswriters to accurately convey the sense of the game being played on the field. When radio came onto the scene, the sportswriters, who by then were accepted and established, groused that broadcasters were simply unable to translate the game audibly as effectively as they were via the printed word. "You might as well," observed one of Roth's characters in *The Great American Novel,* "put an announcer up in the woods in October and have him do a 'live' broadcast of the fall, as describe a game on the radio. 'Well, now, folks, the maples are turning red, and there goes a birch getting yellow,' and so on. Can you imagine nature-lovers sitting all huddled around a dial, following that? No, all radio would do would be to reduce the game to what the gamblers cared about: who scored, how much, and when." His rant concluded: "it might as well be one team of fleas playing another team of fleas, for all such a broadcast had to do with the poetry of the great game itself."[122] The arrival of video, via film and later, television, brought similar complaints. The *Sporting News* portended a dark future for the game due to the arrival of the nascent media: "When Ruth hits a homer . . . a film will catch him in the act, wireless will carry it a thousand miles broadcast and a family sitting in the darkened living room at home will see the scene reproduced simultaneously on the wall. Then what will become of baseball?"[123]

Baseball blogs are different from anything that has come before them in one crucial respect, however: they are the first journalistic medium that is potentially completely outside the control of MLB and the traditional media; they are answerable to no one and pose a unique threat to the game's storytellers. Ever since James made the point through his *Abstracts* that one need not be an insider to understand the game, such a challenge was inevitable. Through the Internet, technology had finally caught up with James's philosophy. Now, anyone with a computer and an Internet connection could practice "outside baseball" and be just as informed and informative as the insiders. In fact, without the pressures and constraints of the traditional media, they could be even more so.

Although not a blogger himself, many of James's *Abstract* articles portended the new journalistic form in tone as well as content. Even after James found a publisher for his *Abstract,* he refused to be edited; he preferred his occasional use of foul language, misspellings, and internal inconsistencies to stay in his text.[124] He remained steadfastly unencumbered, refusing to adhere to preordained publishing standards simply because they had been preordained. As for his occasional potshots toward players and managers, he spent little if any time concerning himself over the possible repercussions because his work did not depend on access. If the recipient of one of his jabs took offense, there was not much in the way of retribution they could do about it. James could, for example, deride Tigers manager Sparky Anderson for his "self-consciously asinine theories about baseball" without fear.[125] His writing was often crude and self-reverential but insightful and thoroughly entertaining. In 1990, he railed against a group of sportswriters, along with Siwoff of Elias, who complained about the *Baseball Encyclopedia*'s decision to fix known errors in old statistics, in an essay whose tone presaged the loose, conversational, and pointedly direct style of many modern blogs: "Among the three of you, I'll bet I could write everything you know about the subject on one piece of paper, and have room left for [my daughter] to cut out a couple of paper dolls and Cher to make a dress for next year's Academy Awards."[126] There was no room for such brashness in the traditional media; one needed to have the stature of James or, later, the freedom of the Internet to express such sentiments.

Some of what was to come with blogs first expressed itself, in more muted tones, in sports talk radio. Like James and the blogs it foreshadowed, sports talk radio thrived largely because it did not depend on access for survival. Despite the constraints placed upon it as, essentially, a traditional media outlet, this freedom allowed it to become brash and opinionated, much to the consternation of both MLB and the sportswriters. In fact, a common theme of many sports talk show hosts was the close relationship between the writers and the players they covered and how this necessarily resulted in a watered-down, censored product. Remarked a Chicago radio host: "if you're a comic and you're making fun of the president or a senator, do you go spend time with the president or the senator?"[127] To the charge levied by many clubs that radio hosts were uninformed simply because they oftentimes chose not to visit the locker rooms, one host fired back, highlighting the dynamics of the locker room as a disincentive for critical analysis: "That's [the locker room] their territory. Of course they want people in their clubhouse, with their public relations people there . . . they're in a position of power if they want us to stand in front of their locker when they've got PR people, media relations people, policing the questions. I don't want to hear that's a sacrosanct even playing field in the locker room."[128] After acknowledging that some of his hosts did not visit the locker rooms regularly, a Philadelphia talk radio general manager highlighted the questionable logic behind an implied assumption that has developed between the players and the media that cover them: "The responsibility of the sports radio station is to voice the opinions of the fans. Our responsibility is to the fan, not the player."[129] Taking access out of the equation made this possible.

In its pure form, the modern blog, untethered from any form of censorship or restraint, is even more liberated than talk radio. In fact, one of the most widely read sports blogs, *Deadspin,* touts this independence as its motto, turning the assumptions inherent within traditional journalism on their head: "Sports news without access, favor or discretion."[130] The *New York Times* would take issue with the merits of at least two of these boasts. But this was precisely the point; *Deadspin,* and other blogs, were proudly antiestablishment. As one *Deadspin* columnist noted, "The inherent catch-22 of a sportswriter's job lies in access. You can't brutally criticize athletes and expect them to give you any access. But, if you go the other way and soften your treatment of athletes in order to maintain access, then you end up looking like a jocksniffer."[131] To bloggers such as this one, traditional journalists, not unlike those who framed the polar images of Williams and DiMaggio, then use access as a sword: "They're effusive in their praise for the handful of guys that give them decent quotes. They save their most gleeful invective for the handful that don't."[132] In the process, slanted, self-interested journalism becomes passed off to the public as critical analysis. "If you take access out of the equation, then favor and discretion never had to come into play. No favoritism. No grudges."[133]

Echoing the predominant theme of sports talk radio, many bloggers contended that their responsibility was to the fans, not the players or the teams. Because they saw the game as fans did—in the stands, on television—they were able to provide content that resonated more deeply with readers than the "privileged sportswriters" who were pampered by teams, provided unusual access in exchange for glowing, effusive articles or stories, and who had become so removed from the game as their readers experienced it as to become virtually irrelevant to them.[134] When the traditional media attempted to fight back, they often stumbled over themselves, inadvertently driving home the points raised by bloggers better than the bloggers could themselves. One particularly uncomfortable moment occurred on HBO in 2008 when, in a segment devoted to the rise of bloggers, sportscaster Bob Costas denigrated them instead by remarking that their opinions were the functional equivalent of what "a cabdriver" thinks about sports.[135] Very quickly the lure of sports blogs was established: despite protestations from established media types like Costas, or perhaps because of them, by 2008 *Deadspin* was drawing an average of six to eight million monthly visitors.[136]

In many ways, by the turn of the twenty-first century, the Internet had become a true alternative media: millions of home computers linked together creating a myriad of social networks outside the traditional power base of the established media. Subject only to the cost of purchasing or using a computer and paying for an Internet connection, anybody was free to say anything they chose, virtually without constraint. In the age of the Internet, the traditional media quickly became less pervasive: newspaper subscriptions declined and many papers struggled as more and more people chose to access their news electronically; television ratings dipped as more, edgier, and better content was found online, through viewer-created and -supported sites such as YouTube and others. After attending an interactive conference in March 2009, a *New York Times* reporter noted that, "the people formerly known as the audience were too busy making content to consume much of it, unless it came from their friends. The medium is not the message; the messages are the media."[137] The traditional definition of "media" was no longer clear; anyone could now become a member regardless of whether they were "right-minded" or otherwise.

The all-encompassing monolith that was the traditional media was clearly losing its grip. Outside the world of baseball, this was becoming obvious: in 2004, presidential candidate Howard Dean financed his campaign largely through donations and support generated by the Internet.[138] Although written off as irrelevant by many within the mainstream media, Dean managed to make himself a viable candidate anyway. Later, he rebuilt the Democratic Party largely through the Internet, remarking that a successful campaign at the highest level could now be built from the ground up. Television ads, once the hallmark of any major campaign, were far less relevant than ever before.[139] In 2008, Barack Obama made significant use of the Internet in his presidential campaign, reaching millions of potential voters who otherwise would have remained on the sidelines had he relied on the traditional media alone to get his message across. On a smaller scale, the power of the Internet was demonstrated in myriad ways. In 2008, a Dartmouth College student was able to win election as county treasurer chiefly through the purchase of a $51 ad taken out on Facebook, leaving her opponent, the sixty-eight-year-old incumbent county treasurer, in the dust.[140] The ability of the traditional media to control the story, to influence the narrative, has never been more in doubt than it is right now.

Regardless, it is hardly powerless. Through the seepage of corporate influence, beneath their rogue veneer, many blogs are starting to look less antiestablishment and more like the traditional media they so fervently criticize. By enticing bloggers with the forbidden fruit—access—the traditional media and corporate world have slowly but surely begun to co-opt this most recent form of alternative media, threatening to transform it into something perhaps different in form from what came before, but no different in content. This is as true in the world of baseball blogs as it is in almost every other corner of the Internet. For just as it had in the fantasy baseball arena, MLB here too has attempted to assert its dominance in its never-ending quest to control the flow of information emanating from the game and, hence, the resulting stories.

Once they finally recognized the challenge blogs represented, MLB and the clubs attempted to rein in this seemingly unstructured journalistic form by approaching the most popular, and therefore the most threatening, bloggers and offering them the competitive advantages of money along with access to players and club personnel (through revenue sharing arrangements and/or salaries, thereby rendering them de facto club employees complete with the perks of locker room and front office access).[141] The Mets and Rangers were two early franchises that recognized the value of co-opting their critics in this manner, while other clubs have attempted to fight the blogosphere by joining in on their own.[142] These "team blogs," however, bear little resemblance to their independent cousins because of their ties to the teams they purport to cover. As a result, many of the constraints present in traditional media formats have returned as these sponsored bloggers are no doubt "right-minded," organization-first individuals who have either internalized the unspoken boundaries of "acceptable" reporting or are destined to be replaced by others who have. A blogger for Reds.com admitted that he was not permitted to use the word "demotion" in his discussion of the team's front office shakeup.[143] Other team-sponsored bloggers reported pressure to remain positive in their postings and to refrain from critical analysis.[144] One MLB.com blogger was told that it was everyone's job to "celebrate baseball," a dictate that influenced the content and nature of the site's postings.[145] These corporate bloggers had access, but at the price of independence.

Even the seemingly independent blogs are not immune to creeping corporate influence. In late 2008, SportsBlog Nation, a network of 274 fan-run sports blogs and growing,[146] was infused with serious capital from venture capitalists with the goal of "connect[ing] fans of teams from all over the country."[147] By offering an administrative infrastructure and technical expertise, SportsBlog Nation lured a multitude of fan bloggers who welcomed the opportunity to focus solely on content while at the same time reaching larger audiences than they could have hoped to attract on their own. However, not all bloggers were welcomed; prospective members were required to achieve and maintain certain "standards" in order to be included. To pay for all this (the venture capitalists' layout reportedly ran into the "mid-seven figures"), SportsBlog Nation turned to advertisers to foot the bill: its chief executive crowed that "[w]e're increasingly a very attractive place to advertise," noting that he hoped to lure traditional sponsors such as car dealerships and beer companies into the fold.[148] Among the venture's investors are the chairman of the FCC and the owner of the NHL's Washington Capitals, who remarked to member bloggers that he hoped he could find enough advertisers to support it "because all of you deserve to be rewarded for what you're doing."[149] Whether bloggers critical of the Capitals or with opinions that scare off valued advertisers would be dismissed from SportsBlog Nation is an open question. Regardless, corporate intervention, whether in the form of MLB or venture capitalists, undoubtedly threatens the impartiality and independence of the blogosphere. If corporate models such as these become the norm, then the democratizing medium of the Internet will be no more; cheaper, more easily accessible corporate blogs will soon dominate the landscape while their independent competitors wither in the competition and ultimately die in obscurity. What will remain will be a blogosphere dominated by insiders rather than outsiders, with the entry barriers no different than those that exist within the traditional media.

The tide has seemingly already begun to turn. Apart from the enticements offered to sports bloggers, successful bloggers of all stripes are drawing the attention of corporate America, which is focusing on those it considers "influencers" and offering them a bevy of free merchandise and services with the expectation of favorable, promotional commentary in return.[150] Products, trips, locker room passes—all of this "access" in one form or another—have been increasingly finding their way to the most powerful bloggers with the promise, either spoken or unspoken, of more to come if their subsequent blog postings meet corporate expectations. The growing prevalence of these "sponsored conversations" (a term generally preferred over "kickbacks" by those engaging in the practice) finally drew the ire of the Federal Trade Commission, which ruled that, as of December 1, 2009, bloggers engaging in such activities were required to disclose these ties in their postings.[151] Beyond the immediate impact of this ruling, the FTC's action was significant in that it demonstrated that, perhaps inevitably, the government was starting to view the Internet as a media outlet no different than the traditional media that preceded it. A professor at New York University stressed this overarching meaning of the ruling: "It crushes the idea that the Internet is separate from the kinds of concerns that have been attached to previous media."[152] In a relatively short time, the Internet has grown up. In the process, dissenting voices are beginning to fade into the background—those who refuse to be co-opted and who suffer from reduced exposure and higher relative costs of production as their acquiescent competitors zoom past them courtesy of SportsBlog Nation and other powerful corporate benefactors.

Eventually, it may very well be the coterie of privileged bloggers who draw the ire of the next media incarnation. Perhaps it will be they who are called out for their biased reporting and who are denigrated for praying at the altar of access at the cost of independence. They, like the sportswriters before them, will be challenged for their willingness to peddle their influence for gold, choosing to "play ball" with their subjects rather than critically analyze them.[153] One day, perhaps very soon, it may very well be the blogosphere that will serve as guardians of the culturally affirming, patriotic stories of baseball—armed to the teeth and willing to destroy anyone who dares Americans to frame the game through an alternative lens.

NOTES

PROLOGUE

1. Jane B. Baron, "Resistance to Stories," 67 *Southern California Law Review*, 255, 261–62 (1994). See also Daniel A. Farber and Suzanna Sherry, "Telling Stories Out of School: An Essay on Legal Narratives," 45 *Stanford Law Review*, 807, 822–23 (1993).
2. See Steven D. Jamar, "Aristotle Teaches Persuasion: The Psychic Connection," 8 *Scribes Journal of Legal Writing*, 61, 62 (2001–2002).
3. See Stephen Johansen, "This Is Not the Whole Truth: The Ethics of Telling Stories to Clients," 38 *Arizona State Law Journal*, 961, 981–82 (2006), for a discussion of the value and impact of fictional stories.
4. See Jamar, "Aristotle Teaches Persuasion," 61–62.
5. See Johansen, "This Is Not the Whole Truth," 981–82.
6. See Richard Delgado, "On Telling Stories in School: A Reply to Farber and Sherry," 46 *Vanderbilt Law Review*, 665, 666–67 (1993).
7. Ibid.
8. Ibid., 674.
9. Ibid., 666–67, 674.
10. Ibid., 667. ("Unless the storyteller is exceptionally ingenious, the scope for change through remonstrance, argument, and other verbal means is much more limited than we like to think.") Richard Delgado and Jean Stefancic coined the term "emphatic fallacy" to describe the erroneous belief that we can somehow overcome our desire to screen and interpret new stories—the counter-stories—through the medium of the old, accepted stories. Through this method of interpretation, we naturally reject those counter-stories that are radical departures from what we previously believed to be true. See Richard Delgado and Jean Stefancic, "Images of the Outsider in American Law and Culture: Can Free Expression Remedy Systemic Social Ills?" 77 *Cornell Law Review*, 1258, 1261, 1278–79 (1992).

CHAPTER 1. A GAME OF THEIR OWN

1. Jules Tygiel, *Past Time: Baseball As History* (New York: Oxford University Press, 2000, 2001), 6.
2. Ibid., 3–4.
3. Benjamin G. Rader, *Baseball: A History* (Urbana: University of Illinois Press, 2002), 1.
4. Jason Kaufman and Orlando Patterson, "Cross-National Cultural Diffusion: The Global Spread of Cricket," *American Sociological Review* 70 (February 2005): 82, 92.
5. Ibid.
6. Ibid.
7. Ibid., 85.
8. Steven A. Riess, *Touching Base: Professional Baseball and American Culture in the Progressive Era* (Urbana: University of Illinois Press, 1999), 7–32.
9. Ibid., 22.
10. Felipe Fernandez-Armesto, *Amerigo: The Man Who Gave His Name to America* (New York: Random House, 2007, 2008).
11. Ibid., 110.
12. Ibid., 194–95.
13. Harold Seymour, *Baseball: The Early Years* (New York: Oxford University Press, 1960, 1989), 15.
14. E. Digby Baltzell, *The Protestant Establishment: Aristocracy and Caste in America* (New York: Vintage Books, 1964, 1966), 112–13.
15. George B. Kirsch, *Baseball and Cricket: The Creation of American Team Sports, 1838–72* (Urbana: University of Illinois Press, 1989, 2007), 97–98.
16. Baltzell, *Protestant Establishment,*136. The discussion of the distinctions between the American and British clubs discussed herein draws primarily from Baltzell's study. See also pp. 124, 135–36.
17. Kaufman and Patterson, *Global Spread of Cricket,* 99.
18. Ibid., 93.
19. Ibid., 98–99, 105.
20. Ibid., 97.
21. This would continue throughout the amateur era of baseball. In fact, the game's first professional baseball player, Jim Creighton, played cricket as well in 1861 and 1862, as did some of his Brooklyn Excelsior teammates. John Thorn, *Baseball in the Garden of Eden: The Secret History of the Early Game* (New York: Simon and Schuster, 2011), 124.
22. In his study of nineteenth-century baseball and cricket, Kirsch notes that in New York, where baseball took early root, "most of the first baseball players were skilled craftsmen, clerks, petty proprietors, or managers." He further notes that "very few unskilled or semi-skilled men played baseball

in New York or Brooklyn before the Civil War . . ." Rather, the game was favored primarily by white-collar workers. Kirsch, *Baseball and Cricket*, 130.

23. Thorn, *Baseball in the Garden*, 26, 38–39. Indeed, William Rufus Wheaton appears to have taken on this task for the Gotham Club, also of New York, in 1838. As Thorn notes, the Knickerbockers were more likely "consolidators rather than innovators" as, rather than create new rules for baseball, they most likely jotted down the rules as they knew them to be at the time.

24. Seymour, *Baseball: The Early Years*, 16.

25. Melven L. Adelman, *A Sporting Time: New York City and the Rise of Modern Athletics, 1820–70* (Urbana: University of Illinois Press, 1986), 122–23.

26. Seymour, *Baseball: The Early Years*, 23.

27. Thorn, *Baseball in the Garden*, 48, 81.

28. Ibid., 111.

29. Ibid., 112.

30. Ibid., 48.

31. Peter Morris, *But Didn't We Have Fun?: An Informal History of Baseball's Pioneer Era, 1843–1870* (Chicago: Ivan R. Dee, 2008), 49–50.

32. Ibid.

33. Riess, *Touching Base*, 32.

34. Ibid., 31–38.

35. Kirsch, *Baseball and Cricket*, 130.

36. Riess, *Touching Base*, 31–38.

37. Ibid., 38.

38. See Kirsch, *Baseball and Cricket*, 155–56. Kirsch notes that, as the nineteenth century progressed, there were ever more blue-collar baseball clubs and even "mixed" clubs with members of varying economic backgrounds. Prior to the Civil War, however, there were far fewer blue-collar players. Between 1850 and '55, 87 percent of New York's baseball players were white-collar workers. By the time of the war era, the percentage of white-collar ballplayers hailing from New York and Brooklyn had dropped to 64 percent. In sum, semiskilled and unskilled workers constituted only a small percentage of baseball players in the antebellum period. Ibid., 130.

39. John Shiffert, *Base Ball in Philadelphia: A History of the Early Game, 1831–1900* (Jefferson, N.C.: McFarland, 2006), 24.

40. *Makers of Philadelphia: An Historical Work Giving Portraits and Sketches of the Most Eminent Citizens of Philadelphia From the Time of William Penn to the Present Day,* ed. Charles Morris (Philadelphia: L.R. Hamersly, 1894), 122 (Profile of Col. Thomas Fitzgerald). Available at *https://secureapps.libraries .psu.edu/digitalbookshelf/bookindex.cfm?oclc=29893541.*

41. Shiffert, *Base Ball in Philadelphia,* 41.

42. Morris, *But Didn't We Have Fun?*, 177–81.

43. Ibid.

44. Ibid., 178.

45. Shiffert, *Base Ball in Philadelphia*, 62.

46. Morris, *But Didn't We Have Fun?*, 177–81.

47. Ibid.

48. Seymour, *Baseball: The Early Years*, 60.

49. Riess, *Touching Base*, 158.

50. Ibid.

51. See Thorn, *Baseball in the Garden*, 85–89.

52. Rader, *Baseball: A History*, 47–48.

53. Seymour, *Baseball: The Early Years*, 80.

54. Mitchell Nathanson, "Gatekeepers of Americana: Ownership's Never-Ending Quest for Control of the Baseball Creed," 15 *NINE: A Journal of Baseball History and Culture*, 68, 71 (Fall 2006).

55. Ibid.

56. Rader, *Baseball: A History*, 49.

57. Ibid., 50.

58. Seymour, *Baseball: The Early Years*, 81.

59. Thorn, *Baseball in the Garden*, 104.

60. "Baseball at Delmonico's," *New York Times*, April 9, 1889, 5.

61. Rader, *Baseball: A History*, 33; Morris, *But Didn't We Have Fun?*, 147–48.

62. Tygiel, *Past Time*, 48.

63. Nathanson, "Gatekeepers of Americana," 74.

64. Ibid.

65. Ibid.

66. Morris, *But Didn't We Have Fun?*, 147–48.

67. Nathanson, "Gatekeepers of Americana," 74.

68. Rader, *Baseball: A History*, 44.

69. Richard Hofstadter, *The Age of Reform* (New York: Vintage Books, 1955), 135–36.

70. Hofstadter refers to these values as the "agrarian myth" and notes the contrast in how the WASP elites identified themselves and their vanishing world with the rapidly growing cities and the men who had overtaken them in both economic and financial status. Hofstadter, *Age of Reform*, 8–46.

71. Robert H. Wiebe, *The Search for Order, 1877–1920* (New York: Hill and Wang, 1967), 45–47. See also Richard Weiss, *The American Success Myth: From Horatio Alger to Norman Vincent Peale* (Urbana: University of Illinois Press, 1988), 100. Weiss notes that despite their name recognition, the business magnates of the Gilded Age "were not the heroes of the popularizers of the mobility ideology." Instead, those who preached tales of American success

during this time idealized the small businessman who valued principles and virtue rather than naked wealth and power.

72. Riess, *Touching Base*, 138–39.

73. Wiebe, *Search for Order*, 56–57.

74. Seymour, *Baseball: The Early Years*, 91.

75. Ibid.; Riess, *Touching Base*, 33.

76. Kirsch, *Baseball and Cricket*, 195–96.

77. Riess, *Touching Base*. Unless otherwise noted, the National League's owners' courtship of the well-heeled draws primarily from this text. See also pp. 37, 51–52.

78. Rader, *Baseball: A History*, 55.

79. See Kirsch, *Baseball and Cricket*, 195–96.

80. Riess, *Touching Base*, 135.

81. Seymour, *Baseball: The Early Years*, 150.

82. Ibid., 144, 150.

83. Nathanson, "Gatekeepers of Americana," 72.

84. Riess, *Touching Base*, 136.

85. Baltzell, *Protestant Establishment*, 58, 138. See also pp. 27–32, 74–75, 98–105, 113–15, 157–75 on his discussion of WASP society, social Darwinism, and the emergence of the new social science discussed herein.

86. Hofstadter, *Age of Reform*, 137.

87. Robert C. Bannister, *Social Darwinism: Science and Myth in Anglo-American Social Thought* (Philadelphia: Temple University Press, 1979), 35. According to Bannister, the term "social Darwinism" has been historically misunderstood, as has much else surrounding mid- to late-nineteenth-century social thought. Ibid., 6–7. Technically, Spencer was not a "social Darwinist," although he expressed many views, some contradictory throughout his lifetime, on social policy. He did spawn many followers who misinterpreted his beliefs, thus giving rise to various forms of "reform Darwinism" that in many ways were likewise inconsistent with the beliefs and teachings of Charles Darwin himself but were nevertheless used to justify the stratification of society and to support various exclusionary and discriminatory practices.

88. For a more complete analysis of the debate between various theories of social Darwinism, see for example, Bannister, *Social Darwinism* and Richard Hofstadter, *Social Darwinism in American Thought* (New York, Beacon Press, 1992). Bannister and Hofstadter differ on the definition of the term, as well as on who wore the moniker. A detailed analysis of their disagreement is beyond the scope of this chapter.

89. See Baltzell, *Protestant Establishment*. Interestingly, Sumner diverged from Spencer in many ways, most fundamentally with regard to Spencer's

Enlightenment belief in universal evolution. Bannister, *Social Darwinism*, 99. In addition, although Sumner was a proponent of individualism and laissez faire, he recognized the necessity of law to protect competition. In this way, he was very much a progressive in spite of his naturalism. Ibid., 100.

90. Wiebe, *Search for Order*, 135. Spencer once described Carnegie as one of his two best American friends. Despite this, Carnegie, as did many others, badly misinterpreted much of Spencer's work. As historian Joseph Wall once wrote, "Carnegie waded bodily into the writings of Herbert Spencer, and with his feet barely wet . . . imagined himself to be swimming in the strong current of a new faith." Joseph Wall, *Andrew Carnegie* (New York: Oxford University Press, 1970), 365.

91. Baltzell, *Protestant Establishment*, 98.

92. Bannister, *Social Darwinism*, 189–90, 196, 198–99.

93. If anything, Galton was convinced that Darwin (who in any event, never intended his theory of "natural selection" to be the final word with regard to human social interactions and policy, Bannister, *Social Darwinism*, 31) was wrong, as discussed herein. Ibid., 168.

94. Baltzell, *Protestant Establishment*, 105.

95. Hofstadter, *Age of Reform*, 138.

96. Baltzell, *Protestant Establishment*, 115.

97. See Baltzell, *Protestant Establishment*, 157, 58; Wiebe, *Search for Order*, 136.

98. Baltzell, *Protestant Establishment*, 167.

99. Ibid., 169.

100. Ibid., 171–73.

101. Riess, *Touching Base*, 29.

102. Rader, *Baseball: A History*, 93.

103. Jeffrey Powers-Beck, *The American Indian Integration of Baseball* (Lincoln: University of Nebraska Press, 2004), 7.

104. Ibid., 38–39.

105. Ibid., 34–35.

106. Ibid., 38–39.

107. Baltzell, *Protestant Establishment*, 274–75; Bannister, *Social Darwinism*, 178–79.

108. Rader, *Baseball: A History*, 36; See also Tygiel, *Past Time*, 47–48.

109. Weiss, *American Success Myth*, 52–60.

110. Although, given the WASP values embraced through the stories as well as their foundation within the agrarian myth, Alger's tales were undoubtedly written for a nativist audience, his appeal broadened significantly after his death. By World War I, aggregate sales of his books had exceeded sixteen million copies. Frank L. Mott, *Golden Multitudes: The Story of Best Sellers in the United States* (New York: Macmillan, 1947), 158–59.

111. Kaufman and Patterson, *Global Spread of Cricket*, 105.

CHAPTER 2. THE SOVEREIGN NATION OF BASEBALL

1. There exists a fundamental difference between the applicability of the law to MLB and to its players. Players have always been subject to the law when acting outside the cocoon of MLB. Once ensconced within it, however, the cloak of immunity typically covers them as well—to the extent that such immunity inures to the benefit of MLB. Indeed, although Pete Rose (whose tribulations with Commissioner Giamatti are discussed herein) served time in jail in 1990, it was for tax evasion (outside the cocoon of MLB, from which, by that point, he had been banned) and for nothing having to do with the allegations that he bet on baseball. The gambling aspect of his tale was handled in-house, with the exception of Rose's attempts (likewise discussed herein) to have Giamatti recused from presiding over his case. See Jill Lieber and Craig Neff, "The Case Against Pete Rose," *Sports Illustrated*, July 3, 1989; Lonnie Wheeler, "Pete Rose Tied to Tax-Evasion Plan," *New York Times*, August 31, 1989. Within the same vein, the 2007 indictment of Barry Bonds, likewise discussed herein, was a result of his alleged activities in connection with BALCO—a San Francisco–area laboratory not affiliated with MLB and which was alleged to have supplied and injected him with illegal steroids. Initially, the federal BALCO investigation targeted athletes not affiliated with MLB (primarily track and field athletes) and Bonds's name was drawn into the investigation after the fact, when it became apparent that he too was a client. See Michael S. Schmidt, "Drug Test Results from 2003 Could Soon Be In Evidence," *New York Times*, May 18, 2008, Sports Sunday, 1 (reporting that the federal government planned to question 104 MLB players who tested positive for performance-enhancing drugs in 2003). The results were intended to be anonymous but, owing to the separate BALCO investigation, the names of some of the players became known to the federal government, which was initially only seeking information pertaining to ten players who were suspected to have perjured themselves before the BALCO grand jury. In the course of its investigation into BALCO's files, the names of all 104 players who tested positive became known. Without the BALCO investigation, it is likely that the anonymity sought by MLB and the Players Association with regard to testing would have been honored by the government. The 2010 indictment of Roger Clemens provides yet another example. There, despite the national conversation generated by the 2007 release of the Mitchell Report and its findings of player activities undertaken in violation of federal law (discussed herein), Congress was content to allow MLB to handle the situation internally. It was only when Clemens insisted upon testifying before a House committee in February 2008, against the advice of congressional leaders who urged him to reconsider, that federal law,

reluctantly, intervened. If he had never testified, it is likely that he never would have experienced the wrath of the law despite his illegal activities, as some lawmakers later stated that they were "inclined to give Clemens the benefit of the doubt." See Katie Thomas, "Clemens, Once Under Oath, Is Now Under Indictment," *New York Times*, August 20, 2010, B10. The dichotomy of treatment by courts and legislatures of players and MLB is a relevant inquiry but one that is outside the scope of this chapter.

2. Of course, baseball and the law have been intertwined in numerous instances throughout the years. See Ross. E. Davies, "The Sport of Courts," 38 *Baseball Research Journal* 59 (Fall 2009). Litigation has ensued over the ownership of home run balls, torts committed within the confines of stadiums, grievances among players and between players and fans, and so forth. In fact, there are literally thousands of cases that touch on baseball players or organizations in one facet or another. This chapter is concerned, however, with those instances where the legal system was asked to confront the business of baseball itself; that is, how the game was to be run and, as such, presented to the public. In those instances, which have been considerably far fewer in number, the legal system has chosen to defer more often than not.

3. Daniel A. Nathan, *Saying It's So: A Cultural History of the Black Sox Scandal* (Urbana: University of Illinois Press, 2005), 15.

4. See generally, Nathanson, "Gatekeepers of Americana."

5. Lowell L. Blaisdell, "The Cobb-Speaker Scandal," 13 *NINE: A Journal of Baseball History and Culture*, 54 (2004).

6. Christopher H. Evans, "The Kingdom of Baseball in America: The Chronicle of an American Theology," in *Faith of 50 Million: Baseball, Religion and American Culture*, ed. Christopher H. Evans and William R. Herzog II (Louisville, Ky.: Westminster John Knox Press, 2002), 38.

7. Blaisdell, "Cobb-Speaker Scandal," 54.

8. Nathan, *Saying It's So*, 15.

9. Ibid., 17–18.

10. Ibid.

11. Ibid.

12. Ibid. See also, Gene Carney, "Uncovering the Fix of the 1919 World Series: The Role of Hugh Fullerton," 13 *NINE: A Journal of Baseball History and Culture*, 39, 42–43 (2004).

13. Nathan, *Saying It's So*, 18.

14. David Q. Voigt, *American Baseball: From the Commissioners to Continental Expansion* (University Park: Pennsylvania State University Press, 1983), 126.

15. Michael W. Klein, comment, "Rose Is In Red, Black Sox Are Blue: A Comparison of Rose v. Giamatti and the 1921 Black Sox Trial," 13 *Hastings Communications and Entertainment Law Journal*, 551, 574 (1991).

16. Ibid., 573–74. See also Nathan, *Saying It's So*, 4.
17. Nathan, *Saying It's So*, 4. See also Carney, "Uncovering the Fix," 45.
18. See Klein, "Rose Is In Red," 558. By refusing to rule on the Federal League's case, Landis forced a settlement between the Federal and Major Leagues that, effectively, dissolved the Federal League. One Federal League team, Baltimore, refused to join in the settlement, however, and pursued its antitrust case against MLB. Eventually, the case reached the United States Supreme Court and became the infamous case in which MLB's antitrust exemption was carved out. See *Federal Base Ball Club of Baltimore, Inc. v. National League of Professional Base Ball Clubs*, 259 U.S. 200 (1922).
19. Matthew B. Pachman, comment, "Limits on the Discretionary Powers of Professional Sports Commissioners: A Historical and Legal Analysis of Issues Raised by the Pete Rose Controversy," 76 *Virginia Law Review*, 1409, 1415 (1990).
20. Klein, "Rose Is In Red," 558.
21. Pachman, "Limits on the Discretionary Powers," 1415.
22. William Marshall, *Baseball's Pivotal Era: 1945–1951* (Lexington: University Press of Kentucky, 1999), 4.
23. Jeffrey A. Durney, comment, "Fair or Foul? The Commissioner and Major League Baseball's Disciplinary Process," 41 *Emory Law Journal*, 581, 585 (1992).
24. Rader, *Baseball: A History*, 120.
25. Nathan, *Saying It's So*, 49.
26. Jonathan M. Reinsdorf, "The Powers of the Commissioner in Baseball," 7 *Marquette Sports Law Journal*, 211, 220–21, 246–47 (1996).
27. Ibid.
28. Ibid.
29. Nathan, *Saying It's So*, 7. See also David Q. Voigt, "The Chicago Black Sox and the Myth of Baseball's Single Sin," in *America Through Baseball* (Chicago: Nelson-Hall, 1976), 65, 73.
30. Ibid.
31. Ibid., 221. See also Pachman, "Limits on the Discretionary Powers," 1415.
32. Major League Agreement art. I §§ 2–4 (1921).
33. Ibid., art. VII, § 2.
34. J. G. Taylor Spink, *Judge Landis and Twenty-Five Years of Baseball* (New York: Amereon), 76.
35. Ibid., 84.
36. Nathan, *Saying It's So*, 5. The discussion of Landis's actions in the Black Sox scandal discussed within this paragraph draws from Nathan's text. See also pp. 31, 50, 62, 130.
37. Ibid., 50.
38. Ibid., 130.

39. Lowell L. Blaisdell, "Judge Landis Takes a Different Approach," 15 *NINE: A Journal of Baseball History and Culture*, 32, 32–33 (2006).

40. Ibid., 41; see also Voigt, "Chicago Black Sox," 73.

41. Blaisdell, "Judge Landis," 32–33. The discussion of Judge Landis's tactics during the hearings concerning the alleged 1917 fix discussed herein draws from Blaisdell's article. See also pp. 36, 41–42.

42. Ibid., 61.

43. Blaisdell, "Cobb-Speaker Scandal," 61. The discussion of Judge Landis's tactics during the hearings concerning the alleged 1919 fix discussed herein draws from Blaisdell's article. See also pp. 65–66.

44. Ibid., 66.

45. See Pachman, "Limits on the Discretionary Powers," 1415–16. These crimes ranged from gambling to a suggestion that a pitcher would leave his club to prevent it from winning the pennant.

46. Ibid.

47. Norman L. Rosenberg, "Here Comes the Judge!: The Origins of Baseball's Commissioner System and American Legal Culture," 20 *Journal of Popular Culture* 140 (Spring 1987).

48. 259 U.S. 200 (1922).

49. For a more detailed examination of *Federal Baseball* and its decision within the context of Progressive Era America, see Mitchell Nathanson, "Law and Politics," in *Understanding Baseball: Approaches to the Scholarly Study of America's Game*, ed. Trey Stecker (Jefferson, N.C.: McFarland, 2012), from which the discussion contained herein originated, in somewhat modified and expanded form.

50. Hofstadter, *Age of Reform*, 246.

51. Ibid., 248.

52. Ibid., 249.

53. Letter from Oliver Wendell Holmes to Sir Frederick Pollock (April 30, 1910), in *Holmes–Pollock Letters: The Correspondence of Mr. Justice Holmes and Sir Francis Pollock, 1874–1932*, ed. Mark DeWolfe Howe, 1:163 (quoted in Samuel A. Alito Jr., "The Origin of the Baseball Antitrust Exemption: Federal Baseball Club of Baltimore, Inc. v. National League of Professional Baseball Players," 38, *Baseball Research Journal*, 86, 87 (Fall 2009).

54. Alito, "Baseball Antitrust Exemption," 87.

55. Wiebe, *Search for Order*, 52–53.

56. *National League of Professional Baseball Clubs, et. al. v. Federal Baseball Club of Baltimore, Inc.*, 269 F.681 (D.C. App., 1921), 687.

57. 269 F. at, 685.

58. *Gardella v. Chandler*, 172 F.2d 402 (2d Cir. 1949).

59. G. Richard McKelvey, *Mexican Raiders in the Major Leagues: The Pasquel Brothers vs. Organized Baseball, 1946* (Jefferson, N.C.: McFarland, 2006), 70.

60. For a detailed discussion of the *Gardella* case within the context of the Sherman Antitrust Act, see Brad Snyder, *A Well-Paid Slave: Curt Flood's Fight for Free Agency in Baseball* (New York: Viking Penguin, 2006), 25–27, 101.

61. *Gardella,* 172 F.2d, 409. The subsequent trial over this issue never took place because Gardella subsequently settled his case for $60,000, along with reinstatement in MLB.

62. 346 U.S. 356 (1953) (per curiam).

63. 407 U.S. 258 (1972).

64. Ibid.

65. Ibid., 282.

66. Brad Snyder's *A Well-Paid Slave* contains a lively retelling of the inner workings of the Court in the deliberation and preparation of the Flood case and opinion. See pp. 283–312.

67. 407 U.S. 282–83.

68. 49 F.2d 298 (E.D. Ill. 1931).

69. Ibid., 300–302.

70. Ibid., 299.

71. Ibid., 302.

72. Ibid., 303.

73. Ibid.

74. See Pachman, "Limits on the Discretionary Powers," 1416–17.

75. Ibid.

76. See *Finley v. Kuhn,* 569 F.2d, 527, 530–32 (7th Cir. 1978).

77. Ibid.

78. Ibid., 537.

79. Ibid.

80. Ibid.

81. Ibid., 541.

82. Ibid., 536–37.

83. Ibid.

84. Ibid.

85. *Landis,* 303.

86. *Finley,* 544.

87. Ibid.

88. Ibid.

89. Ibid., 539.

90. 432 F. Supp. 1213 (N.D. Ga., 1977).

91. *Finley v. Kuhn,* No. 76C-2358 (N.D. Ill., September 7, 1976).

92. *Atlanta,* 1218.

93. 373 F. Supp. 946 (W.D. Tex., 1974).

94. Ibid., 949.

95. Ibid. The relevant portion of the ABA's bylaws (Art. IV, § 5) stated: "The Commissioner shall hear and finally decide any dispute to which a player or a coach is a party. In all matters pertaining to the eligibility of players and all disputes arising between clubs relative to title to players' contracts, the Commissioner shall make such investigation, and call such witnesses and demand such papers as he deems necessary, and his decision in such matters shall be final."

96. Ibid., 950.

97. Ibid.

98. Ibid., 951.

99. *Atlanta*, 1219.

100. *Finley*, 544.

101. Nathan, *Saying It's So*, 185.

102. See Klein, "Rose is in Red," 570.

103. Ibid.

104. See Ronald J. Rychlak, "Pete Rose, Bart Giamatti, and the Dowd Report," 68 *Mississippi Law Journal*, 889, 891 (1999).

105. See Klein, "Rose is in Red," 575–76.

106. Ibid.

107. See ibid.

108. See ibid., 576.

109. See ibid., 580–81. See also *Rose v. Giamatti*, no. A8905178, 1989WL 111447 (Ohio Ct. C.P., Hamilton Co., June 26, 1989).

110. Ibid. See also *Rose v. Giamatti*.

111. See Durney, "Fair or Foul?" 592. See also *Rose v. Giamatti*.

112. See Klein, "Rose is in Red," 580–81. See also *Rose v. Giamatti*.

113. See *Rose v. Giamatti*.

114. See Klein, "Rose is in Red," 584.

115. *Rose v. Giamatti*, 721 F. Supp. 906, 916-19 (S.D. Ohio, 1989).

116. See Klein, "Rose is in Red," 586.

117. Ibid.

118. See Rychlak, "Rose, Giamatti, and the Dowd Report," 895.

119. Ibid. During the question and answer session of the announcement of the agreement between MLB and Rose, Giamatti's response to the first question posed to him ("Did Rose bet on Baseball?") was: "In the absence of a hearing and therefore in the absence of evidence to the contrary . . . I am confronted by the factual record of Mr. Dowd. On the basis of that, yes, I have concluded that he bet on baseball."

120. See Nathan, *Saying It's So*, 187.

121. See Rychlak, "Rose, Giamatti, and the Dowd Report," 900.

122. *Finley*, 569 F. 2d, 544.

123. See Durney, "Fair or Foul?" 609–10. See also *Automotive Serv. Councils of Michigan v. Secretary of State*, 267 N.W. 2d 698, 705 (Mich. App. 1978). The court quoted a well-known treatise on administrative law when it wrote: "The danger of unfairness is particularly great in an agency in which there is a high degree of concentration of both prosecuting and judicial functions, especially where the functions are combined in the same men. The courts have pointed out that in such situations the agency members must be zealous in the recognition and preservation of the right to a hearing by impartial triers of the facts, and such fusion of functions has been subjected to considerable criticism." 1 *American Jurisprudence* 2d Administrative Law § 78.

124. See *Commonwealth Coatings Corp. v. Continental Casualty Co.*, 393 U.S. 145, 149 (1968) ("We should . . . be even more scrupulous to safeguard the impartiality of arbitrators . . . since [they] have completely free reign to decide the law as well as the facts and are not subject to appellate review.")

125. See Durney, "Fair or Foul?" 610–11.

126. Bill Madden, *Steinbrenner: The Last Lion of Baseball* (New York: Harper, 2010), 306–8.

127. Dave Anderson, "A Good Day for Baseball, And a Better One Looms" *New York Times*, November 18, 2007, Sports Sunday 11.

128. Ibid.

129. Ibid.

130. Alan Schwarz, "Prosecution's Best Pitch Is Precision, Experts Say," *New York Times*, Nov. 17, 2007, *http://www.nytimes.com/2007/11/17/sports/baseball/17/perjury.html*. "Bonds's situation and Libby's situation are particularly similar, in regard to the denials of any kind of wrongdoing," according to Peter Keane, a professor at Golden Gate University School of Law.

131. George J. Mitchell, "Report To The Commissioner of Baseball Of An Independent Investigation Into The Illegal Use Of Steroids And Other Performance Enhancing Substances By Players In Major League Baseball," December 13, 2007.

132. Bill Pennington, "Selig Says Report 'Is a Call to Action' And Vows to Act Swiftly," *New York Times*, December 14, 2007, D1.

133. Selig's insistence that the problems in baseball unearthed during his reign were confined to a defined "steroid era" was crystallized with his statement in response to Mark McGwire's January 2010 admission that he took steroids throughout his career. With McGwire's announcement, Selig pronounced the steroid era over, a statement that Travis Tygart, the head of the United States Anti-Doping Agency, found astonishing. "He said that?" replied Tygart. "If so, it sounds like the same stick-your-head-in-the-

sand approach that led to this whole mess. I find it hard to believe that is what he said." Michael S. Schmidt, "Selig Says Steroid Era is Basically Over," *New York Times,* January 12, 2010, B13.

134. Michael S. Schmidt, "Players in Mitchell Report Unlikely to be Punished," *New York Times,* April 11, 2008, D5. As the title of this article indicates, after the Players Association objected to this suggestion, Selig backed down.

135. Mitchell Report, 2.

136. Mitchell Report, Summary and Recommendations (SR) 10–11.

137. Ibid., SR 11.

138. Francis T. Vincent Jr. Memorandum to All Major League Clubs Re: Baseball's Drug Policy and Prevention Program, June 7, 1991, 2.

139. Murray Chass, "Mitchell Report Revealed Little New Work," *New York Times,* December 18, 2007, D5.

140. Federal Food, Drug and Cosmetic Act, c. 675, 52 Stat. 1040 (codified as amended at 21 U.S.C. § 353 (b)(1)(B) (2004)). See also Mitchell Report, 18.

141. Anabolic Steroids Control Act of 1990, Pub. L. No. 101-647, 101 Stat. 4789 (1990).

142. See Arturo J. Marcano Guevara and David P. Fidler, *Stealing Lives: The Globalization of Baseball and the Tragic Story of Alexis Quiroz* (Bloomington: University of Indiana Press, 2002), 185, 190–91. The authors cite a judgment of a Venezuelan labor law court against the New York Yankees in 2000 that went ignored by the team. In response, the Commissioner's Office "reminded its teams that they should obey local laws in the foreign jurisdictions in which they operate." This, apparently, did not convince the Yankees to honor the court's ruling in that case, however.

143. Phil Sheridan, "Baseball Turned a Blind Eye—And Saw Cash," *Philadelphia Inquirer,* November 18, 2007, E1.

144. Mitchell Report, 61–66.

145. Ibid., 66–67. Phillies general manager Lee Thomas suspected Dykstra of abusing performance-enhancing drugs but never pursued it beyond asking Dykstra if he had used steroids (Dykstra denied using them). In addition, Phillies trainer Jeff Cooper stated that an unnamed player's use of steroids was "obvious" and that he confronted Thomas with his suspicions. Thomas told Cooper to confront the player. Cooper did, the player said "it was none of his business," and the matter was dropped.

146. Ibid., 69.

147. Ibid., 69–70.

148. Ibid., 70.

149. Mitchell Report, appendix C.

150. Ibid., 71.

151. Allan H. "Bud" Selig and Robert D. Manfred Jr., "The Regulation of Nutritional Supplements in Professional Sports," 15 *Stanford Law and Policy Review,* 35, 35–36 (2004).

152. Ibid.

153. Mitchell Report, 290–91.

154. Ibid., 292.

155. Ibid.

156. Ibid., 290–91.

157. For example, in 2010, the owner of the NFL's Houston Texans ordered a sweep of his players' locker room to ensure that none of them were using banned substances. See "Owner Ordered Search of Locker Rooms," *New York Times,* October 30, 2010, B10. The NFL Players Association did not challenge the search as violative of the league's collective bargaining agreement.

158. Mitchell Report, 285–306.

159. Statement of Commissioner Allan H. Selig before the House Committee On Oversight and Government Reform, January 15, 2008, 9–10, 15. "I am here to ask for your assistance in this fight. The illegal use of performance enhancing substances is a problem for Baseball—but it is a social problem that extends beyond this sport or any sport. It is a societal issue. Senator Mitchell's report identified the difficulties inherent in any attempt, whether by Baseball, by other professional sports, or by the Olympics, to stop by itself the use of illegal performance enhancing substances. We welcome your participation in attacking the problem at its source. There are a number of bills that have been introduced that we wholly support, including Representative Lynch's bill (HR 4911) and Senator Schumer's bill (Senate Bill 877) to make HGH a Schedule III Controlled Substance, Senator Grassley's bill (Senate Bill 2470) to prohibit the sale of DHEA to minors, and Senator Biden's bill (Senate Bill 2237) to crackdown on the sale of controlled substances over the Internet."

CHAPTER 3. RICKEY, RACE, AND "ALL DELIBERATE SPEED"

1. See, for example, Joshua Fleer, "The Church of Baseball and the U.S. Presidency," 16 *NINE: A Journal of Baseball History and Culture,* 51 (2007); Roberta Newman, "The American Church of Baseball and the National Baseball Hall of Fame," 10 *NINE: A Journal of Baseball History and Culture,* 46 (2001).

2. Rader, *Baseball: A History,* 156.

3. 347 U.S. 483 (1954).

4. 163 U.S. 537 (1896).

5. Baltzell, *Protestant Establishment,* 83 (". . . anyone involved in the study of minority relations in this country knows that all hyphenated Americans [and

Negroes as well] tend to share a more or less common marginal situation and feel, in turn, that a breakthrough for one group is a break for all").

6. See Howard Zinn, *The Twentieth Century*, (New York: Harper Perennial 1998, 2003), viii. "The treatment of heroes (Columbus) and their victims (the Arawaks)—the quiet acceptance of conquest and murder in the name of progress—is only one aspect of a certain approach to history, in which the past is told from the point of view of governments, conquerors, diplomats, leaders. It is as if they, like Columbus, deserve universal acceptance, as if they—the Founding Fathers, Jackson, Lincoln, Wilson, Roosevelt, Kennedy, the leading members of Congress, the famous Justices of the Supreme Court—represent the nation as a whole."

7. Lee Lowenfish, *Branch Rickey: Baseball's Ferocious Gentleman* (Lincoln: University of Nebraska Press, 2007), 358.

8. See, for example, ibid., 369–70. This sentiment is expressed in virtually every discussion of Rickey and/or the integration of baseball.

9. Marshall, *Baseball's Pivotal Era*, 126.

10. Ibid., 127.

11. Rick Swaine, *The Black Stars Who Made Baseball Whole* (Jefferson, N.C.: McFarland, 2006), 12.

12. Ibid., 13.

13. Tygiel, *Past Time*, 158. It is worth noting that, by the end of his life, Robinson regretted his decision to testify in rebuttal to Robeson. See William C. Rhoden, "A Way to Mark Robinson's 90th Birthday," *New York Times*, January 26, 2009, D5.

14. Tygiel, *Past Time*, 158.

15. Robert Nowatzki, "Foul Lines and the Color Line: Baseball and Race at the Turn of the Twentieth Century," 11 *NINE: A Journal of Baseball History and Culture*, 82, 82–83 (2002). See also Gerald Early, "Performance and Reality: Race, Sports and the Modern World," *The Nation*, August 10–17, 1998, 11–15.

16. Irwin Silber, *Press Box Red: The Story of Lester Rodney, the Communist Who Helped Break the Color Line in American Sports* (Philadelphia: Temple University Press, 2003), 51.

17. Rader, *Baseball: A History*, 59–60.

18. Seymour, *Baseball: The Early Years*, 334–35.

19. Ibid.

20. Rader, *Baseball: A History*, 59.

21. 163 U.S. 537 (1896).

22. Powers-Beck, *American Indian Integration of Baseball*, 162. Landis hoped to avoid a repeat of a 1901 incident where Baltimore Orioles manager John McGraw attempted to convince his Major League brethren that his new second baseman, Charlie Grant, was in actuality "Chief Tokahoma."

Chicago owner Charles Comiskey exposed the ruse and Grant was released from the Orioles. Landis interrogated both Yellow Horse and his manager extensively on the issue of Yellow Horse's heritage, attended a few of his games, and then pronounced himself "pleased" with his performance, apparently convinced that he was not, after all, an African American in disguise.

23. Lowenfish, *Branch Rickey*, 351.

24. At the time, some within the alternative press initially misunderstood Landis's statement and took it to mean that Landis had announced a shift in MLB's policy with regard to race; that in the aftermath of the Durocher incident, club owners were now freed to sign anyone irrespective of the color of their skin. A headline in the black newspaper, the *Pittsburgh Courier,* hailed the statement as "Commissioner Landis's Emancipation Proclamation," while the communist *Daily Worker* ran several articles in its aftermath announcing that the integration of MLB was on the horizon. Very quickly, however, reality set in: no black players were signed and Landis's statement was exposed for what it was: "ritualistic, meaningless boilerplate." Henry D. Fetter, "The Party Line and the Color Line: The American Communist Party, the Daily Worker, and Jackie Robinson," 28 *Journal of Sport History,* 375, 381–82 (Fall 2001).

25. Marshall, *Baseball's Pivotal Era,* 79–80.

26. Ibid.

27. Rader, *Baseball: A History,* 163–64.

28. Bryan Booker, *African Americans in the United States Army in World War II* (Jefferson, N.C.: McFarland, 2008), 16. The discussion of African American military involvement draws primarily from this text. See also pp. 2, 20–33, 41–49, 84–85, 171, 277.

29. Ibid., 33.

30. Rader, *Baseball: A History,* 164.

31. Ibid., 164.

32. Ibid.

33. Lowenfish, *Branch Rickey*, 359.

34. Silber, *Press Box Red,* 49.

35. According to Rodney, most people were very receptive to the information contained in the leaflets: "People would say, 'Gee, I never thought of that.' And then they'd say, 'Yeah, I think if they're good enough then they should have a chance.' We wound up with at least a million and a half signatures that we delivered straight to the desk of [baseball commissioner] Judge Landis." Dave Zirin, "Lester Speaks: An Interview with 'Red' Rodney," *Counterpunch,* Weekend Edition, April 3–5, 2004.

36. Silber, *Press Box Red,* 64–74.

37. Lowenfish, *Branch Rickey*, 352.

38. Ibid., 352–53; Marshall, *Baseball's Pivotal Era*, 122.

39. Lowenfish, *Branch Rickey*, 353.

40. See, for example, Lowenfish, *Branch Rickey*, 361–62; Rader, *Baseball: A History*, 165.

41. See, for example, Lowenfish, *Branch Rickey*, 363; Swaine, *Black Stars*, 69.

42. Neil Lanctot, *Negro League Baseball: The Rise and Ruin of a Black Institution* (Philadelphia: University of Pennsylvania Press, 2004), 275.

43. Lowenfish, *Branch Rickey*, 377.

44. Marshall, *Baseball's Pivotal Era*, 128.

45. Lowenfish, *Branch Rickey*, 377.

46. Ibid., 378–79.

47. Ibid.

48. Tygiel, *Past Time*, 110–11.

49. Lee Lowenfish, "When All Heaven Rejoiced: Branch Rickey and the Origins of the Breaking of the Color Line," 11 *NINE: A Journal of Baseball History and Culture*, 1, 7 (2002).

50. Ibid., 9; Lowenfish, *Branch Rickey*, 349.

51. Lowenfish, *Branch Rickey*, 349.

52. Tygiel, *Past Time*, 112.

53. Ibid.

54. Rader, *Baseball: A History*, 156.

55. Lowenfish, *Branch Rickey*, 379.

56. Ibid.

57. Marshall, *Baseball's Pivotal Era*, 123.

58. Although most accounts date the Rickey-Thomas incident to 1904, Ohio Wesleyan did not travel to South Bend to play Notre Dame during the 1904 season. The two teams played on May 12, 1903, however, and it was during this trip when the facts that gave rise to the story most likely occurred.

59. See, for example, Lowenfish, *When all Heaven Rejoiced*, 10; Marshall, *Baseball's Pivotal Era*, 123.

60. Lowenfish traces the story to two sources: Arthur Mann, "The Life Story of Branch Rickey," *LOOK*, August 20, 1957, and Mark Harris, "Branch Rickey Keeps His 40 Year Promise," *NEGRO DIGEST*, September, 1947, 4–7. Marshall follows the story back to several sources, all post-1947, the earliest of which being Carl T. Rowan and Jackie Robinson, *Wait Till Next Year*, 105–106 (New York: Random House, 1960). Lowenfish notes evidence of the relationship between Rickey and Thomas in Rickey's letters dating back to 1921 but these letters do not refer to the specific incident in South Bend. See Letters of Branch Rickey and Charles Thomas, 10/26/21, 11/1/21 located in the Branch Rickey Papers, Library of Congress, Washington, D.C. Subsequent research conducted in conjunction with the writing of *A People's History of Baseball* uncovered an October 24, 1945, Associated Press

article in the *Zanesville (Ohio) Times-Recorder* that referenced Rickey's remarks in an April 1945 talk to a Brooklyn Rotary group. See Gayle Talbot, "Montreal Signs First Negro To Organized Baseball," *Zanesville Times-Recorder*, October 24, 1945, 8. See also Howard Spencer, "The Signal of Sports," *Zanesville Times-Recorder*, October 24, 1945, 9, which likewise referenced Rickey's remarks regarding Thomas.

61. Lowenfish, *When All Heaven Rejoiced*, 9–10.
62. Ibid.
63. Lowenfish, *Branch Rickey*, 351. Rickey did become close with some black sportswriters, particularly Wendell Smith of the *Pittsburgh Courier*. It was the agitation and constant pressure placed on people like himself by those in the black and communist press that he found troubling.
64. Ibid., 595.
65. See generally, Lowenfish, et al.
66. Louis Lusky, "Racial Discrimination and the Federal Law: A Problem in Nullification," 63 *Columbia Law Review*, 1163, 113–64 (1963).
67. See Robert L. Carter, "The Warren Court and Desegregation," 67 *Michigan Law Review*, 237, 247 (1968).
68. Ibid.
69. Ibid.
70. Lowenfish, *When All Heaven Rejoiced*, 12.
71. Marshall, *Baseball's Pivotal Era*, 125–26.
72. Lowenfish, *Branch Rickey*, 379.
73. Ibid., 379–80; Marshall, *Baseball's Pivotal Era*, 129.
74. Lowenfish, *Branch Rickey*, 365–66.
75. Ibid., 367.
76. Ibid., 367–68.
77. Ibid.
78. Lowenfish, *When All Heaven Rejoiced*, 12.
79. Rader, *Baseball: A History*, 165–66.
80. Ibid.
81. Lowenfish, *When All Heaven Rejoiced*, 11–12.
82. Ibid.
83. Ibid.
84. Ibid.
85. Zirin, "Lester Speaks."
86. Swaine, *Black Stars*, 16.
87. Ibid.
88. John Bauman, *Public Housing, Race and Renewal* (Philadelphia: Temple University Press, 1987), 124. George Nesbitt, race relations officer for the Federal Housing and Home Finance Administration, commented during a 1954 tour of a proposed integrated housing development in Philadelphia

that "Philadelphia happens to be a city with a distinctly favorable level of readiness for racially unrestricted housing development."

89. Of the 566 players who saw action during the 1947 season, 150 (26.5 percent) hailed from one of the eleven former Confederate states. See "Major League Players by Birthplace During the 1947 Season," *Baseball Almanac.com*. Available at: http://www.baseball-almanac.com/players/birthplace.php?y=1947.

90. Ibid. In fact, these four states alone were the birthplaces of 197 (35 percent) of the players who played during the 1947 season.

91. Swaine, *Black Stars*, 19.

92. Ibid., 88.

93. Silber, *Press Box Red*, 100–101.

94. See, for example, Malcolm X's November 30, 1963, open letter to Robinson as published in the *Amsterdam News* in *First Class Citizenship: The Civil Rights Letters of Jackie Robinson*, ed. Michael G. Long (New York: Henry Holt, 2007), 182–86.

95. See Zirin, "Lester Speaks." As Rodney noted, "Some people are thrust into roles in history that they didn't seek or maybe even comprehend. Jackie was different. He was a fiercely intelligent man. He knew exactly what he was doing."

96. Rader, *Baseball: A History*, 167.

97. Marshall, *Baseball's Pivotal Era*, 344–46.

98. As stated herein, there is no evidence that suggests Robinson, as opposed to Rickey, is any less heroic for his actions. To the contrary (and as stated herein), his willingness to endure the wrath of fans, players, and members of his own race are testament to his heroism in light of the dearth of options available to him. Moreover, the stresses imposed on him may very well have contributed to his later health problems that ultimately shortened his life. The point is, rather, that many more Americans, at least outside the South, were apparently willing (either begrudgingly or more freely) to accept at least some movement toward integration than the Rickey story assumes. Regardless, hard-core racists existed then as they do today and it is folly to suggest that Rickey's managed portrait of the integration issue had any effect on swaying these entrenched racists even minimally. To the extent he was addressing his message to them, this was foolhardy; to the extent he was addressing his message to those who were either in favor of at least some strides toward integration or were simply ambivalent on the issue, the benefits of his message must be weighed against the costs, which, as discussed herein, were significant in that it was very likely detrimental to the integration movement in the long run.

99. Marshall, *Baseball's Pivotal Era*, 213–14, 285.

100. 349 U.S. 294 (1955).

101. 347 U.S. 483 (1954).

102. 163 U.S. 537 (1896).
103. 347 U.S. at 495.
104. Charles Black, "The Unfinished Business of the Warren Court," 46 *Washington Law Review,* 3, 19–20 (1970).
105. Ibid.
106. 349 U.S. 294 (1955).
107. Ibid., 299.
108. Ibid., 300 (emphasis added).
109. Lusky, "Racial Discrimination," 1171–72.
110. Ibid.
111. Ibid. See also Carter, "Warren Court," 245.
112. Carter, "Warren Court," 244.
113. James R. Dunn, "Title VI, The Guidelines and School Desegregation in the South," 53 *Virginia Law Review,* 42, 42 (1967).
114. Lusky, "Racial Discrimination," 1171.
115. Ibid.
116. Carter, "Warren Court," 243.
117. Ibid.
118. Ibid.
119. Black, "The Unfinished Business," 22.
120. Ibid.
121. Carter, "Warren Court," 243.
122. Louis Lusky, "The Stereotype: Hard Core of Racism," 13 *Buffalo Law Review,* 450, 459 (1963).
123. 349 U.S., 300.
124. Lusky, "The Stereotype," 458.
125. Ibid., 459.
126. Carter, "Warren Court," 245.
127. *Griffin v. Prince Edward Board of Education,* 377 U.S. 216, 234 (1964).
128. *Bradley v. School Board of Richmond,* 382 U.S. 103, 105 (1965).
129. Carter, "Warren Court," 245.
130. Ibid.
131. L. A. Powe Jr., "The Road to *Swann:* Mobile County Crawls to the Bus," 51 *Texas Law Review,* 505, 505–6 (1973).
132. Lusky, "Racial Discrimination," 1163–64.
133. Carter, "Warren Court," 246–47.
134. Ibid., 247.
135. Ibid. See also Lusky, "Racial Discrimination," 1164.
136. See Carter, "Warren Court," 247; Lusky, "Racial Discrimination," 1164.
137. Ibid.
138. See Steve Treder, "The Persistent Color Line: Specific Instances of Racial Preference in Major League Player Evaluation Decisions after 1947," 10 *NINE: A Journal of Baseball History and Culture,* 1, 27 (2001).

139. Ibid., 25.

140. Swaine, *Black Stars,* 49.

141. Ibid.

142. Treder, "Persistent Color Line," 2–3.

143. Ibid. See also Swaine, *Black Stars,* 70; Lowenfish, *Branch Rickey,* 483.

144. Treder, "Persistent Color Line," 19–20.

145. Swaine, *Black Stars,* 242.

146. Lowenfish, *Branch Rickey,* 527–28.

147. Fidler and Marcano Guevara, *Stealing Lives,* 30–31.

148. Ibid., 41, 44. In addition, Carrasquel was not provided with a copy of the contract. Carrasquel was eventually sold to the Chicago White Sox, where he became a star.

149. Richard J. Puerzer, "Engineering Baseball: Branch Rickey's Innovative Approach to Baseball Management," 12 *NINE: A Journal of Baseball History and Culture,* 72, 79–80 (2003).

150. Swaine, *Black Stars,* 103.

151. Ibid., 127.

152. Silber, *Press Box Red,* 45–46.

153. Ibid., 127–28.

154. Mark Armour, "The Effects of Integration, 1947–1986," 36 *Baseball Research Journal,* 53, 54–55 (2007).

155. Tygiel, *Past Time,* 160.

156. Ibid.

157. Armour, "Effects of Integration," 55.

158. Michael J. Haupert, "A Look at Player Pay During the Integration Era," *Outside the Lines* ESPN), October 19, 2008 1, 18.

159. Ibid., 19.

160. Swaine, *Black Stars,* 84; Treder, "Persistent Color Line," 18.

161. See generally Armour, "Effects of Integration."

162. Treder, "Persistent Color Line," 10–11.

163. See Andrew Hazucha, "Leo Durocher's Last Stand," 15 *NINE: A Journal of Baseball History and Culture,* 1, 7 (2006).

164. Ibid., 7–8.

165. Ibid., 8.

166. Treder, "Persistent Color Line," 14–15.

167. Ibid., 16–17.

168. Swaine, *Black Stars,* 164–65.

169. Ibid., 175. Although Power eventually found a home with the Minnesota Twins, here too he was subjected to the quota system; in 1964, Power was traded to the Los Angeles Angels when the Twins called up the black Cuban slugger Tony Oliva to take his place in the outfield. Combined with shortstop Zoilo Versalles and catcher Earl Battery, the Twins, who already

fielded more black or dark-skinned players than most other American League teams, had exceeded their quota with the call-up of Oliva. Ibid., 168.

170. Ibid., 164–65.

171. Treder, "Persistent Color Line,16–17.

172. Swaine, *Black Stars*, 173.

173. Ibid., 107.

174. Rader, *Baseball: A History*, 168.

175. Ibid.

176. Richard Lapchick, The 2009 Racial and Gender Report Card: Major League Baseball, appendix I, table 15 (April 15, 2009). Available at: http://tidesport .org/RGRC/2009/2009_MLB_RGRC_PR_Final_rev.pdf. It should be noted that the entirety of the blame should not fall upon the shoulders of MLB, as stacking is undoubtedly a problem that reaches down as far as Little League, with black children often (and perhaps subconsciously) steered toward positions other than pitcher and catcher. As a consequence, there are far fewer black prospects at these positions at the high school and collegiate levels.

177. John Helyar, "Robinson Would Have Mixed View of Today's Game," ESPN .com, April 9, 2007. Available at: http://sports.espn.go.com/mlb/jackie/ news/story?id=2828584. The nine were: Darren Oliver (Relief Pitcher), Edwin Jackson (Starting Pitcher), C. C. Sabathia (SP), Arthur Rhodes (RP), Dontrelle Willis (SP), Ray King (RP), Tom Gordon (RP), Ian Snell (SP), and LaTroy Hawkins (RP).

178. Michael S. Schmidt and Andrew Keh, "Stranded at First Base," *New York Times*, August 12, 2010, B13.

179. Ibid.

180. Lapchick, appendix I, table 8.

181. Ibid., appendix I, table 9.

182. Ibid., appendix I, table 1. In 2008, this percentage rose to 10.2.

183. Tom Gage, "National Pastime Strikes Out With Black Athletes," *Detroit News*, April 10, 2005, available at http://www.detnews.com/2005/ specialreport/0504/10/A01B-145339.htm.

184. Tygiel, *Past Time*, 142.

185. Tom Verducci, "Blackout: The African-American Baseball Player is Vanishing. Does He Have a Future?" *Sports Illustrated*, July 7, 2003, available at: http://sportsillustrated.cnn.com/vault/article/magazine/ MAG1029117/2/index.htm.

CHAPTER 4. TEARING DOWN THE WALLS

1. For a more in-depth discussion of the PCL challenge and MLB's response, see Mitchell Nathanson, *The Fall of the 1977 Phillies: How a Baseball Team's Collapse Sank a City's Spirit* (Jefferson, N.C.: McFarland, 2008), 89–92.

2. Rader, *Baseball: A History*, 188.

3. Lowenfish, *Branch Rickey*, 544–45.

4. Tygiel, *Past Time*, 186.

5. Leonard Koppett, *Koppett's Concise History of Major League Baseball* (New York: Carroll and Graf, 2004), 272–73.

6. Lowenfish, *Branch Rickey*, 546.

7. "Press Release Issued By William Shea, July 27, 1959," in *Late Innings: A Documentary History of Baseball, 1945–1972*, ed. Dean A. Sullivan (Lincoln: University of Nebraska Press, 2002), 141.

8. Tygiel, *Past Time*, 186–87.

9. Mitchell Nathanson, "The Irrelevance of Baseball's Antitrust Exemption: A Historical Review," 58 *Rutgers Law Review*, 1, 37–38 (2005).

10. "Continental Loop Threatens War," *Los Angeles Times*, April 15, 1960, A1.

11. Michael Shapiro, *Bottom of the Ninth: Branch Rickey, Casey Stengel, and the Daring Scheme to Save Baseball From Itself* (New York: Henry Holt, 2009), 30.

12. Ibid.

13. Press Release by William Shea, in Sullivan, ed., *Late Innings*, 143.

14. Shapiro, *Bottom of the Ninth*, 30.

15. Ibid., 207.

16. Nathanson, "Irrelevance of Baseball's Antitrust Exemption," 38–39.

17. "Sports Bill Pigeonholed; Continental Dealt Jolt," *Los Angeles Times*, June 28, 1960, C1, 6.

18. *Joint Major League Committee, Report of Major League Steering Committee for Submission to the National and American Leagues at their Meetings in Chicago* (1946). Available at *http://www.businessofbaseball.com/docs .thm#steeringcommittee*.

19. Robert M. Lipsyte, "Loop Affiliation Remains in Doubt," *New York Times*, July 19, 1960, 33.

20. Koppett, *Koppett's Concise History*, 293.

21. Ibid., 296–97.

22. Ibid., 385, 399, 428.

23. For a more detailed examination of the impact of the corporate revolution on MLB as well as the changing face of baseball (on both the owners' as well as the players' side) from the 1960s onward, See Mitchell Nathanson, "Truly Sovereign At Last: *C.B.C. Distribution v. MLB AM* and the Redefinition of the Concept of Baseball," 89 *Oregon Law Review* 581 (2010), from which these discussions contained herein originated, in somewhat modified and expanded form.

24. John Helyar, *Lords of the Realm: The Real History of Baseball* (New York: Villard Books, 1994), 51.

25. Roger G. Noll, "Major League Team Sports," in *The Structure of American Industry*, ed. Walter Adams, 5th ed. (New York: MacMillan, 1977), 365.

26. Helyar, *Lords of the Realm*, 13.

27. For an analysis of the economics of the era and the nature of the choices available to ownership, *see* Nathanson, *The Fall of the 1977 Phillies*, 62–64.

28. Ibid.

29. Helyar, *Lords of the Realm*, 89–90.

30. Koppett, *Koppett's Concise History*, 194–95.

31. Mark Gallagher, *The Yankees Encyclopedia* (New York: Sports Publishing, 4th ed., 2000), 325–29; see also Baltzell, *Protestant Establishment*, 298.

32. Shapiro, *Bottom of the Ninth*, 76.

33. Ibid., 183.

34. "Powel Crosley Jr.," in *Ohio History Central: An Online Encyclopedia of Ohio History, http://www.ohiohistorycentral.org/entry.php?rec=63&nm=Powel-Crosley-Jr.*

35. Richard M. Abrams, *America Transformed: Sixty Years of Revolutionary Change, 1941–2001* (New York: Cambridge University Press, 2006), 97. The discussion of the concentration of American business in the middle of the twentieth century, herein, draws primarily from Abrams's text. See also pp. 98–102.

36. Ibid., 97.

37. Koppett, *Koppett's Concise History*, 469.

38. Charles P. Korr, *The End of Baseball As We Knew It: The Players Union, 1960–81* (Urbana: University of Illinois Press, 2002), 79.

39. Koppett, *Koppett's Concise History*, 469–70.

40. Ibid., 428.

41. Tygiel, *Past Time*, 81–85.

42. See, for example, Frank Gifford and Peter Richmond, *The Glory Game: How the 1958 NFL Championship Changed Football Forever* (New York: Harper, 2008); Lou Sahadi, *One Sunday in December: The 1958 NFL Championship Game and How it Changed Professional Football* (New York: Lyons Press, 2008).

43. Tygiel, *Past Time*, 154.

44. Ibid.

45. Voigt, *American Baseball*, 283.

46. Koppett, *Koppett's Concise History*, 291.

47. Ibid., 293.

48. In his memoir, *The Crowd Sounds Happy* (New York: Vintage Books, 2008), 237, Nicholas Dawidoff, who was raised in a household that did not have a television set, remarked on the shortcomings of the game on television when he finally was able to watch it with regularity: "The field became reduced to the fragment that fit on the screen, minimizing the game into a fraction of itself, implying that everything happening off-camera was irrelevant. The players were minimized as well, because they did not exist unless the ball came their way. Then the lens swooped into their faces and there was too much of them—which weirdly created distance. Following

the game on the radio, by contrast, what I saw was up to me, and the basic rhythms and landscape of the game remained intact."

49. Nathanson, *Fall of the 1977 Phillies*, 102.

50. Ibid., 73.

51. Rader, *Baseball: A History*, 221.

52. Korr, *End of Baseball*, 188.

53. Helyar, *Lords of the Realm*, 317.

54. Ibid.

55. Ibid.

56. Baltzell, *Protestant Establishment*, 380 (quoting Aristotle).

57. Marshall, *Baseball's Pivotal Era*, 301–3.

58. Technically, the players are still paid only throughout the season. However, after the birth of free agency, player salaries were in accordance with expectations for year-round employment rather than seasonal work.

59. Marshall, *Baseball's Pivotal Era*, 308.

60. Ibid.

61. Ibid., 309.

62. Ibid., 266. Widmar threatened to sue baseball if he did not receive a raise upon his promotion to the Major Leagues. Eventually, Commissioner Happy Chandler intervened on Widmar's behalf and Widmar did indeed receive his raise.

63. Ibid., 299.

64. Tygiel, *Past Time*, 94–95.

65. Korr, *End of Baseball*, 240.

66. Marshall, *Baseball's Pivotal Era*, 300. It should be noted, however, that the average Major League salary as noted here is a bit skewed by the few players earning significantly more than $11,000 annually. The vast majority of players hovered around the Major League minimum of $6,000.

67. Ibid.

68. Koppett, *Koppett's Concise History*, 260.

69. Ibid.

70. Ibid.

71. "Major League Baseball Players' Association Constitution, Bylaws, and Articles of Association," in *Late Innings*, 82.

72. "Salary Report for Major League Baseball Players," in *Late Innings*, 131–34.

73. Abrams, *America Transformed*, 203–5. The discussion of the New Left, herein, draws primarily from Abrams's text.

74. Ibid., 204–5.

75. Ibid., 42; Voigt, *American Baseball*, 281.

76. George H. Knoles, *The Presidential Campaign and Election of 1892* (Palo Alto, Calif.: Stanford University Press, 1942), 179.

77. Hofstadter, *Age of Reform*, 149.

78. Ibid., 149–51.
79. Ibid., 247.
80. Ibid., 169–70.
81. David Brody, *Labor Embattled: History, Power, Rights* (Urbana: University of Illinois Press, 2005), 100.
82. Ibid., 123. Brody speaks specifically of the judicial creation of the labor injunction in the 1890s, which effectively stymied labor's ability to conduct an organized boycott. Without such a remedy, one court wrote, the employer "is certainly remediless, because an action at law, in most cases, would do no good, and ruin would be accomplished before and adjudication could be reached." *Emack v. Kaine*, 34 F. 46 (Ill., 1888).
83. Bannister, *Social Darwinism*, 81.
84. Ibid., 109.
85. Ibid., 126.
86. See Brody, 24. As Brody notes, by 1938 the ACLU, which was initially opposed to the Wagner Act on libertarian grounds, had equated labor and civil rights.
87. Ibid., 26.
88. Ibid., 35.
89. Ibid., 36–37.
90. Ibid., 31.
91. Voigt, *American Baseball*, 281.
92. Zinn, *Twentieth Century*, 150.
93. Ibid. 6,770,000 workers struck during that time.
94. Brody, *Labor Embattled*, 130.
95. Voigt, *American Baseball*, 281.
96. See Scott D. Peterson, "Red Press Nation: The Baseball Rhetoric of Lester Rodney," in *The Politics of Baseball: Essays on the Pastime and Power at Home and Abroad*, ed. Ron Briley (Jefferson, N.C.: McFarland, 2010), 38.
97. Terry H. Anderson, *The Movement and the Sixties: Protest in America From Greensboro to Wounded Knee* (New York: Oxford University Press, 1995), 62.
98. Ibid., 63–64.
99. Ibid., 64. Irrespective of the Port Huron Statement, strands of the New Left did, at times, attempt to challenge various tenets of capitalism.
100. Ibid., 87.
101. Anderson, *Movement and the Sixties*, 97–99.
102. Ibid.
103. Ibid., 98.
104. Baltzell, *Protestant Establishment*, 358.
105. Ibid., 345.
106. Anderson, *Movement and the Sixties*, 196.
107. Ibid., 386–89.

108. Rader, *Baseball: A History,* 204; Korr, *End of Baseball,* 62–64.
109. Rader, *Baseball: A History,* 205.
110. Koppett, *Koppett's Concise History,* 337, 366.
111. Ibid., 367.
112. Korr, *End of Baseball,* 93–94.
113. Koppett, *Koppett's Concise History,* 367.
114. Ibid., 339.
115. Boswell, *Inside Sports,* July 1980.
116. Korr, *End of Baseball,* 5.
117. Ibid., 6.
118. Nathanson, "Gatekeepers of Americana," 81–82.
119. Korr, *End of Baseball,* 242.
120. Ibid., 84.
121. Ibid., 97.
122. Ibid., 96–97. See also Snyder, *A Well-Paid Slave.*
123. Anderson, *Movement and the Sixties,* 248.
124. Korr, *End of Baseball,* 209.
125. Ibid., 189.
126. Ibid., 209.

CHAPTER 5. "WAIT 'TIL NEXT YEAR" AND THE DENIAL OF HISTORY

1. Edward Sagarin, "Who Roots for the Underdog?" 4 *Journal of Popular Culture,* 425 (1970).
2. Ibid.
3. Todd Wilkinson, "Individual Differences and Sports Fans: Who Roots for the Underdog?" Ph.D. diss., University of Minnesota, 2006, 6–7.
4. Philip Roth, *The Great American Novel* (New York: Vintage International, 1973), 142.
5. Sagarin, "Who Roots for the Underdog?" 428.
6. Ibid.
7. Voigt, *American Baseball,* 280–81.
8. Abrams, *America Transformed,* 220.
9. Anderson, *Movement and the Sixties,* 4–5.
10. Ibid.
11. Wilkinson, "Individual Differences and Sports Fans."
12. Ibid., 104.
13. Ibid.
14. Joe Queenan, *True Believers: The Tragic Inner Life of Sports Fans* (New York: Henry Holt, 2003), 60.
15. Ibid., 235–36.
16. *The Underdog.* Available at *http://convictcreations.com/culture/underdog.htm.*

17. Ibid.

18. This is the definition supplied by the *Dictionary of Americanisms on Historical Principles*. See also, Sagarin, "Who Roots for the Underdog?" 426–27.

19. Ibid., 427.

20. Ibid., 430–31.

21. Nadav Goldschmied, "The Appeal of the Underdog: Definition of the Construct and Implications for the Self," Ph.D. diss., University of South Florida, 2007.

22. Ibid., 29.

23. Ibid., 30.

24. Ibid., 79.

25. The disconnect between beliefs and actions is not limited to Americans. According to a 2010 British study across eighty-two countries, self-professed liberals were actually quite conservative when measured by their stances on specific issues. See James Rockey, "Who Is Left Wing, And Who Just Thinks They Are?" (Department of Economics, University of Leicester, UK, 2010). Available at *http://econpapers.repec.org/RePEc:lec:leecon:09/23*.

26. Goldschmied, "Appeal of the Underdog," 78.

27. Sagarin, "Who Roots for the Underdog?" 431.

28. Ibid.

29. *Ideology, Revolution and Utopia in Marx.* Available at *http://mindsmeaningmorals.wordpress.com*.

30. Donald Meyer, *The Positive Thinkers* (Middletown, Ct.: Wesleyan University Press, 1988), 315, 317, 322.

31. Ibid., 322.

32. Roth, *Great American Novel*, 381.

33. Morris, *But Didn't We Have Fun?*, 120–21.

34. Ibid.

35. See, for example, Wiebe, *The Search for Order*, 45.

36. George Beard, American Nervousness (New York: G.P. Putnam's Sons, 1881), vi.

37. Meyer, *Positive Thinkers*, 131–32. See also Wiebe, *Search for Order*, 44.

38. Ibid., 132.

39. Beard, *American Nervousness*, 98–99.

40. Meyer, *Positive Thinkers*, 25–26.

41. Ibid., 29.

42. Wiebe, *Search for Order*, 63.

43. See Beard, *American Nervousness*, 10, for a list of the "symptoms" of the disease.

44. Tygiel, *Past Time*, 18.

45. Ibid., 18–22.

46. Meyer, *Positive Thinkers*, 26–27. The discussion of George Beard, herein, draws primarily from Meyer's study. See also pp. 28–31, 77–78.

47. Weiss, *American Myth of Success*, 52–60.

48. Ibid., 131.

49. Ralph Waldo Trine, *In Tune with the Infinite* (New York: Thomas Y. Crowell, 1898), 176.

50. Meyer, *Positive Thinkers*, 81.

51. Bannister, *Social Darwinism*, 125.

52. Ibid., 136–40.

53. Ibid.

54. Weiss, *American Myth of Success*, 140.

55. Ibid.

56. Ibid., 141. As Weiss notes, to those within the New Thought movement, because scientists could not conclusively prove that one's existence terminated at death, "their position rested on no firmer ground than the idealists." As a result, "immortality was a fact because men had always believed it to be so."

57. Ibid., 133.

58. Wiebe, *Search for Order*, 44–45; Weiss, *American Myth of Success*, 115–16.

59. Weiss, *American Myth of Success*, 162.

60. Bannister, *Social Darwinism*, 162. Spencer's criticism was of Henry Drummond and his work, *The Ascent of Man*.

61. Ibid., 219. His book, *The Genius*, expands upon this point in general as well as his interest in Christian Science. See Theodore Dreiser, *The Genius* (Urbana: University of Illinois Press, 2008).

62. Meyer, *Positive Thinkers*, 109.

63. Frank Haddock, *The Power of Will* (Auburndale, Mass.: Powerbook Library, 1907), 163.

64. Meyer, *Positive Thinkers*, 43–44.

65. Ibid., 167.

66. Ibid., 98–99.

67. "Napoleon Hill," Wikipedia, available at *http://en.wikipedia.org/wiki/Napoleon_Hill*.

68. Napoleon Hill, *Think and Grow Rich* (Radford, Va.: Wilder Publications, 2007).

69. Meyer, *Positive Thinkers*, 168.

70. William Sadler, *Worry and Nervousness* (Chicago: A.C. McClurg, 1915), 48.

71. Meyer, *Positive Thinkers*, 207.

72. Ibid., 44.

73. Ibid., 121–22.

74. Norman Vincent Peale, *The Power of Positive Thinking* (New York: Prentiss-Hall, 1952).

75. Weiss, *American Myth of Success*, 223–24.

76. Meyer, *Positive Thinkers*, 262.

77. Ibid., 282.

78. Norman Vincent Peale and Smiley Blanton, *Faith is the Answer* (New York: Abingdon Press, 1940), 49.

79. Abrams, *America Transformed*, 284–85.

80. Christopher Lehmann-Haupt, "Reverend Ike Dies at 74; Didn't See Money as Evil," *New York Times*, July 30, 2009, A22.

81. Laurie Goodstein, "Even in Recession, Believers Invest in the Gospel of Getting Rich," *New York Times*, August 16, 2009, 1, 22.

82. Indeed, as a nation, the United States is, and has been, an outlier when it comes to religion overall. A 2010 Gallup report of more than one hundred countries showed that although, in general, religiosity is highly correlated with poverty (that is, poorer nations tend to be more religious than richer ones), in the United States the opposite seems to be true—65 percent of Americans stated that religion was "an important part of their lives." See Charles M. Blow, "Religious Outlier," *New York Times*, September 4, 2010, A15.

83. This continues into the present, as the phenomenal successes of Rhonda Byrne's *The Secret* (New York: Atria Books, 2006), which sold more than nineteen million copies, and *The Power* (New York: Atria Books, 2010), which likewise spent significant time on best-seller lists, attest. Both books draw on the tradition of placing faith in "a godlike agent that provides whatever we desire," reality notwithstanding. Christopher Chabris and Daniel Simons, "Fight the Power," *New York Times Book Review*, September 26, 2010, 27.

84. Zinn, *Twentieth Century*, 411 (quoting Alan Bloom, *The Closing of the American Mind* [New York: Simon and Schuster, 1987]).

85. Positive thinkers can be found on both sides of the popular political spectrum. Although many of the most notable positive thinkers have been Republicans, Democrats too have been accused of ignoring reality for the rosier portrait of what could be. See David Brooks, "No Second Thoughts," *New York Times*, October 25, 2010. http://www.nytimes.com/2010/10/26/opinion/26brooks.html.

86. Abrams, *America Transformed*, 279.

87. Anderson, *Movement and the Sixties*, 8.

88. Abrams, *America Transformed*, 222.

89. Anderson, *Movement and the Sixties*, 11.

90. Marshall, *Baseball's Pivotal Era*, 243.

91. Ron Briley, *Class at Bat, Gender on Deck and Race in the Hole* (Jefferson, N.C.: McFarland, 2003), 59.

92. Snyder, *Well-Paid Slave*, 26.

93. Korr, *End of Baseball*, 43.

94. Marshall, *Baseball's Pivotal Era*, 398.

95. Meyer, *Positive Thinkers*, 171–72.

96. Ibid.

97. These stories were later collected in *100 Stories of Business Success* by the Editors of *Fortune Magazine* (New York: Simon and Schuster, 1954).

98. Meyer, *Positive Thinkers*, 172.

99. Korr, *End of Baseball*, 44.

100. Ibid., 242.

101. Ibid.

102. Zinn, *Twentieth Century*, 71.

103. Ibid.

104. See Brody, *Labor Embattled*, 20, 24.

105. Helyar, *Lords of the Realm*, 96–99.

106. Korr, *End of Baseball*, 37.

107. Ibid., drawing from Bavasi's May 22, 1967, *Sports Illustrated* article.

108. Buzzi Bavasi, "Money Makes the Player Go," *Sports Illustrated*, May 22, 1967, 44.

109. Korr, *End of Baseball*, 60.

110. Ibid., 9, 93; See also Helyar, *Lords of the Realm*, 10.

111. Helyar, *Lords of the Realm*, 91–92, remarking that the *Sporting News*, generally considered "the baseball bible," received a small subsidy from the commissioner's office and was "vitriolically anti-Miller." Owners used the paper to send their message to the baseball public (through the *Sporting News*'s writers) that the players were privileged and pampered.

112. Thomas Frank, *What's The Matter With Kansas?: How Conservatives Won the Heart of America* (New York: Henry Holt, 2004), 193.

113. Orestes Swett Marden, *Every Man a King, or Might in Mind Mastery* (New York: Thomas Y. Crowell, 1906).

114. Weiss, *American Myth of Success*, 225.

115. Frank, *What's The Matter With Kansas?*, 23, 192. The "elitist" label has dogged President Obama throughout his tenure, with his intellectualism dismissed as snobbery in the eyes of critics seeking to portray him as out of touch with "average" Americans. See "The Charge that Obama Can't Shake: Why the Elitism Tag Carries Power This Year," *New York Times*, October 31, 2010, Week In Review 1, 6.

116. Anderson, *Movement and the Sixties*, 149. See also Brody, *Labor Embattled*, 20 (noting that labor leaders are routinely "among the least admired in every public opinion poll").

117. Korr, *End of Baseball*, 245.

118. William W. Wright and Mick Cochrane, "The Uses of History in Baseball Labor Disputes," in Paul D. Staudohar, ed., *Diamond Mines: Baseball and Labor* (Syracuse, N.Y.: Syracuse University Press, 2000), 62, 68.

119. Ibid., 69.
120. Korr, *End of Baseball*, 126.
121. Ibid., 126.
122. Ibid., 238.
123. Bowie Kuhn, *Hardball: The Education of a Baseball Commissioner* (Lincoln: University of Nebraska Press, 1997), 77.
124. Korr, *End of Baseball*, 237.
125. 407 U.S. 258 (1972). See also, Nathanson, "Truly Sovereign At Last," where this analysis originated, in modified form.
126. Ibid., 263–64.
127. Ibid., 282.
128. Ibid., 266–67.
129. Ibid., 286 (Douglas, J. dissenting) (footnote omitted).
130. Ibid., 287.
131. Korr, *End of Baseball*, 82.
132. Abrams, *America Transformed*, 281.
133. Anderson, *Movement and the Sixties*, 250.
134. Abrams, *America Transformed*, 286.
135. Ibid., 294.
136. This disparity continues today. See Charles M. Blow, "The Prurient Trap," *New York Times*, June 27, 2009, A17, which summarizes recent studies showing the disparity between the thoughts and actions of American social conservatives. One study, entitled "Red Light States: Who Buys Online Adult Entertainment?" found that subscriptions to online pornography sites were "more prevalent in states where surveys indicate conservative positions on religion, gender roles, and sexuality," and in states where "more people agree that 'I have old-fashioned values about family and marriage.'" Others found that divorce rates and teen pregnancy rates were highest in the traditional "red" states that have historically voted for socially conservative candidates preaching traditional family values.
137. Abrams, *America Transformed*, 294.
138. Wright and Cochrane, "Uses of History in Baseball Labor Disputes," 66.
139. Robert Lipsyte, "In Memoriam," *New York Times*, September 15, 1994, A1.
140. George Weigel, "Politically-Correct Baseball," *Commentary*, November 1994. Available at *http://www.commentarymagazine.com*.
141. Wright and Cochrane, "Uses of History in Baseball Labor Disputes," 78–79.
142. Ibid.
143. *Field of Dreams*, dir. Phil Alden Robinson, 107 min., Universal 1989, motion picture.
144. In the book upon which the film was based, *Shoeless Joe*, Jones's character, Terence Mann, was the white writer J. D. Salinger. W. P. Kinsella, *Shoeless Joe* (New York: Mariner Books, 1999).
145. Wright and Cochrane, "Uses of History in Baseball Labor Disputes," 78.

146. See Tim Arango, "Myth of Baseball's Creation Endures, With a Prominent Fan," *New York Times,* November 13, 2010, B9.

147. Bernard-Henri Levy, *American Vertigo: Traveling America in the Footsteps of Tocqueville* (New York: Random House, 2007), 28.

148. Ibid.

149. Wright and Cochrane, "Uses of History in Baseball Labor Disputes," 79.

CHAPTER 6. THE STORYTELLERS

1. Thorn, *Baseball in the Garden,* 102–4. Cauldwell discussed baseball in a May 1, 1853, column and later reported on a July game between the Knickerbockers and the Gothams.

2. Andrew J. Schiff, *The Father of Baseball* (Jefferson, N.C.: McFarland, 2008), 8.

3. Ibid.

4. Ibid.

5. Ibid., 18.

6. Morris, *But Didn't We Have Fun?,* 40–41.

7. Thorn, *Baseball in the Garden,* 42.

8. Schiff, *Father of Baseball,* 7.

9. Kaufman and Patterson, *Global Spread of Cricket,* 82, 92.

10. Thorn, *Baseball in the Garden,* 86, 99.

11. Schiff, *Father of Baseball,* 17.

12. Ibid., 26–27.

13. Ibid., 173–74.

14. Thorn, *Baseball in the Garden,* 110–14.

15. Schiff, *Father of Baseball,* 42.

16. See Peterson, "Red Press Nation," 40.

17. Morris, *But Didn't We Have Fun?,* 66.

18. Ibid.

19. Schiff, *Father of Baseball,* 48. Technically speaking, credit for the nine-inning and ninety-foot rules should go to Louis Wadsworth, a player who spent time with both the Gotham as well as the Knickerbocker clubs. See Thorn, *Baseball in the Garden,* 50–54. Chadwick's role as the "voice of the game," discussed herein, draws primarily from Schiff's text. See also pp. 59, 68, 105, 161.

20. Ibid., 70–71. See also Michael Lewis, *Moneyball: The Art of Winning an Unfair Game* (New York: W.W. Norton, 2003), 70.

21. Lewis, *Moneyball,* 69–70; Schiff, *Father of Baseball,* 83.

22. Schiff, *Father of Baseball,* 83.

23. Ibid.

24. Ibid., 79.

25. Ibid., 85.

26. Lewis, *Moneyball,* 70–71.
27. Schiff, *Father of Baseball,* 86. Chadwick's use of statistics and other means to promote baseball, as well as his influence on the emerging field of baseball journalism, discussed herein, draws primarily from Schiff's text. See also pp. 117, 156–58, 221.
28. Ibid., 88–89.
29. Ibid., 221.
30. Morris, *But Didn't We Have Fun?,* 147–48, 151.
31. Rader, *Baseball: A History,* 35.
32. Ibid., 174–75.
33. Peterson, "Red Press Nation," 39.
34. Rader, *Baseball: A History,* 133–34.
35. Wilborn Hampton, *Babe Ruth: A Twentieth Century Life* (New York: Viking, 2009), 12. In truth, Ruth was a troubled youth whose parents placed him in a reform school for delinquents and orphans at the age of seven.
36. Rader, *Baseball: A History,* 133–34.
37. Tygiel, *Past Time,* 77–79.
38. Ibid., 61.
39. Queenan, *True Believers,* 16. In fact, a well-traveled myth has it that the term "Black Sox" originated not from the 1919 World Series scandal but from the White Sox players' habitually dirty uniforms. In their book *Freakonomics,* Steven Levitt and Steven Dubner investigated this claim and found it to be without significant foundation. See Steven Levitt and Steven Dubner, *Freakonomics: A Rogue Economist Explores the Hidden Side of Everything,* rev. ed. (New York: William Morrow, 2006), 266–68.
40. Voigt, *American Baseball,* 237.
41. John Heidenry, *The Gashouse Gang* (New York: Public Affairs, 2007), 149–50.
42. Ibid., 129.
43. Marshall, *Baseball's Pivotal Era,* 334–35.
44. Ibid., 336.
45. Ibid., 337.
46. Rader, *Baseball: A History,* 176–77.
47. Heidenry, *Gashouse Gang,* 32.
48. Tony Silvia, "The Art and Artifice of Early Radio Baseball Re-Creations," 15 *NINE: A Journal of Baseball Culture and History,* Spring 2007, 87.
49. Although the FCC required broadcasters to inform listeners that the games were re-creations, this was often done quietly and with a fanciful nod to the contrary, such as Nat Allbright's "Welcome to Ebbetts Field!" See, for example, Douglas Martin, "Nat Allbright, 87, Voice of Dodgers Games He Did Not See," *New York Times,* August 16, 2011, B16.
50. Silvia, "Art and Artifice," 89.

51. Voigt, *American Baseball,* 269.

52. Silvia, "Art and Artifice," 91–92.

53. Ibid., 93.

54. Ibid.

55. Edward S. Herman and Noam Chomsky, *Manufacturing Consent: The Political Economy of the Mass Media* (New York: Pantheon Books, 1988, 2002), lix.

56. Ibid., lx.

57. Ibid.

58. Korr, *End of Baseball,* 8.

59. Ibid., 119.

60. "Cardinals' Owner Lectures Players on Virtues of Proposed Pension Plan," *Late Innings,* 273.

61. George Castle, *Baseball and the Media: How Fans Lose in Today's Coverage of the Game* (Lincoln: University of Nebraska Press, 2006), 38.

62. Guevara and Fidler, *Stealing Lives,* 48. Guevara and Fidler's book focused on the Chicago Cubs' baseball academy in the Dominican Republic. Although members of the Cubs organization would not confirm much of the worst that was reported within their study (Oneri Fleita, the Cubs' director of player development/Latin American operations at the time, replied to the allegations made by a former player at the academy by saying that "[t]here was a general feeling that you can please some of the people some of the time, but never all the people."), a 2003 investigation conducted by the *Chicago Tribune* corroborated many of the allegations. See Gary Marx, "Cubs Odyssey Was Bad Trip, He Claims," *Chicago Tribune,* June 29, 2003. Available at http://articles.chicagotribune.com/2003–06–29/sports/0306290354_1_dominican-republic-cubs-officials-cubs-director. The *Tribune* likewise noted that a confidential MLB report similarly supported the charges made within the book. David Wilder, the former minor-league director for the Cubs, acknowledged the conditions in general at these baseball academies: "It's a Third World country, and that's the way [the clubs] treated it."

63. Ibid., 69.

64. Of course, not everyone within the media has ignored the exploitation inherent within the Latin American baseball academies. Steve Fainaru of the *Washington Post* has written numerous critical articles on the topic. See, for example, Steve Fainaru, "Baseball's Minor Infractions: In Latin America, Young Players Come at a Bargain Price," *Washington Post,* October 26, 2001, D1. Fainaru's perspective is a dissenting one, however.

65. Ibid., 50.

66. Samuel O. Regalado, *Viva Baseball! Latin Major Leaguers and their Special Hunger,* 3d ed. (Urbana: University of Illinois Press, 1998, 2008), 172.

67. Ibid., 208.

68. Ibid., 123.

69. Ibid., quoting Phil Musick, *Who Was Roberto? A Biography of Roberto Clemente* (New York: Doubleday, 1974), 126.

70. Ibid., 60, quoting Jerry Izenberg, *Great Latin Sports Figures: The Proud People* (New York: Doubleday, 1976), 79.

71. Castle, *Baseball and the Media*, 106–7, 167.

72. Herman and Chomsky, *Manufacturing Consent*, 4.

73. Ibid., 14.

74. Zirin, "Lester Speaks."

75. Silber, *Press Box Red*, 35.

76. For example, in 1945 the *Daily Worker* sold for five cents; the *New York Times* three cents. Although this difference seems a pittance today, in 1945 it was the difference between spending the equivalent of $5.90 for the *Daily Worker* and $3.40 for the *New York Times* when those 1945 figures are adjusted for inflation into 2009 dollars.

77. Herman and Chomsky, *Manufacturing Consent*, 14.

78. Ibid.

79. Ibid., 21–22.

80. Castle, *Baseball and the Media*, 153–54, 164–65.

81. Ibid.

82 Ibid., 105.

83. Herman and Chomsky, *Manufacturing Consent*, 305–6.

84. Ibid., xii, 302.

85. Alan Schwarz, "When a Secret Opened the Door to Candid Sports Reporting," *New York Times*, September 14, 2008, N2.

86. Ibid.

87. See Leonard Koppett, "Eager Beavers +Pack Rats = Chipmunks: Youth, Hustle, Irreverence Mark New Writing Breed," *Sporting News*, April 16, 1966.

88. Wiebe, *Search for Order*, 147.

89. Voigt, *American Baseball*, 238–40.

90. Ibid.

91. Larry Merchant, "The Record Business," *New York Post*, April 23, 1970.

92. Scott Gray, *The Mind of Bill James: How a Complete Outsider Changed Baseball* (New York: Doubleday, 2006), 15. Unless otherwise noted, the discussion of Bill James draws primarily from Gray's text. See also pp. 26–34, 40–42, 60, 78, 85, 117.

93. Tygiel, *Past Time*, 213.

94. Ibid.

95. Ibid., 219.

96. Gray, *Mind of Bill James*, 72.

97. Ibid.

98. Ibid., 71–72.

99. See http://www.retrosheet.org/.

100. Gray, *Mind of Bill James*, 74–75.

101. See Tyler Kepner, "Use of Statistics Helps Greinke to Cy Young," *New York Times*, November 18, 2009, B13; Kepner, "A New Generation of Statistics Redefines Baseball," *New York Times*, November 22, 2009, Sports Sunday 1. This trend continued in 2010 when Seattle's Felix Hernandez won the AL Cy Young Award with only thirteen victories—the lowest total ever for a Cy Young–winning starting pitcher in a nonstrike season. See Ross Newhan, "Why Winning Isn't the Only Thing," *New York Times*, November 21, 2010, Sports Sunday 5.

102. Gray, *Mind of Bill James*, 88.

103. Isaac Gewirtz, *Kerouac At Bat: Fantasy Sports and the King of the Beats* (New York: New York Public Library, 2009), 31.

104. Ibid., 7, 36.

105. Ibid., 7.

106. Ibid., 46.

107. Charles McGrath, "Another Side of Kerouac: The Dharma Bum as Sports Nut," *New York Times*, May 16, 2009, C1, 8.

108. "Baseball Seminar: The First Fantasy Baseball Game?" *Late Innings*, 256–57.

109. Ibid.

110. Tygiel, *Past Time*, 199–200.

111. Ibid., 198.

112. Surina Mann, Comment, "*C.B.C. Distribution And Marketing, Inc. V. Major League Baseball Advanced Media, L.P.*: The First Amendment Versus The Right of Publicity in the Eighth Circuit," 31 *Hastings Communications and Entertainment Law Journal*, 303, 313 (2009).

113. Gray, *Mind of Bill James*, 55, 56.

114. Ibid., 150.

115. Mann, "*C.B.C. v. MLB AM*," 313.

116. Stacey B. Evans, comment, "Whose Stats are they Anyway? Analyzing the Battle Between Major League Baseball and Fantasy Game Sites," 9 *Texas Review of Entertainment and Sports Law*, 335, 339 (2008).

117. Ibid., 339.

118. *C.B.C. Distribution and Marketing, Inc. v. Major League Baseball Advanced Media, L.P.*, 443 F.Supp.2d 1077 (2006).

119. Ibid., *C.B.C. Distribution and Marketing, Inc. v. Major League Baseball Advanced Media, L.P.*, 505 F.3d 818 (2007).

120. 505 F.3d. 823–24, quoting *Gionfriddo v. Major League Baseball*, 94 Cal. App.4th 400, 411 (2001).

121. Nicholas D. Kristof, "The Daily Me," *New York Times*, March 19, 2009, A27.

122. Roth, *Great American Novel*, 90–91.

123. Tygiel, *Past Time*, 85–86.

124. Gray, *Mind of Bill James,* 55.

125. Ibid., 59.

126. Ibid., 147.

127. Castle, *Baseball and the Media,* 193.

128. Ibid.

129. Ibid., 203.

130. http://www.deadspin.com.

131. Balls Deep, "Ricky Reilly, Billy Simmons, and the Follies of Privileged Sportswriting," Available at http://www.deadspin.com.

132. Ibid.

133. Ibid.

134. Ibid.

135. Dave Zirin, "Blogged Down: The Seduction of Buzz Bissinger," Available at http://edgeofsports.com.

136. Ibid.

137. David Carr, "Here the Messages Are the Media (Tweet, Tweet)," *New York Times,* March 18, 2009, C1, 5.

138. Matt Bai, "The Other Winner," *New York Times Magazine,* November 16, 2008, 11; "From Dean to Obama: Four Years in the Internet Revolution," available at http://www.netrootsnation.org.

139. Ibid.

140. Katie Zezima, "Dartmouth Junior Wins County Election and Starts Town vs. Gown Dispute," *New York Times,* November 13, 2008, A18.

141. Tim Arango, "Tension Over Sports Blogging," *New York Times,* available at http://www.nytimes.com.

142. Ibid.

143. Castle, *Baseball and the Media,* 244.

144. Ibid., 244–45.

145. Ibid.

146. Lou Dubois, "The Evolution of Sports Blog Nation," Inc., August 20, 2010, available at: http://www.inc.com/news/articles/2010/08/interview-with-jim-bankoff-ceo-of-sbnation.html.

147. Kim Hart, "A New Arena for Hard-Core Sports Fans," *Washington Post,* February 9, 2009, available at http://www.washingtonpost.com/wp-dyn/content/article/2009/02/08/AR2009020801725.html.

148. Ibid.

149. Ibid.

150. Pradnya Joshi, "When a Blogger Voices Approval, A Sponsor May Be Lurking," *New York Times,* July 13, 2009, B1.

151. Tim Arango, "Soon, Bloggers Must Give Full Disclosure," *New York Times,* October 6, 2009, B3.

152. Ibid.

153. See Zirin, Blogged Down."

BIBLIOGRAPHY

BOOKS

Abrams, Richard M. *America Transformed: Sixty Years of Revolutionary Change, 1941–2001.* New York: Cambridge University Press, 2006.

Adelman, Melven L. *A Sporting Time: New York City and the Rise of Modern Athletics, 1820–70.* Urbana: University of Illinois Press, 1986.

Anderson, Terry. *The Movement and the Sixties: Protest in America From Greensboro to Wounded Knee.* New York: Oxford University Press, 1995.

Baltzell, E. Digby. *The Protestant Establishment: Aristocracy and Caste in America.* New York: Vintage Books, 1964, 1966.

Bannister, Robert C. *Social Darwinism: Science and Myth in Anglo-American Social Thought.* Philadelphia: Temple University Press, 1979.

Bauman, John. *Public Housing, Race and Renewal.* Philadelphia: Temple University Press, 1987.

Beard, George. *American Nervousness.* New York: G.P. Putnam's Sons, 1881.

Booker, Bryan. *African Americans in the United States Army in World War II.* Jefferson, N.C.: McFarland, 2008.

Briley, Ron. *Class at Bat, Gender on Deck and Race in the Hole.* Jefferson, N.C.: McFarland, 2003.

Brody, David. *Labor Embattled: History, Power, Rights.* Urbana: University of Illinois Press, 2005.

Byrne, Rhonda. *The Secret.* New York: Atria Books, 2006.

———. *The Power.* New York: Atria Books, 2010.

Castle, George. *Baseball and the Media: How Fans Lose in Today's Coverage of the Game.* Lincoln: University of Nebraska Press, 2006.

Chomsky, Noam. *Media Control: The Spectacular Achievements of Propaganda.* 2d ed. New York: Seven Stories Press, 1991, 2002.

Dawidoff, Nicholas. *The Crowd Sounds Happy.* New York: Vintage Books, 2008.

Dreiser, Theodore. *The Genius.* Urbana: University of Illinois Press, 2008.

Fernandez-Armesto, Felipe. *Amerigo: The Man Who Gave His Name to America.* New York: Random House, 2007, 2008.

Frank, Thomas. *What's The Matter With Kansas?: How Conservatives Won the Heart of America.* New York: Henry Holt, 2004.

Gallagher, Mark. *The Yankees Encyclopedia.* 4th ed. New York: Sports Publishing, 2000.

Gewirtz, Isaac. *Kerouac At Bat: Fantasy Sports and the King of the Beats.* New York: New York Public Library, 2009.

Gifford, Frank, and Peter Richmond. *The Glory Game: How the 1958 NFL Championship Changed Football Forever.* New York: Harper, 2008.

Gray, Scott. *The Mind of Bill James: How a Complete Outsider Changed Baseball.* New York: Doubleday, 2006.

Haddock, Frank. *The Power of Will.* Auburndale, Mass.: Powerbook Library, 1907.

Hampton, Wilborn. *Babe Ruth: A Twentieth Century Life.* New York: Viking, 2009.

Heidenry, John. *The Gashouse Gang.* New York: Public Affairs, 2007.

Helyar, John. *Lords of the Realm: The Real History of Baseball.* New York: Villard Books, 1994.

Herman, Edward S., and Noam Chomsky. *Manufacturing Consent: The Political Economy of the Mass Media.* New York: Pantheon Books, 1988, 2002.

Hill, Napolean. *Think and Grow Rich.* Radford, Va.: Wilder Publications, 2007.

Hofstadter, Richard. *The Age of Reform.* New York: Vintage Books, 1955.

———. *Social Darwinism in American Thought.* New York, Beacon Press, 1992.

Izenberg, Jerry. *Great Latin Sports Figures: The Proud People.* New York: Doubleday, 1976.

Kinsella, W. P. *Shoeless Joe.* New York: Mariner Books, 1999.

Kirsch, George B. *Baseball and Cricket: The Creation of American Team Sports, 1838–72.* Urbana: University of Illinois Press, 1989, 2007.

Knoles, George H. *The Presidential Campaign and Election of 1892.* Palo Alto, Calif.: Stanford University Press, 1942.

Koppett, Leonard. *Koppett's Concise History of Major League Baseball.* New York: Carroll and Graf, 2004.

Korr, Charles P. *The End of Baseball As We Knew It: The Players Union, 1960–81.* Urbana: University of Illinois Press, 2002.

Kuhn, Bowie. *Hardball: The Education of a Baseball Commissioner.* Lincoln: University of Nebraska Press, 1997.

Lanctot, Neil. *Negro League Baseball: The Rise and Ruin of a Black Institution.* Philadelphia: University of Pennsylvania Press, 2004.

Levitt, Steven, and Steven Dubner. *Freakonomics: A Rogue Economist Explores the Hidden Side of Everything.* Rev. ed. New York: William Morrow, 2006.

Levy, Bernard-Henri. *American Vertigo: Traveling America in the Footsteps of Tocqueville.* New York: Random House, 2007.

Lewis, Michael. *Moneyball: The Art of Winning an Unfair Game*. New York: W.W. Norton, 2003.

Long, Michael G., ed. *First Class Citizenship: The Civil Rights Letters of Jackie Robinson*. New York: Henry Holt, 2007.

Lowenfish, Lee. *Branch Rickey: Baseball's Ferocious Gentleman*. Lincoln: University of Nebraska Press, 2007.

Madden, Bill. *Steinbrenner: The Last Lion of Baseball*. New York: Harper, 2010.

Marcano Guevara, Arturo J., and David P. Fidler. *Stealing Lives: The Globalization of Baseball and the Tragic Story of Alexis Quiroz*. Bloomington: University of Indiana Press, 2002.

Marden, Orestes Swett. *Every Man a King, or Might in Mind Mastery*. New York: Thomas Y. Crowell, 1906.

Marshall, William. *Baseball's Pivotal Era: 1945–1951*. Lexington: University Press of Kentucky, 1999.

McKelvey, Richard G. *Mexican Raiders in the Major Leagues: The Pasquel Brothers vs. Organized Baseball, 1946*. Jefferson, N.C.: McFarland, 2006.

Meyer, Donald. *The Positive Thinkers*. Middletown, Ct.: Wesleyan University Press, 1988.

Morris, Peter. *But Didn't We Have Fun?: An Informal History of Baseball's Pioneer Era, 1843–1870*. Chicago: Ivan R. Dee, 2008.

Mott, Frank L. *Golden Multitudes: The Story of Best Sellers in the United States*. New York: Macmillan, 1947.

Musick, Phil. *Who Was Roberto? A Biography of Roberto Clemente*. New York: Doubleday, 1974.

Nathan, Daniel A. *Saying It's So: A Cultural History of the Black Sox Scandal*. Urbana: University of Illinois Press, 2005.

Nathanson, Mitchell. *The Fall of the 1977 Phillies: How a Baseball Team's Collapse Sank a City's Spirit*. Jefferson, N.C.: McFarland, 2008.

Peale, Norman Vincent. *The Power of Positive Thinking*. New York: Prentiss-Hall, 1952.

Peale, Norman Vincent, and Smiley Blanton. *Faith is the Answer*. New York: Abingdon Press, 1940.

Powers-Beck, Jeffrey. *The American Indian Integration of Baseball*. Lincoln: University of Nebraska Press, 2009.

Queenan, Joe. *True Believers: The Tragic Inner Life of Sports Fans*. New York: Henry Holt, 2003.

Rader, Benjamin G. *Baseball: A History of America's Game*. Urbana: University of Illinois Press, 2002.

Rampersad, Arnold. *Jackie Robinson: A Biography*. New York: Ballantine Books, 1998.

Regalado, Samuel O. *Viva Baseball!: Latin Major Leaguers and their Special Hunger*. Urbana: University of Illinois Press, 1998, 2008.

Riess, Steven A. *Touching Base: Professional Baseball and American Culture in the Progressive Era.* Urbana: University of Illinois Press, 1999.

Robinson, Jackie, and Alfred Duckett. *I Never Had It Made: An Autobiography of Jackie Robinson.* New York: Harper Perennial, 2003.

Roth, Philip. *The Great American Novel.* New York: Vintage International, 1973.

Rowan, Carl T., and Jackie Robinson. *Wait Till Next Year.* New York: Random House, 1960.

Sadler, William. *Worry and Nervousness.* Chicago: A.C. McClurg, 1915.

Sahadi, Lou. *One Sunday in December: The 1958 NFL Championship Game and How it Changed Professional Football.* New York: Lyons Press, 2008.

Schiff, Andrew J. *The Father of Baseball.* Jefferson, N.C.: McFarland, 2008.

Seymour, Harold. *Baseball: The Early Years.* New York: Oxford University Press, 1960, 1989.

———. *Baseball: The Golden Age.* New York: Oxford University Press, 1971, 1989.

Shapiro, Michael. *Bottom of the Ninth: Branch Rickey, Casey Stengel, and the Daring Scheme to Save Baseball From Itself.* New York: Henry Holt, 2009.

Shiffert, John. *Base Ball in Philadelphia: A History of the Early Game, 1831–1900.* Jefferson, N.C.: McFarland, 2006.

Silber, Irwin. *Press Box Red: The Story of Lester Rodney, the Communist Who Helped Break the Color Line in American Sports.* Philadelphia: Temple University Press, 2003.

Snyder, Brad. *A Well-Paid Slave: Curt Flood's Fight for Free Agency in Baseball.* New York: Viking Penguin, 2006.

Spink, J. G. Taylor. *Judge Landis and Twenty-Five Years of Baseball.* New York: Amereon,1947.

Sullivan, Dean A., ed. *Late Innings: A Documentary History of Baseball, 1945–1972.* Lincoln: University of Nebraska Press, 2002.

Swaine, Rick. *The Black Stars Who Made Baseball Whole.* Jefferson, N.C.: McFarland, 2006.

Thorne, John. *Baseball in the Garden of Eden: The Secret History of the Early Game.* New York: Simon and Schuster, 2011.

Tilly, Charles. *Democracy.* New York: Cambridge University Press, 2007.

Trine, Ralph Waldo. *In Tune with the Infinite.* New York: Thomas Y. Crowell, 1898.

Tygiel, Jules. *Baseball's Great Experiment: Jackie Robinson and his Legacy.* New York: Oxford University Press, 1983, 2008.

———. *Past Time: Baseball As History.* New York: Oxford University Press, 2000, 2001.

Voigt, David Q. *American Baseball: From the Commissioners to Continental Expansion.* University Park: Pennsylvania State University Press, 1983.

Wall, Joseph. *Andrew Carnegie.* New York: Oxford University Press, 1970.

Weiss, Richard. *The American Myth of Success: From Horatio Alger to Norman Vincent Peale*. Urbana: University of Illinois Press, 1988.

Wiebe, Robert H. *The Search for Order, 1877–1920*. New York: Hill and Wang, 1967.

Zinn, Howard. *The Twentieth Century: A People's History*. New York: Harper Perennial, 1998, 2003.

———. *A People's History of the United States*. New York: Harper Perennial, 2010.

ARTICLES, CHAPTERS IN BOOKS, PAPERS, AND THESES

Alito, Samuel A., Jr. "The Origin of the Baseball Antitrust Exemption: *Federal Baseball Club of Baltimore, Inc. v. National League of Professional Baseball Players*." 38, *Baseball Research Journal* 86 (Fall 2009).

Armour, Mark. "The Effects of Integration, 1947–1986." 36 *Baseball Research Journal*, 53 (2007).

Baron, Jane B. "Resistance to Stories." 67 *Southern California Law Review*, 255 (1994).

Bavasi, Buzzi. "Money Makes the Player Go." *Sports Illustrated*, May 22, 1967, 44.

Black, Charles. "The Unfinished Business of the Warren Court." 46 *Washington Law Review*, 3 (1970).

Blaisdell, Lowell L. "The Cobb-Speaker Scandal." 13 *NINE: A Journal of Baseball History and Culture*, 54 (2004).

———. "Judge Landis Takes a Different Approach." 15 *NINE: A Journal of Baseball History and Culture*, 32 (2006).

Carney, Gene. "Uncovering the Fix of the 1919 World Series: The Role of Hugh Fullerton." 13 *NINE: A Journal of Baseball History and Culture*, 39 (2004).

Carter, Robert L. "The Warren Court and Desegregation." 67 *Michigan Law Review*, 237 (1968).

Davies, Ross E. "The Sport of Courts." 38 *Baseball Research Journal*, 59 (Fall 2009).

Delgado, Richard. "On Telling Stories in School: A Reply to Farber and Sherry." 46 *Vanderbilt Law Review*, 665 (1993).

Delgado, Richard, and Jean Stefancic. "Images of the Outsider in American Law and Culture: Can Free Expression Remedy Systemic Social Ills?" 77 *Cornell Law Review*, 1258 (1992).

Dunn, James R. "Title VI, The Guidelines and School Desegregation in the South." 53 *Virginia Law Review*, 42 (1967).

Durney, Jeffrey A. "Fair or Foul? The Commissioner and Major League Baseball's Disciplinary Process." 41 *Emory Law Journal*, 581 (1992).

Early, Gerald. "Performance and Reality: Race, Sports and the Modern World." *The Nation*, 11 (August 10–17, 1998).

Evans, Christopher H. "The Kingdom of Baseball in America: The Chronicle of an American Theology." In *Faith of 50 Million: Baseball, Religion and American Culture*. Louisville, Ky.: Westminster John Knox Press, 2002.

Evans, Stacey B. "Whose Stats are they Anyway? Analyzing the Battle Between Major League Baseball and Fantasy Game Sites." 9 *Texas Review of Entertainment and Sports Law*, 335 (2008).

Farber, Daniel A., and Suzanna Sherry. "Telling Stories Out of School: An Essay on Legal Narratives." 45 *Stanford Law Review*, 807 (1993).

Fetter, Henry D. "The Party Line and the Color Line: The American Communist Party, the Daily Worker, and Jackie Robinson." 28 *Journal of Sport History*, 375 (Fall 2001).

Fleer, Joshua. "The Church of Baseball and the U.S. Presidency." 16 *NINE: A Journal of Baseball History and Culture*, 51 (2007).

Goldschmied, Nadev. "The Appeal of the Underdog: Definition of the Construct and Implications for the Self." Ph.D. diss., University of South Florida, 2007.

Harris, Mark. "Branch Rickey Keeps His 40 Year Promise." *Negro Digest*, September 1947.

Haupert, Michael J. "A Look at Player Pay During the Integration Era." *Outside the Lines: A Publication of the SABR Business of Baseball Committee*, 1 (October 19, 2008).

Hazucha, Andrew. "Leo Durocher's Last Stand." 15 *NINE: A Journal of Baseball History and Culture*, 1 (2006).

Jamar, Steven D. "Aristotle Teaches Persuasion: The Psychic Connection." 8 *Scribes Journal of Legal Writing*, 61 (2001–2002).

Johansen, Stephen. "This Is Not the Whole Truth: The Ethics of Telling Stories to Clients." 38 *Arizona State Law Journal*, 961 (2006).

Kaufman, Jason, and Orlando Patterson. "Cross-National Cultural Diffusion: The Global Spread of Cricket." *American Sociological Review*, 70 (February 2005).

Klein, Michael W. "Rose Is In Red, Black Sox Are Blue: *A Comparison of Rose v. Giamatti* and the 1921 Black Sox Trial." 13 *Hastings Communication and Entertainment Law Journal*, 551 (1991).

Lieber, Jill, and Craig Neff. "The Case Against Pete Rose." *Sports Illustrated*, July 3, 1989.

Lowenfish, Lee. "When All Heaven Rejoiced: Branch Rickey and the Origins of the Breaking of the Color Line." 11 *NINE: A Journal of Baseball History and Culture*, 1 (2002).

Lusky, Louis. "Racial Discrimination and the Federal Law: A Problem in Nullification." 63 *Columbia Law Review*, 1163 (1963).

————. "The Stereotype: Hard Core of Racism." 13 *Buffalo Law Review*, 450 (1963).

Mann, Arthur. "The Life Story of Branch Rickey." *LOOK*, August 20, 1957.

Mann, Surina. "*C.B.C. Distribution And Marketing, Inc. V. Major League Baseball Advanced Media, L.P.*: The First Amendment Versus The Right of Publicity in the Eighth Circuit." 31 *Hastings Communications and Entertainment Law Journal*, 303 (2009).

Mitchell, George J. "Report to the Commissioner of Baseball of an Independent Investigation into the Illegal Use of Steroids and Other Performance

Enhancing Substances by Players in Major League Baseball." December 13, 2007.

Nathanson, Mitchell. "Gatekeepers of Americana: Ownership's Never-Ending Quest for Control of the Baseball Creed." 15 *NINE: A Journal of Baseball History and Culture*, 68 (Fall 2006).

———. "The Irrelevance of Baseball's Antitrust Exemption: A Historical Review." 58 *Rutgers Law Review*, 1 (2005).

———. "Law and Politics." In *Understanding Baseball: Approaches to the Scholarly Study of America's Game*, ed. Trey Stecker. Jefferson, N.C.: McFarland, 2012.

———. "Truly Sovereign At Last: C.B.C. Distribution v. MLB AM and the Redefinition of the Concept of Baseball." 89 *Oregon Law Review*, 581 (2010).

Newman, Roberta. "The American Church of Baseball and the National Baseball Hall of Fame." 10 *NINE: A Journal of Baseball History and Culture*, 46 (2001).

Noll, Roger G. "Major League Team Sports." In *The Structure of American Industry*, ed. Walter Adams, 5th ed. New York: MacMillan, 1977.

Nowatzki, Robert. "Foul Lines and the Color Line: Baseball and Race at the Turn of the Twentieth Century." 11 *NINE: A Journal of Baseball History and Culture*, 82 (2002).

Pachman, Matthew B. "Limits on the Discretionary Powers of Professional Sports Commissioners: A Historical and Legal Analysis of Issues Raised by the Pete Rose Controversy." 76 *Virginia Law Review*, 1409 (1990).

Peterson, Scott D. "Red Press Nation: The Baseball Rhetoric of Lester Rodney." In *The Politics of Baseball: Essays on the Pastime and Power at Home and Abroad*, ed. Ron Briley. Jefferson, N.C.: McFarland, 2010.

Powe, L. A., Jr. "The Road to Swann: Mobile County Crawls to the Bus." 51 *Texas Law Review*, 505 (1973).

Puerzer, Richard J. "Engineering Baseball: Branch Rickey's Innovative Approach to Baseball Management." 12 *NINE: A Journal of Baseball History and Culture*, 72 (2003).

Reinsdorf, Jonathan M. "The Powers of the Commissioner in Baseball." 7 *Marquette Sports Law Journal*, 211 (1996).

Rosenberg, Norman L. "Here Comes the Judge!: The Origins of Baseball's Commissioner System and American Legal Culture." 20 *Journal of Popular Culture*, 140 (Spring 1987).

Rychlak, Ronald J. "Pete Rose, Bart Giamatti, and the Dowd Report." 68 *Mississippi Law Journal*, 889 (1999).

Sagarin, Edward. "Who Roots for the Underdog?" 4 *Journal of Popular Culture*, 425 (1970).

Selig, Allan H. "Bud," and Robert D. Manfred Jr. "The Regulation of Nutritional Supplements in Professional Sports." 15 *Stanford Law and Policy Review*, 35 (2004).

Silvia, Tony. "The Art and Artifice of Early Radio Baseball Re-Creations." 15 *NINE: A Journal of Baseball Culture and History*, 87 (Spring 2007).

Treder, Steve. "The Persistent Color Line: Specific Instances of Racial Preference in Major League Player Evaluation Decisions after 1947." 10 *NINE: A Journal of Baseball History and Culture,* 1 (2001).

Vincent, Fay, "Memorandum To All Major League Clubs Re: Baseball's Drug Policy and Prevention Program." June 7, 1991.

Voigt, David Q. "The Chicago Black Sox and the Myth of Baseball's Single Sin." In *America Through Baseball,* 65. Chicago: Nelson-Hall, 1976.

Wilkinson, Todd. "Individual Differences and Sports Fans: Who Roots for the Underdog?" Ph.D. diss., University of Minnesota, 2006.

Wright, William. W., and Mick Cochrane. "The Uses of History in Baseball Labor Disputes." In *Diamond Mines: Baseball and Labor,* ed. Paul D. Staudohar. Syracuse, N.Y.: Syracuse University Press, 2000, 62.

Zirin, Dave. "Lester Speaks: An Interview with 'Red' Rodney." *Counterpunch,* Weekend Edition, April 3–5, 2004.

WEB SITE SOURCES

Balls Deep, "Ricky Reilly, Billy Simmons, and the Follies of Privileged Sportswriting," *Deadspin.* Available at http://www.deadspin.com.

Baseball Almanac.com. Available at: http://www.baseball-almanac.com.

Baseball Reference.com. Available at: http://www.baseball-reference.com.

Dubois, Lou. "The Evolution of Sports Blog Nation." *Inc.,* August 20, 2010. Available at: http://www.inc.com/news/articles/2010/08/interview-with-jim-bankoff-ceo-of-sbnation.html.

"From Dean to Obama: Four Years in the Internet Revolution." *Netrootsnation.* Available at http://www.netrootsnation.org.

Helyar, John. "Robinson Would Have Mixed View of Today's Game." *Espn.com,* April 9, 2007. Available at: http://sports.espn.go.com/mlb/jackie/news/story?id=2828584.

Ideology, Revolution and Utopia in Marx. Available at http://mindsmeaning morals.wordpress.com.

Joint Major League Committee, Report of Major League Steering Committee for Submission to the National and American Leagues at their Meetings in Chicago (1946). Available at http://www.businessofbaseball.com/docs.thm# steeringcommittee.

Lapchick, Richard. *The 2009 Racial and Gender Report Card: Major League Baseball.* Appendix I, table 15 (April 15, 2009). Available at http://tidesport .org/RGRC/2009/2009_MLB_RGRC_PR_Final_rev.pdf.

Morris, Charles, ed. *Makers of Philadelphia: An Historical Work Giving Portraits and Sketches of the Most Eminent Citizens of Philadelphia From the Time of William Penn to the Present Day.* Philadelphia: L.R. Hamersly, 1894. Available at https://secureapps.libraries.psu.edu/digitalbookshelf/bookindex.cfm ?oclc=29893541.

"Napoleon Hill." Wikipedia, available at http://en.wikipedia.org/wiki/ Napoleon_Hill.

"Powel Crosley Jr." In *Ohio History Central: An Online Encyclopedia of Ohio History*. Available at http://www.ohiohistorycentral.org/entry.php?rec= 63&nm=Powel-Crosley-Jr.

Retrosheet. Available at http://www.retrosheet.org.

Rockey, James. "Who Is Left Wing, And Who Just Thinks They Are?" Department of Economics, University of Leicester, UK, 2010. Available at http://econpapers.repec.org/RePEc:lec:leecon:09/23.

The Society for American Baseball Research. Available at http://www.sabr.org.

The Underdog. Available at http://convictcreations.com/culture/underdog.htm.

Verducci, Tom. "Blackout: The African-American Baseball Player is Vanishing. Does He Have a Future?" *Sports Illustrated*, July 7, 2003. Available at http://sportsillustrated.cnn.com/vault/article/magazine/MAG1029117/2/index .htm.

Weigel, George. "Politically-Correct Baseball." *Commentary*, November 1994. Available at http://www.commentarymagazine.com.

Zirin, Dave. "Blogged Down: The Seduction of Buzz Bissinger." Available at http://edgeofsports.com.

NEWSPAPERS

Baltimore Afro-American
Boston Globe
Chicago Defender
Chicago Herald-Examiner
Chicago Tribune
Daily Worker
Detroit News
Los Angeles Times
New York Daily Mirror
New York Daily News
New York Post
New York Times
People's Voice
Philadelphia Inquirer
Pittsburgh Courier
Sporting News
USA Today
Washington Post
Zanesville (Ohio) Times-Recorder

INDEX

Abrams, Cal, 100, 103
Alger, Horatio/Alger tales, 26, 153, 155, 158, 159, 195, 226n110
American Association, 17–18
Anderson, Sparky, 213
Angell, Roger, 208
Anson, Adrian "Cap," 71
Aristotle, xiii, 130
Athletics Base Ball Club (nineteenth century edition), 9–11
Atlanta National League Baseball Club v. Kuhn, 48–51, 62

"backyard rebellions," 140
Bakker, Jim, 175
Bankhead, Dan, 91
Banks, Ernie, 104
Barber, Red, 191
Barnhill, Dave, 77
baseball academies, Latin American, 195, 256n62, 256n64
baseball creed, the, 3, 21–27, 29–30, 37, 157, 180, 182, 184; and fantasy baseball, 208, 209; and Bill James, 202–3; and the Players Association, 171, 172; and Jackie Robinson, 69; and underdogs/positive thinking, 147, 151, 154
Bavasi, Buzzi, 168
Beard, George, 155–58, 162, 163, 170, 174, 183
Bernier, Carlos, 100
Bisher, Furman, 166
Black, Joe, 101
Blackmun, Justice Harry, 43–44, 47, 172–73
Black Sox scandal: and Judge Landis,

29–35; origin of the nickname "Black Sox," 255n39
blogs, baseball and, 211–19
Bloom, Allan, 163–64
Boas, Franz, 23
Bonds, Barry, 57–59, 60, 64, 227n1
Bostic, Joe, 78, 81
Bouton, Jim, 127, 141
Boyer, Clete, 127
Breadon, Sam, 82
Brock, Lou, 168
Brooklyn Brown Dodgers, 86–87
Brown v. Board of Education (Brown 1), 68, 93, 94–97, 98
Brown v. Board of Education (Brown 2), 93, 94–97, 98
Brush, John, 26
Buckley, William F., Jr., 164
Burger, Justice Warren, 43
Burns, Ken, 177
Busch, Gussie, 122, 168

Campanella, Roy, 77, 87, 89, 99, 102
Candelaria, John, 101
Cannon, Jimmy, 190
Canseco, Jose, 63
Carlisle Indian Industrial School, 24–25
Carnegie, Andrew, 19, 161, 167, 226n90
Carpenter, Robert, 120
Carrasquel, Chico, 101, 242n148
Carter, Jimmy, 175
Cauldwell, William, 181, 254n1
Cavaretta, Phil, 103
C.B.C. Distributing and Marketing Inc., v. MLB AM, 209–11
Celler, Emanuel, 114

Cepeda, Orlando, 195
Chadwick, Edwin, 183, 185–86
Chadwick, Henry, 180, 181–88, 193, 211; and the baseball creed, 157, 182–88, 201; and fantasy baseball, 208; and statistics, 183–87, 200, 204
Chadwick, James, 182
Chandler, Albert "Happy," 42, 93, 165
Chinese Exclusion Act of 1882, 20
"chipmunk" journalists, 199–200, 203
Chomsky, Noam, 198
Cincinnati Red Stockings, 10, 11
Clemens, Roger, 58, 64, 227n1
Clemente, Roberto, 100, 176, 195–96
Cobb, Ty, 30, 36–37
Collins, Joe, 103
Comiskey, Charles, 190
Congress of Racial Equality (CORE), 78
Continental League, 112–17, 122, 123
Copeland, Kenneth, 163
Corporate Revolution, 117–23
Costas, Bob, 215
Crosby, Bing, 92
Crosley, Powel, 120
Currier and Ives, 1

Darrow, Clarence, 22
Darwin, Charles, 19
Davis, Benjamin B., 78–79
Deadspin, 214–15
Dean, Dizzy, 190, 191
Dean, Howard, 216
Dean, Paul, 190
Dewey, John, 22, 160
DeWitt, William O., 131
DiMaggio, Joe: and the media/contrast with Ted Williams, 190–91, 215; and praise for Satchel Paige, 90, 196
Dobson, H. A., 186
Doby, Larry, 89, 106
Doubleday, Abner, 178
Douglas, William O., 173–74
Dowd, John, M., 52, 56
Downing, Al, 127
Dreiser, Theodore, 160
Dropo, Walt, 103
Drysdale, Don, 140
Duren, Ryne, 127, 199
Durocher, Leo, 72, 104
Dykstra, Lenny, 63, 234n145

Easter, Luke, 103
Edwards, Bruce, 99
Eisenhower, Dwight, 75
Epstein, Theo, 206
eugenics movement, 20, 23, 24
evolutionary environmentalism, 22–26, 160, 184

Fainaru, Steve, 199
Fair Employment Practices Act of 1941, 75, 76, 97
Falwell, Jerry, 164, 175
fantasy baseball, 206–11
Federal Baseball Club Supreme Court decision, 37–42, 173, 229n18
Federal League, 37–38, 229n18
Feeney, Chub, 141
Field of Dreams, 177–78
Finley, Charles O., 46–47
Finley v. Kuhn, 46–48, 49, 51, 53, 55–56, 62
Fisher, Jack, 142
Flood, Curt, 43, 129, 142–45, 172–73
Flood v. Kuhn, 43–44, 172–74
Food, Drug and Cosmetic Act of 1938, 62
Ford, Henry, 167
Foster, George, 202
Frick, Ford, 46, 115
Fullerton, Hugh: and the baseball creed, 23; and the Black Sox scandal, 31–32, 33, 190, 199

Galton, Francis, 20, 226n93
Gamble, Oscar, 104
Gammons, Peter, 63
Gamson, William, and the Baseball Seminar, 207–8
Gardella, Danny, 42, 165
Gervin, George, 49
Giamatti, A. Bartlett, 51, 52–56, 232n119
Giles, Bill, 129
Gingrich, Newt, 177–79
Goldwater, Barry, 174
Graham, Billy, 164
Greinke, Zack, 206

Haddock, Frank, 160
Harwell, Ernie, 208
Henry, John, 206
Hill, Napoleon, 161

Holmes, Justice Oliver Wendell, 39–41
Holschuh, John D., 54, 56
Houk, Ralph, 199
Howard, Elston, 105
Howsam, Bob, 142

Jackson, "Shoeless" Joe, 52, 59
James, Bill, 180, 200–206, 213; and the
    baseball creed, 202–3; and *C.B.C.
    Distribution and Marketing, Inc. v.
    MLB AM*, 210; and Henry Chadwick,
    201, 203–5; and fantasy baseball, 209;
    and Internet blogs, 213; and Project
    Scoresheet, 205
James, William, 153–54, 159
Jethroe, Sam, 100
Johnson, Ban, 14, 31, 109, 111
Johnson, Lou, 104

Kefauver, Estes, 114, 115–16
Kelly, Ned 150
Kerouac, Jack, and fantasy baseball, 207
Kiner, Ralph, 132
Knickerbocker Base Ball Club, 7, 8, 13,
    183, 223n23
Koppett, Leonard, 194, 199
Koufax, Sandy, 140
Kuhn, Bowie: and *Atlanta National
    League Baseball Club v. Kuhn*, 48, 50;
    and defense of the owners in labor
    negotiations, 142; and *Finley v. Kuhn*,
    47; and Marvin Miller, 171

Lacy, Sam, 78, 79
LaGuardia, Fiorello, 76, 79, 81, 84, 85
Landis, Judge Kenesaw Mountain: and
    the Black Sox scandal, 29–35; and the
    Federal League, 112, 229n18; and his
    judicial career, 32; and *Milwaukee AA
    v. Landis*, 44–46, 51; and other base-
    ball scandals, 35–37; and his powers as
    Commissioner of Baseball, 33–37; and
    the protection of MLB's color line,
    71–72, 78, 84, 236n22, 237n24; and the
    "single sin" myth, 33
Lane, Frank, 166–67
Lardner, Ring, 189
Larsen, Don, 127
Lewis, J. Norman, 132
Lewis, John L., 136

Lincecum, Tim, 206
Lipsyte, Robert, 176–77
Lopez, Hector, 127
Louis, Joe, 74
Low, Nat, 77
Lurie, Bob, 48

Malcolm X, 91
Mantle, Mickey, 105, 131, 176
Maris, Roger, 127, 168, 202
Martin, Billy, 105, 131
Matthews, Gary, 48
Mays, Willie, 104, 176
McGwire, Mark, 57, 58, 233n133
McLendon, Gordon, 192
McNally, Dave, 108, 144
McNamee, Graham, 191
McPhail, Larry, 72, 79, 125
McPhail, Lee, 105
Messersmith, Andy, 108, 144
Mexican League, 112
Miller, Marvin, 110, 111, 112, 122, 129,
    130, 133, 140–41, 142, 166, 252n111;
    and the baseball creed, 172; and be-
    nevolent paternalism, 168–69, 171;
    and communism, 165, 171; and posi-
    tive thinking, 170–72
*Milwaukee American Association v. Lan-
    dis*, 44–46, 47, 51, 62, 83
mind cure, 158, 160, 162, 169, 171, 174,
    175, 179
Minoso, Minnie, 101, 105–6
Mitchell, George, 59, 60, 65
Mitchell Report, 59–66, 194, 235n159
Mize, Johnny, 127
Moreno, Omar, 101
Moss, Dick, 143
Munsey, Frank, 167
Murcer, Bobby, 127
Murphy, Robert, 130
"Murphy money," 130, 132
Musial, Stan, 168

NAABP (National Association of Ama-
    teur Base Ball Players), 11
NABBP (National Association of Base
    Ball Players), 11
National Association (National Associa-
    tion of Professional Base Ball Players),
    11–12

Newcombe, Don, 87, 89, 101, 102
New Thought movement, 159–60, 250n56
Nightengale, Bob, 63–64
Nixon, Richard, 165

Obama, Barack, 216, 252n115
Okrent, Daniel, and Rotisserie League Baseball, 208, 209
O'Malley, Walter, 130, 143, 165
Owens, Jesse, 74

Pacific Coast League, possible promotion to a third major league, 112–13
Pafko, Andy, 103
Paige, Satchel, 90, 196
Palmeiro, Rafael, 58
Parker, Dan, 105
Peale, Norman Vincent, 162–63, 166, 169
Pena, Tony, 101
Pendleton, Jim 103
Peters, Ron, 52–53
Plessy v. Ferguson, 68, 71, 84, 91, 94
Porter, William Trotter, 13
Port Huron Statement, 138
Powell, Adam Clayton, 78, 84
Power, Vic, 104–5, 242n169
Pratt, Richard Henry, 24–25
Pro Sports Ltd. v. Virginia Squires et. al., 49–51, 53, 232n95

Quinn-Ives Act, 76–77, 79, 81, 85–86, 90, 97

Reach, Al, 10
Reagan, Ronald: and positive thinking, 174, 175; and radio broadcast recreations, 192
Red Summer of 1919, 74
Reid, Daniel, 120
Reverend Ike, 163
Reynolds, Allie, 132
Rice, Grantland, 189
Richards, Paul, 101
Rickey, Branch: and the Brooklyn Brown Dodgers, 86–87; and Roy Campanella, 99; and communism, 83, 165; and the Continental League, 113–15; and contract negotiation, 131; and the integration of MLB, xii, 68–69, 78, 79–94, 97–103, 180, 240n98; and Milwaukee

AA v. Landis, 45, 83; and the Quinn-Ives Act, 81, 85–86, 97; and Jackie Robinson, xii, 68–69, 87–88, 90–93, 240n98; and television, 125; and tenure as GM of the Pittsburgh Pirates, 100; and Charles "Tommy" Thomas, 81–82, 100, 238n58, 238n60
Roberts, Curt, 100
Robertson, Pat, 164, 175
Robeson, Paul, 69, 78
Robinson, Jackie: and Leo Durocher, 104; and influence on the Players Association movement, 144; and integration, xii, 81, 82, 88–93, 102, 107, 236n13, 240n98; and the Kansas City Monarchs, 87; and Malcolm X, 91; and military court martial, 75–76; and Vic Power, 105; and Branch Rickey's "Great Experiment," 68, 69, 70, 88–93, 107
Robison, Frank and Stanley, 26
Rodney, Lester, 77, 91, 101–2, 137, 196–97, 237n35
Roosevelt, Franklin, 75, 161
Roosevelt, Theodore, 39–40, 135, 136, 167
Rose, Pete, 46, 51, 52–56, 227n1, 232n119
Roth, Philip, 147–48, 149, 154, 212
Rotisserie League Baseball, 208, 209
Rubin, Carl, 53
Runyon, Damon, 189
Ruth, Babe, 57, 124, 176, 189, 212, 255n35

SABR (Society for American Baseball Research), 206
Sadler, William, 161, 178
Saigh, Fred, 165
Sain, Johnny, 127
Sanguillen, Manny, 101
Savio, Mario, 138
Schecter, Leonard, 199
Seitz, Peter, 108, 144
Selig, Allan H. "Bud": and the Mitchell Report, 59–66, 194, 233n133, 235n159; and positive thinking, 178; and Pete Rose, 55
Shantz, Bobby, 127
Shea, William, 114–15
Shuba, George 100
"single sin myth": and Judge Landis, 33, 35–36, 60; and Bud Selig, 59–60
Siwoff, Seymour, 201, 213

Skowron, Bill, 105
Slaughter, Enos, 127
Smith, Red, 194, 199
Smith, Wendell, 77, 78
Smith, Willie, 104
social Darwinism, 19–23, 24, 25, 225n87, 225n88; and Henry Chadwick, 183; and relationship with New Thought movement, 159–60
Sosa, Sammy, 57, 58, 195
Spalding, Albert, 16, 17, 24
Speaker, Tris, 30, 36–37
Spencer, Herbert, 19, 160, 161
Spira, Howie, 56
SportsBlog Nation, 217–18, 219
sports talk radio, 213–14
"stacking," 6, 106
Steinbrenner, George, 56
Stendhal, 156
Stengel, Casey, 104–5
Stennett, Rennie, 101
Steroid Control Act of 1990, 62, 63
Stewart, Justice Potter, 43
Stockton, Roy, 190
Stottlemyre, Mel, 127
Strong, Josiah, 156
Sumner, William Graham, 19, 22, 135, 225n89
Swaggart, Jimmy, 175
Swett-Marden, Orestes, 169

television revolution, 123–29
Terry, Ralph, 128
Thomas, Charles "Tommy," 81–82, 83, 100, 238n58, 238n60
Toolson v. New York Yankees, 42, 173
Topping, Dan, 120
Trine, Ralph Waldo, 158
Turley, Bob, 127
Turner, Ted, 48–49, 50

Ueberroth, Peter, 52
Union Association, 17

Valenzuela, Fernando, 195
Veeck, Bill, 129
Versalles, Zoilo, 196
Vespucci, Amerigo, 4
Vincent, Fay, 56, 61–62, 66

Wagner, George and J. Earl, 26
Wagner, Robert, 113
Wagner Act, 136–37, 247n86
Waitkus, Eddie, 103
Walsh, Christy, 190
Ward, Arch, 189
Ward, John Montgomery, 132
Washington, Kenny, 90
Weaver, Buck, 36, 52, 59
Weaver, James, 134–35
Webb, Del, 120, 130
Weiss, George, 131
Westlake, Wally, 91
Whitman, Walt, 1, 2, 156
Widmar, Al, 131, 246n62
Williams, Serena and Venus, 107
Williams, Ted: and the media/contrast with Joe DiMaggio, 190–91, 215; and the Players Association, 141
Wilson, Woodrow, 40, 41, 161
Winfield, Dave, 56
Woods, Tiger, 107
Wrigley, Philip, 118
Wrigley, William, 161

Yawkey, Tom, 120, 139, 207
Yellow Horse, Moses, 72, 236n22
Young, A. S. "Doc," 87
Young, Dick, 141

Zinn, Howard, 236n6

MITCHELL NATHANSON is a professor of legal writing at Villanova University School of Law and the author of *The Fall of the 1977 Phillies: How a Baseball Team's Collapse Sank a City's Spirit.*

The University of Illinois Press
is a founding member of the
Association of American University Presses.

Designed by Kelly Gray
Composed in 10/14 Chaparral Pro Regular
with Trade Gothic LT Std and Marcelle Script display
by Barbara Evans
at the University of Illinois Press
Manufactured by Sheridan Books, Inc.

University of Illinois Press
1325 South Oak Street
Champaign, IL 61820-6903
www.press.uillinois.edu